Yale Studies in Political Science, 16
Published under the Direction of the Department of
Political Science

SYMBOLS OF AMERICAN COMMUNITY

1735–1775

BY RICHARD L. MERRITT

NEW HAVEN AND LONDON, YALE UNIVERSITY PRESS, 1966

To my parents,
Ray and Sarah Merritt,
who taught me American history and the
value of community

Contents

Contents

Preface

People give the greatest amount of support to those governments that respond to their needs and assure them a measure
of internal peace. Among these needs, whether dimly felt or
explicitly stated, an adequate allocation of resources and goods,
links of social communication, opportunities for participation
in communal life, and processes facilitating peaceful and or-
derly change rank high. In some places at some times, quite
often during periods of temporary instability and stress, still
other needs are paramount—protection from an external enemy, for instance, or perpetuation of existing social customs
and classes. In either event the pursuit of such needs usually
complements and facilitates the maintenance of internal peace.
Such interaction is a hallmark of the integrated community,
regardless of how that community's political institutions and
processes are organized.

In spite of a common desire for internal peace, however,
people often have differing perceptions of their needs and of
the means to satisfy them. It is not always the case that a
community's government can adjust such conflicting demands
in a context of domestic tranquillity. When segments of the
population feel that the creation of a new and independent

government, or association with another government, would meet their needs better or at least not worse than existing political institutions, the integration of the community breaks down. Secession, revolution, or even civil war may ensue.

This book is about political disintegration and integration. In a narrow sense it focuses upon disintegrative and integrative trends in colonial America. But, in applying the test of empirical data to some alternative views about the separation of the colonies from the eighteenth-century British Empire and their subsequent union as a separate political entity, it has a much broader scope. The study points to a more generalized theory of political integration, that is, the development of political communities based on a high degree of mutual interaction, together with expectations of peaceful relations among their members.

One important approach to the study of political integration —whether in the local or international sphere—stresses the conscious basis of demands for political change in a society. In a sense it is the more direct approach to problems of integration, and the one most often followed by students of political communities. Scholars and students favoring such an approach generally concentrate upon the nature of the social system in which demands for change are made, the goals projected by persons or groups making demands for change, the intensity with which the politically relevant strata of the populations concerned support the demands, the relative strength of competing demands, the means to effect changes, and the conditions that favor certain patterns of demands and strategies above others.

Underlying this approach is the psychological issue of expected rewards and deprivations. The type of demands for loyalty or change that a person makes in the political sphere, so the argument runs, as well as the strategies that he chooses to achieve his goals, are tied directly to his expectations of economic, political, social, or psychological gains and losses.

A second approach disputes the notion that demands for political change are solely functions of expected rewards and deprivations. Conscious motivating factors are indeed important, but they do not tell the whole story. Alone they do not account for the specific nature of demands for political change. Nor do they tell us much about the timing of successful demands. The demand for colonial union voiced at the Albany Congress of 1754, for example, fell for the most part upon deaf ears. What was it that made similar demands so attractive to colonial patriots two decades later?

The essential argument of the second approach is that unconscious elements of behavior—perceptions, moods, habits, climates of opinion—are significant determinants in the patterns of shifting demands. Explicitly stated demands for change are formulated in terms of these unconscious elements. What a person perceives when he looks at himself and his environment, as well as the attitudes and values held by his contemporaries, plays an important role in creating his own demands, therefore shaping what he considers to be rewards or deprivations.

The second approach to the study of political integration, then, concentrates upon the ecology of demands for change, on the relationship of the demands themselves to the environment of perspectives, values, and attitudes in which they take place. It is particularly concerned with the question of timing: why a demand, unimportant or possibly even obnoxious at a given point in time, becomes acceptable to the politically relevant strata of a population at a later date. It seeks to answer one central question: What is it that produces a climate of opinion or a mood favorable to change?

In studying community development in colonial America,

this book concentrates upon the ecology of demands for political change, that is, the relationship of the demands to the environment in which they occurred. This is not to say, however, that I shall ignore the approach to political integration that stresses the conscious elements of demands for political change. Such an omission would be as undesirable as it is impossible. Indeed, the evidence for evaluating alternative theories about the unconscious processes will also be useful in formulating hypotheses about the role in community building of expected rewards and deprivations.

The methodology used in the study is a quantitative symbol analysis of the colonial press. Since symbol analysis and, more generally, content analysis are fairly new techniques for the investigation of historical processes and events, a few words on their assumptions, uses, and limitations are appropriate here.[1] The specific procedure used in this book is described in the Appendix.

In brief, content analysis is the systematic examination of style in communications. The unit of analysis is the message: a newspaper editorial, speech, painting, book, letter, prayer, and so forth. The method provides a quantitative means to characterize persistent patterns in the message: logical structure, mode of reasoning, syntax, diction, intonation, gestures, shading, particular constellations of words, images, or concepts. With the characterization of the message's style in hand, the analyst may proceed to make qualitative inferences about the source of the message or about its effect upon its recipient. As one of several forms of content analysis, symbol analysis

[1] For a fuller discussion of the value of symbol analysis for the study of political processes in colonial America, see Richard L. Merritt, "The Emergence of American Nationalism: A Quantitative Approach," *American Quarterly,* 17 (1965), 319–35. Cf. also Harold D. Lasswell, Daniel Lerner, and Ithiel de Sola Pool, *The Comparative Study of Symbols: An Introduction,* Hoover Institute Studies, Series C, No. 1 (Stanford, Stanford University Press, 1952).

focuses upon the words (or symbols) used in communicating.

Since the message itself is the unit of analysis, the difference between the conscious and unconscious elements that make up its style is often quite unimportant (although it would be possible, through content analysis, to discern such differences). To some extent the selection of words by a communicator is a conscious process: he may consciously "stylize" his messages to create a particular effect or even to disguise his true feelings. Ultimately, however, it is the mass of unconscious elements—and most particularly word usage, syntax, and contextual configurations—that define the person's style. Indeed, the unconscious or latent structure of a message may even outweigh its manifest content. If, for instance, with the passage of time a Tory newspaper in colonial America, such as the *Massachusetts Gazette,* devoted an increasing share of its space to news of the American colonies, or if it increasingly identified its readers as "Americans" rather than as "His Majesty's subjects" or even "colonists," we might say that, despite its pro-British point of view, the latent content of the *Gazette* encouraged its readers to think of themselves as members of a distinctly American community and to turn their thoughts inward toward that American community.

At the heart of symbol analysis is its systematic procedure. It is useful only when the researcher has questions of a quantitative nature—how often? how much? how many? with what covariance?—that can be answered by systematically counting the appearance of a limited number of symbols in a given body of data. The symbol analyst's first step, then, is to frame his questions (or formulate his hypotheses) so that quantitative data can answer them clearly, directly, and simply. Next he must outline the technical aspects of his project, determining how to count which symbols in what body of data, covering what time period. Objectivity requires that these technical aspects of the symbol analysis be specified in advance, and that throughout the analysis there be strict adherence to the coding procedure. If this requirement is met, an independent research project should be able to verify the findings of a symbol analysis by applying the analyst's coding procedures to the original body of data. If it is impossible or impractical to analyze all the data, the analyst must utilize a sampling technique, designed to produce a representative sample or reproduction in miniature of the entire body, or universe, of relevant items. After a pretest or "dry run," in which he subjects a small portion of his sample to analysis, the researcher can usually see where he must eliminate and where he must add categories to his symbol list, or where he must make changes in his hypotheses or coding procedures.

The value of content analysis data rests solely upon the uses to which they are put, upon the inferences that can be drawn from them.[2] In this regard such information is not at all dissimilar from any other piece of concrete evidence used in the study of American history or processes of community-building. In another sense, however, such data are quite different from the standard materials of American history: they

[2] The process of analysis and inference is of course cyclical and raises some important theoretical issues: What is the relationship between the characteristics of an individual's personality and the messages that he communicates? What is the relationship between the characteristics of a society and its public messages (e.g. in newspapers, official documents, public speeches)? What is the relationship between the personality characteristics of an individual and the societal communication media? What is the level of "interaction" between the opinions and values expressed in a newspaper and those of its readers? What is the relationship among societal communication media? What effect does a communication have upon its recipient? How accurately is the "objective" style of a communication (as determined through a systematic content analysis) perceived subjectively by its individual recipients? To go into such questions here would take us too far afield; for a beginning, see Richard L. Merritt, "The Representational Model in Cross-National Content Analysis," in Joseph L. Bernd, ed., *Mathematical Applications in Political Science* (Dallas, Texas, Southern Methodist University Press, 1966).

are quantitative in nature, based on standard statistical tests of reliability and verification. The information yielded is both impersonal and objective, that is, an independent researcher could get similar results by following the same procedures. The fact that symbol analysis produces trend information bears two important implications for research: it encourages us to fit single pieces of evidence into continuing patterns, thereby giving us a better understanding of the relevance of single bits of information as well as enriching our understanding of the patterns; and it helps us to focus our attention upon years or months of particular importance in such long-run processes as the political integration of the eighteenth-century American colonies.

Since the effectiveness of symbol analysis depends in large part upon sharply defined symbol categories, a note on my use of terms is also appropriate here. The term "continental," for instance, means many things to many people. To the eighteenth-century European it referred most directly to the European continent. To the writer in the American colonies, however, it most often referred to his own continent, North America. It was in the latter sense that the term was used in forming a "Continental Congress" in 1774, and a "Continental Army" during the course of the following year. And the term "continentals" in the colonial press after 1774 referred most often to the colonial troops, and not to those from Europe. One important category of symbols analyzed in this study comprises what I have termed "continental symbols." Such symbols, then, are those referring to the American continent as a whole. In discussing symbols of the European continent, I have used the term "European symbols."

The terms "sense of community" and "community awareness" are used to connote aspects of the American community. In referring to the ties of community binding the eighteenth-century American colonies to the mother country, I have used the terms "sense of Anglo-American community" and "Anglo-American community awareness."

Throughout this study I have relied upon the type of statistical tests known as "nonparametric statistics." Nonparametric statistics does not require the assumption that the data in the colonial newspapers were, in a statistical sense, distributed "normally," that the variance was normal, and so forth. Since it most often entails the ranking of frequencies rather than inferences based upon numerically exact frequencies, nonparametric statistics is relatively simple to compute, particularly for small samples.

Many people have been very helpful to me in the preparation of this study. I would like to thank most particularly the three members of my dissertation committee at Yale University, to which I submitted an earlier version of the study. The director of the committee was Harold D. Lasswell. I have profited immensely from his pioneering work in the techniques of symbol analysis as well as in the field of political behavior; I appreciated the time that he took out from his own research activities to counsel me and assist me with my project. Karl W. Deutsch was in a sense the guiding light of the project. It was as his research assistant that I undertook the study of symbols of American community in the colonial era. Throughout the months spent in research, Mr. Deutsch provided helpful advice and warm encouragement, and was instrumental in securing needed financial support. The student of political communities, in reading this book, will not fail to note the extent of my reliance upon the important theoretical work performed by Mr. Deutsch. I am also indebted to Edmund S. Morgan for his generous and helpful assistance. I drew extensively upon his knowledge of American colonial history in the preparation of the study.

Preface

In acknowledging my indebtedness to Messrs. Lasswell, Deutsch, and Morgan, I should not like to saddle them with the responsibility for shortcomings in this study of symbols of American community. This responsibility I alone bear.

Others have assisted me in particular aspects of the study. Eugene C. McCreary of the Carnegie Institute of Technology not only performed the symbol counting for the Massachusetts newspapers, but also gave me valuable criticisms of early drafts of the study. Eugene Royster of Temple University assisted me in all of the statistical aspects of the study. Hayward R. Alker, Jr., of Yale University not only suggested but helped to carry out the computer analysis of intercolonial attention patterns. Leonard W. Labaree of Yale University took time out from editing the papers of Benjamin Franklin on a number of occasions to offer me advice on certain problems in American history. Louis P. Galambos of Johns Hopkins University scrutinized several chapters in manuscript form, saving me from many a misleading statement and factual as well as stylistic error. I am also grateful to the staff of the Sterling Memorial Library of Yale University (and particularly Miss Marjorie Wynne of the Beinecke Rare Book and Manuscript Library) for their many helpful services. To Mrs. Lucile Seibert and Mrs. Barbara Bruns I am indebted for producing a well-typed manuscript out of masses of typewritten and scribbled notes.

A special note of thanks goes to Miss Eileen Grady, formerly of the Sterling Memorial Library, for the many courtesies that she has extended to me in the past few years; Miss Grady is indeed the ideal librarian for research scholars.

Grants from the Carnegie Corporation of New York enabled the completion of the project. I would like to take this opportunity to express my gratitude to the Carnegie Corporation for this assistance.

Preface

Chapter 5 has previously appeared in the *William and Mary Quarterly;* some of the material has been published in *American Quarterly, Public Opinion Quarterly, General Systems Yearbook, 1963* and *General Systems Yearbook, 1964,* and Karl W. Deutsch and William J. Foltz, eds., *Nation-Building* (New York, Atherton, 1963).

It would be difficult in this brief note to acknowledge the extent to which my wife, Anna, assisted in this enterprise. Without her cheerful help and gentle encouragement, and her ability to translate jargon into English, the study and I would have suffered considerably.

R. L. M.

Morgan Point, Connecticut
April 1964

List of Tables

List of Tables

List of Figures

List of Figures

CHAPTER ONE

The Integration of the American Community

The seventeenth-century American colonies existed in a state of semi-isolation, separated from one another in many cases by stretches of uninhabited wilderness and more generally by inadequate systems of intercolonial transportation and communication. Contacts with the mother country were often easier to maintain, and perhaps more fruitful, than those with neighboring colonies. To the extent that there was any coordination among separate colonial administrations, it was the result, not of the colonists' cooperation, but of the efforts of His Majesty's Government in England. Even as late as the middle of the eighteenth century the colonists were unable to organize an effective intercolonial defense against marauding Indians on the western frontiers; and some voices expressed fears of armed conflict among certain colonies.

By the early nineteenth century, however, the United States of America comprised an integrated political community. The American people possessed a sense of national community and a set of political structures sufficient to maintain a high degree of mobility as well as a large volume of mutual transactions, to ensure expectations of peaceful relations within the Ameri-

I

can Union, and to enable the achievement or at least the satisfactory pursuit of common national interests. The national government had successfully protected those common interests, battling the world's most important maritime power (1812–15) and resisting attacks upon the national unity by northern secessionists (1815). The American republic was unified by 1820 and, with the voluntary and often enthusiastic support of its population of almost ten million persons, master in its own house.[1]

The rise of an integrated political community on the North American continent is a challenging topic for study. What factors explain this dramatic change in the fabric of American society? Which of the processes that led to an eighteenth-century American Union were more, and which less, instrumental? The scholar who would answer such questions faces a broad panorama of events: the receding but still present threat of Indian attacks; the promises and dangers of the unexplored western lands; wars against the French; the Molasses Act, the Stamp Act, and other British parliamentary measures to control colonial trade; the development of facilities for and habits of intercolonial communications; the growth of an interlocking elite among the Americans; a rebellion against parliamentary acts considered unjust by some colonists; the creation of a Continental Congress and a Continental Army; the development of a governmental system; a confederation of the colonies and, eventually, a federation. These events, familiar enough to us all, provide the basic stuff out of which scholars must fashion meaningful patterns and relationships that help us to understand how the semi-isolated and self-concerned population clusters of 1700 became the nucleus of a political

---

1. 1820 was also a milestone—perhaps the first overt manifestation—of a sectional rivalry that was to divide the Union four decades later. The term "political community" is discussed at greater length in Chapter 2.

community that was to become, two and one-half centuries later, a dominant force in world politics.

The emergence of an integrated American political community is not, however, solely of intrinsic interest. It is an important example of the more general process by which political communities are formed. Students and proponents of international organizations and polities have found eighteenth-century American history particularly rich in parallels to the modern, multistate world. The thirteen colonies were distinct entities, separate in many ways, divided to some extent by suspicion and petty jealousies. And yet they had some things, such as language and political heritage, in common, and possessed a certain number of common interests—control over the frontier lands, the maintenance of peaceful relations among themselves, and a desire to have commercial opportunities unrestricted by British navigation laws, to name but a few. Similarly, the countries of today's world have many things in common in their diversity. The more optimistic advocates of a world government have predicted that modern nation-states will eventually follow the path taken by the colonies three centuries ago. Carl Van Doren has perhaps most dramatically underlined the influence of the American example of federalism. Writing in 1948 and referring specifically to the newly formed United Nations, he argued that the making and ratifying of the federal Constitution was "a rehearsal for the federal governments of the future." [2]

In the many studies that have chronicled and analyzed the growth of the American community, three concepts of political integration, in part complementary and in part mutually contradictory, recur time and again. The first of these is that the

2. Carl Van Doren, *The Great Rehearsal: The Story of the Making and Ratifying of the Constitution of the United States* (New York, Viking, 1948), p. x.

creation of common political structures (a parliament to legislate for the entire community, for instance, or a unified army under a command based on professional rather than territorial qualifications) produces a climate of opinion conducive to high levels of integration among otherwise mutually disinterested or even antagonistic groups. This theory is typical of many "world government" movements. They assert that, if the leaders of the world would only sit down together at a table and draft a constitution embodying an effective set of transnational institutions, the binding ties creating a single world community and outmoding war would follow as a matter of course.

A variation of this theory is the "functionalist" approach to political integration. It argues that common formal experiences even without enforcement procedures will produce a sense of community among diverse peoples. Accordingly, by delegating a limited number of governmental functions to an intergovernmental agency, and by giving such agencies real powers in their limited spheres of action, a climate of mutual responsiveness and eventually an international sense of community and political consensus can be nurtured.[3]

Historians of eighteenth-century America who present this position generally do not argue that outright hostility fragmented the colonies (although some, with considerable justification, dwell upon the issues that occasionally pitted colony against colony). Indeed, the fact that the colonists lived in a geographic and political environment that in many ways was quite uniform is a commonplace in these many studies. What such writers find more persuasive is the argument that the colonists, separated by the lack of communication facilities and walls of indifference, had no inkling of the extent to which

3. Cf. for example, Ernst B. Haas, *The Uniting of Europe: Political, Social, and Economic Forces, 1950–1957* (Stanford, Stanford University Press, 1958), particularly pp. 526–27.

they shared a common way of life and a common fate.[4] When representatives of the individual colonies met at intercolonial congresses, they behaved more as ambassadors of sovereign nations than as compatriots, and seemed more interested in preserving than breaking down existing barriers.

The relative ease and the wide range of transactions between the individual colonies and the mother country, according to this line of reasoning, made the intercolonial barriers doubly apparent and effective. Unstable currencies and the virtual absence of intercolonial credit facilities increased the colonists' reliance upon London merchants and bankers. For political ideas and cues, the colonists looked, not to their fellow colonists in other parts of the continent, but to English thinkers and

4. Quoting the eighteenth-century Boston patriot, Josiah Quincy, the historian Evarts Boutell Greene suggests that "there was a 'prevalent and extended ignorance' in the colonies about one another's concerns, while mutual prejudices and clashing interests also worked against a common American feeling." *The Revolutionary Generation, 1763–1790* (New York, Macmillan, 1943), p. 185. Merrill Jensen, after describing the colonies' relations with one another as "nationalistic," notes that each delegate to the first Continental Congress in 1774 "thought of his own colony as his country, as an independent nation in its dealings with England and with its neighbors," despite "social, racial, and economic affinities and the cohesive force of the British connection." *The Articles of Confederation: An Interpretation of the Social–Constitutional History of the American Revolution, 1774–1781* (Madison, University of Wisconsin Press, 1940), p. 56. John C. Ranney went so far as to write: "Separated as they were by vast distances and abominable roads, unaccustomed to travel in other states or to communicate with their inhabitants, living in isolated communities which of necessity approximated to self-sufficiency, they had little interest in and little knowledge of their neighbors." "The Bases of American Federalism," *The William and Mary Quarterly* (3d series), 3 (1946), 2–3. Perhaps the strongest statement of intercolonial antipathy stemmed from the Loyalist Jonathan Boucher of Philadelphia. In a sermon delivered on the eve of the Revolution, Boucher described the New Englanders as "the Goths and Vandals of America," and concluded: "O 'tis a monstrous and an unnatural coalition; and we should as soon expect to see the greatest contrarieties in Nature to meet in harmony, and the wolf and the lamb to feed together, as Virginians to form a cordial union with the saints of New England." *Reminiscences of an American Loyalist, 1738–1789*, ed. Jonathan Bouchier (Boston, Houghton Mifflin, 1925), pp. 132–33, 134; cf. generally pp. 130–36.

parliamentarians. Even local news, some writers point out, reached England before nearby colonies.[5]

Not until the colonists severed their ties with the mother country and formed their own unified political system, this argument continues, did the barriers of indifference separating them begin to fall away. For such writers as Edward Frank Humphrey, Kenneth C. Wheare, and, more recently, Esmond Wright, the Revolution was but the beginning of the process of American community development.[6] Accordingly, it was only after widespread functional amalgamation of political structures that the great bulk of Americans was willing to submerge particularistic sentiments and loyalties in a truly national feeling or sense of community.

A second concept of political integration suggests that single events or series of events, or even the memory of these events, lead to dramatic changes in a population's mood and pattern

5. Virginia D. Harrington, *The New York Merchant on the Eve of the Revolution* (New York, Columbia University Press, 1935), pp. 103–22. Clarence P. Gould, *Money and Transportation in Maryland, 1720–1765* (Baltimore, Johns Hopkins Press, 1915), pp. 160–61.

6. According to Humphrey, the colonies "had existed up to the time of the Revolutionary War as thirteen separate and distinct political units. Nor had they seriously attempted to break down the social, economic, educational or religious barriers which separated them. They seemed to dread unification. . . . The Declaration of Independence but cleared the way for the creation of whatever spirit or form of institutions the colonists might elect to produce." *Nationalism and Religion in America, 1774–1789* (Boston, Chipman, 1924), pp. 2–4. Humphrey's first chapters nonetheless discuss the intercolonial aspects of religion prior to the Revolution. Writing in 1955 on the ways "in which, through federation, new nations have been brought into existence," Wheare suggested that the American case was one "where people of differing nationality are prepared to join in a federation, but they do not yet feel a sense of common nationality." "Federalism and the Making of Nations," in Arthur W. Macmahon, ed., *Federalism, Mature and Emergent* (Garden City, N. Y., Doubleday, 1955), p. 33. According to Wright, the Revolution was not "a single 'national' movement," but thirteen separate revolutions conducted differently by the individual colonies. *Fabric of Freedom, 1763–1800* (New York, Hill and Wang, 1961), p. 20.

6

of demands. Examples of such events include the invention of a new weapon, the death of a great leader, or the enactment of some item of legislation. Their effects may be diverse. They may make strong ties of community even firmer, strengthen newly formed ties or those weakened by the passage of time, jolt a population (or part of it) into an awareness of significant differences between it and another population (or segment of the population), or, finally, force upon the members of different groups the realization that a closer union among them, or even political amalgamation, would better meet their needs (for mutual contracts, processes of peaceful change, and so forth) than would their continued separation. In all cases, a formative event is one that dramatically catches the imagination of the population, an event that makes a firm impression on the minds of the people.

In the modern world, according to such a theory, a thermonuclear holocaust, or even the threat of mutual annihilation, could lead at least some of the states of the world to an awareness of their interdependence and their common stake in the maintenance of international peace and security. As it was only after the tragic death of their children that Capulet and his "brother Montague" could extend their hands in friendship to each other, so on the verge of another great disaster, in the darkest days of World War II, Great Britain's Prime Minister Winston Churchill proposed a plan of virtual union with the French. And with every increase in the tension of today's "cold war," such as the failure of a summit conference or a Soviet breach of the moratorium on testing atomic bombs, responsible statesmen and journalists alike point out that the deepening of the bipolar split only serves to increase "western unity." In jest, some commentators have hoped for an invasion from Mars that would unite the countries of our world in a permanent alliance; others have seriously proposed "peace races"—wars on poverty, disease, ignorance, and technological backwardness—as means to the goal of international integration.

Perhaps most historians interested in the formation of the eighteenth-century American political community belong to this school of thought. Many have tried to define precisely the point in time at which the colonists began to develop a collective sense of community. Very few writers, it must be added, have pointed to significant events occurring prior to the Stamp Act crisis. Albert Harkness, Jr., was one of these. He argued that the use of the terms "Americans" and "Europeans" to differentiate the colonists from their English brethren stemmed from the War of Jenkins' Ear, which began in 1739.[7] And Max Savelle found a growing "national" feeling among Americans during the six years between the end of King George's War (1748) and the outbreak of the French and Indian War.[8] Carl Lotus Becker selected a later date for the separation of Americans from Englishmen but, like Harkness, attributed the rise of a feeling of community consciousness to the forced association of Americans and Englishmen in time of war. "From the experience of the last French war [1754–63] there emerged something of that sublime self-confidence which stamps the true American," Becker wrote, "and in that war was generated a sense of spiritual separation from Eng-

7. Albert Harkness, Jr., "Americanism and Jenkins' Ear," *Mississippi Valley Historical Review*, 37 (1950), 61–90, particularly pp. 89–90.

8. Max Savelle, *Seeds of Liberty: The Genesis of the American Mind* (New York, Knopf, 1948), p. 555. He adds: "It would of course be a mistake to suggest that . . . the appearance of the new American loyalty . . . was fully self-conscious in the year 1750. But the new loyalty was beginning to show itself, as the bases of economic, social, political, and intellectual homogeneity were being more clearly drawn and firmly laid. Thereafter the dramatic flowering of American nationalism between 1765 and 1770 and the conflict between the new loyalty and the old were only a matter of growth." Ibid., p. 561.

land never quite felt before." [9] Another, and much larger, set of historians, including such prominent scholars as Carl Bridenbaugh, Bernhard Knollenberg, John C. Miller, Edmund S. Morgan, and Allan Nevins, has argued that the sharp increase in the American sense of community came during the critical decade that began with the passage of the Stamp Act and ended with the creation of the first Continental Congress in 1774.[10] As Carl Bridenbaugh has written,

9. Carl Lotus Becker, *Beginnings of the American People* (Boston, Houghton Mifflin, 1915), pp. 191–93. In a brilliant essay, Becker later recounted the tale of one Jeremiah Wynkoop "from the beginning of the quarrel in 1763 to the final breach in 1776." "The Spirit of '76," in Carl Becker, J. M. Clark, and William E. Dodd, *The Spirit of '76 and Other Essays* (Washington, Robert Brookings Graduate School of Economics and Government, 1927), pp. 10, 14. Cf. also Lawrence Henry Gipson, "The American Revolution as an Aftermath of the Great War for the Empire, 1754–1763," *Political Science Quarterly*, 65 (1950), 86–104.

10. Carl Bridenbaugh, *Cities in Revolt: Urban Life in America, 1743–1776* (New York, Knopf, 1955), p. 424. Bernhard Knollenberg, in considering the repeal of the Stamp Act in March 1766, writes: "Thus, though the Act and the colonial measures to annul it had excited fears and animosities on both sides of the water which were never wholly dispelled, the most important cause and the threat of immediate colonial rebellion were removed." *Origin of the American Revolution, 1759–1766* (rev. ed. New York, Collier, 1961), p. 218. This statement, which did not appear in the first edition of the book (New York, Macmillan, 1960), is particularly curious in view of Knollenberg's introductory remarks: "My conclusion and thesis are that, while the British Stamp Act of 1765 greatly contributed to and touched off the colonial uprising of 1765–1766, the colonists had been brought to the brink of rebellion by a number of other provocative British measures from 1759 to 1764, most of which persisted after the Stamp Act was repealed in 1766 and contributed to the mounting colonial discontent culminating in the American Revolution of 1775–1783." Ibid., p. 1 in first edition, p. 11 in revised edition. John C. Miller suggests: "It was not until after the passage of the Stamp Act that [the] real menace" of the earlier trade restrictions was perceived. *Origin of the American Revolution* (Boston, Little, Brown, 1949), p. 22. According to Edmund S. Morgan, "The British efforts to curb a supposed drive toward independence united Americans in a common sense of grievance and alarm, nourishing a sense of togetherness that grew steadily toward nationality." He adds, "our nation was the child, not the father, of our revolution." *The Birth of the Republic, 1763–89* (Chicago, University of Chicago Press, 1956), p. 101. Allan Nevins points out: "Till a few years before the Revolution, no real

"the contest of the sixties forced the citizens to a recognition of the differences between Englishmen and Americans." [11]

A third view of political integration regards informal processes of a long-run nature as the most important in creating a climate of opinion favorable to political change. An increase in communication loads (that is, a greater volume of transactions among the groups, a broadened scope of the commitments involved in the transactions, and the arousing of expanded expectations among the participants) together with an increase in communication and decision-making capabilities (including, in particular, complementary habits and facilities of communication and decision making) and a high rate of rewarding or mutually beneficial transactions to the total number of transactions push independent groups toward the threshold of integration.

The proponents of this position do not ignore the role of formal institutions and formative events in their emphasis upon gradual integrative processes. It is less a question of which of these processes by itself clinches the integration of a political community than a question of which is more important at a given stage in the community's development.

---

sense of American nationality existed among the colonists. They often called themselves Englishmen or British subjects; they were Carolinians, Pennsylvanians, or New Englanders; but they felt little need for a term applicable to all the colonists, and the colonists alone." *The American States During and After the Revolution, 1775–1789* (New York, Macmillan, 1924), p. 544.

11. Bridenbaugh, *Cities in Revolt*, p. 424. He adds: "Through constant communication and interchange," the major urban centers of colonial America "moved with rapid strides toward the integration of colonial culture, a culture that had diverged sufficiently from the English standard by 1776 to be recognized as American. To this end, since 1761, many individuals had been more or less unwittingly directing their talents and energy, but as each new political crisis arose, the word *American* was pronounced more often and with growing conviction. . . . As the realization of nationality spread, the citizens pronounced it good, and their collective self-confidence soared." *Ibid.*, p. 417.

Accordingly, the gradual processes of integration—shared foci of attention, common perceptions of the community and its inhabitants, complementary habits and facilities of communication and decision making, and so forth—would have to cross a certain threshold before the "formative events" would be perceived by the participants in a common or mutually compatible manner. And both rewarding mutual transactions and common perceptions of important events would have to proceed some distance before common political institutions, whether limited to simple functions or carrying on the most important functions of government, would become acceptable to or be actively sought by the politically relevant strata of the populations concerned. Thus, policy planners interested in increasing the level of international political integration in the atomic age should aim at an increased mutual responsiveness among the different countries, greater capabilities (that is, enhanced political and economic strength), a greater range of mutual transactions, more and stronger links of social communication, and a greater mobility of persons.[12]

That the growth of an American community was a gradual process, resulting not only from the unique conditions affecting the colonists (such as the presence of the frontier) but also from increasing intercolonial communication of all sorts, is a prominent theme in some histories of the eighteenth-century colonies. The colonists, according to this idea, were conscious of one another's existence and problems long before such events as the Stamp Act crisis. They were alert to the interests that they held in common. And, although remaining loyal to the British Crown, they nonetheless appreciated the

12. Cf. Karl W. Deutsch, Sidney A. Burrell, Robert A. Kann, Maurice Lee, Jr., Martin Lichterman, Raymond E. Lindgren, Francis L. Loewenheim, Richard W. Van Wagenen, *Political Community and the North Atlantic Area: International Organization in the Light of Historical Experience* (Princeton, Princeton University Press, 1957).

differences between themselves and their English brethren. The growing amount and range of intercolonial communication transactions of all kinds at once reflected and helped to shape the bonds of American community.

The emphasis here is upon political integration as a process of growth, with the colonists moving away from their absorption with local affairs, or with their ties to the mother land, toward genuinely intercolonial communication and attention patterns. Hence the argument of the Bancroft school of historians, that the colonists were united from the outset by a common devotion to such political principles as liberty, is not appropriate.[13] More to the point are the writings of such historians as James Truslow Adams, Charles M. Andrews, Oscar Handlin, Michael Kraus, and Howard H. Peckham.[14] Other studies have concentrated upon particular aspects of the growth of intercolonial communication transactions: William B. Weeden, in his economic and social analysis of colonial New England, emphasized the importance of "the coasting trade, knitting together the several communities in different colonies with gossamer webs stronger than hooks [sic] of steel";[15] Robert K. Lamb dealt with family and business re-

13. George Bancroft, *History of the United States* (10 vols. Boston, Bowen, and Little, Brown, 1834–74).

14. James Truslow Adams, *The March of Democracy: The Rise of the Union* (New York, Scribner's, 1932), pp. 54, 74–75. Charles M. Andrews, "The American Revolution: An Interpretation," *American Historical Review,* 31 (1926), 219–32. Oscar Handlin, *This Was America: True Accounts of People and Places, Manners and Customs, as Recorded by European Travelers to the Western Shore in the Eighteenth, Nineteenth, and Twentieth Centuries* (Cambridge, Mass., Harvard University Press, 1949), p. 7. Michael Kraus, *Intercolonial Aspects of American Culture on the Eve of the Revolution, with Special Reference to the Northern Towns* (New York, Columbia University Press, 1928). Howard H. Peckham. *The Colonial Wars, 1689–1762* (Chicago and London, University of Chicago Press, 1964), pp. 219–21.

15. William B. Weeden, *Economic and Social History of New England, 1620–1789* (2 vols. Boston, Houghton Mifflin, 1891), 2, 592.

lationships, as well as ties of friendship, extending across colonial boundaries;[16] Charles Beard considered the growth of an interlocking colonial elite;[17] and still others, such as Wheaton J. Lane, have discussed facets of intercolonial transportation.[18] But it was John Adams who perhaps best summed up the argument that extensive intercolonial contacts and the growth of a sense of community preceded the outbreak of revolution and the creation of amalgamated political structures. "The Revolution was effected before the war commenced," he remarked in 1816; the "radical change in the principles, sentiments, and affections of the people was the real American Revolution." [19]

The record left by historians provides support for all three possible interpretations of the integration of the American political community. It leaves the main questions, however, unanswered: Does a sense of political community among separate and mutually indifferent groups or states follow the creation of common structures designed to perform certain political functions? Or is the process reversed, with the development of some degree of community consciousness preceding the desire to set up common structures? Did the Declaration of Independence and the Constitution of 1787 create Americans, or did Americans draft these documents? How important

16. Robert K. Lamb, "The Entrepreneur and the Community," in William Miller, ed., *Men in Business: Essays in the History of Entrepreneurship* (Cambridge, Harvard University Press, 1952); see also his summary and diagram in Karl W. Deutsch, *Nationalism and Social Communication: An Inquiry into the Foundations of Nationality* (Cambridge, and New York, Massachusetts Institute of Technology Press and Wiley, 1953), pp. 15–21. Cf. Harrington, *The New York Merchant*, pp. 225–29, for a discussion of the intercolonial contacts of New York businessmen.

17. Charles A. Beard, *An Economic Interpretation of the Constitution of the United States* (New York, Macmillan, 1914), pp. 149–51, 324–25.

18. Wheaton J. Lane, *From Indian Train to Iron Horse: Travel and Transportation in New Jersey, 1620–1860* (Princeton, Princeton University Press, 1939), p. 55.

19. Cited in Bridenbaugh, *Cities in Revolt*, p. 425.

were formative events, relative to the steady increase of mutually beneficial communication transactions, in leading to a sense of colonial community? Were such outbursts as the Stamp Act crisis of 1765 a result of a well-developed community consciousness, or did they first make the colonists aware of and interested in one another and their common problems?

Is it possible that a reanalysis of some of the standard materials of American history, using the newer concepts and empirical methods of the social sciences, might shed more light upon the development of the American political community? One particularly useful way of looking at the emergence of an American union is in terms of the group concept: When did the idea that the Americans comprised a single group, different from other national groups and with a fairly well-defined set of group interests, begin to appeal to the eighteenth-century colonists? What is the process by which groups become integrated political communities?

CHAPTER TWO

Political Communities and Integrative Processes

The concept of the "group" has come to have a flexible meaning in everyday usage. Essentially, however, groups are sets of objects (or variables) united by some form of regular interaction. This interaction has its stationary as well as its dynamic elements. In a forest, for example, where the trees are organized in an immobile spatial relationship and where the boundary between the forest and the pasture is fairly clear, the stationary aspect of interaction may be said to predominate. The interaction is nonetheless dynamic to the extent that old trees decay, die, and are replaced by new ones.

Highly dynamic patterns of interaction generally characterize groups of human beings, whether they be stamp-collecting clubs or large-scale political communities. Through their perceptions of and their behavior toward each other and the group itself, members of a group distinguish themselves from nonmembers. Six aspects of these perceptual and behavioral patterns are particularly important. Although some may not appear until late in the process by which groups are formed, all six are present in the well-integrated group.

One set of attributes constitutes what may be called group awareness. (1) There is an external perception of the group's existence, that is, people who are not members of the group recognize its existence and differentiate it from other groups (or even from themselves) through their terminology. (2) Balancing the external perception or label is the recognition of the group's existence as an entity apart from other such groups by its own members, who begin to use certain collective terms in reference to their group. (3) The members of the group share patterns of attention. When they pay heed to the same things and events (and, particularly, to the group as a whole), they may be said to have parallel patterns of attention; and these patterns are symmetrical to the extent that the attention paid to one another by the members of the group is balanced. In considering group awareness, whether or not the individual members are aware of the implications of group membership is less important than their awareness that they comprise a part of the group.

The form of interaction characterizing a social group also encompasses an internalization of group interests. (4) There is a recognition that certain events or objectives are of common interest to members of the group. This recognition implies more than the presence of common attention patterns, that is, a number of people observing the same events and processes more or less simultaneously. It suggests a perception that the events and processes affect all of them in a similar way and hence are of importance to them collectively. In this sense there will be an expectation of rewards for successful group behavior, for a common or mutually compatible response to such events and processes. In a well-knit group, group interests are a concatenation of the members' values, faiths, and loyalties pertaining to politics, ethics, economics, religion, and other aspects of social life. (5) There is some probability that the members will in fact be able to coordinate their behavior in an effort to promote their common interests. This is a two-pronged process. There must be, on the one hand, an expectation that the promotion of common interests will be mutually beneficial and, on the other, an ability to fulfill the need for coordination in terms of actual performance. Linguistic, ethnic, or other barriers may prevent people from realizing what they may perceive to be of common interest. The more highly integrated the group, however, the more likely it is that its members will be able to coordinate their activities to extend even beyond those of immediate necessity to the group. (6) Certain persistent structures or processes, whether amalgamated or pluralistic but parallel, exist to perform functions in the group interest. In an informal group, such as a stamp-collectors' club, the structures and processes may be little more than a network of interlocking roles (such as the relationship between leaders and followers). Constitutions, however, or even years of habit may systematize such an informal division of labor. In some cases, such as political communities or businesses, elaborate and complex machinery of government may emerge.

The essential role that communication plays in the internalization of group interests should also be noted. Where there is no communication whatsoever among its members, we might anticipate a low consensus on the nature of group interests, as well as a division of labor or degree of cooperation inadequate to achieve them. A greater amount of communication encompassing an increasingly wide range of topics might produce two types of results. First, it could lead to a higher degree of understanding of and consensus on such vital matters as values, goals, and strategies for attaining them. In such an event, the members of the group would be more conversant with other members than with persons outside the group on matters related to the group interests. Second, increased communication could create an awareness that the basic needs and interests of the members are in fact incompatible. If this conflict of interests is extreme, disintegration rather than integration may ensue. Alternatively, if there is a high degree of consensus among the majority, it seems likely that those with conflicting interests, and who are unable or unwilling to force changes in the group's conception of its interests, would dissociate themselves from that group. Thus the two types of results produced by increasing communication within a group are not at all dissimilar: a growing consensus on group interests (albeit possibly among a smaller number of people).

A political community is a territorially based social group in which both the level of group awareness and the internalization of group interests are high. As a social group it has inclusive as well as exclusive aspects. Broadly speaking, on the one hand, membership is open to any who can voluntarily, spontaneously, and in the spirit of free partnership join in the effort to further the community interests; but, on the other hand, the community may exclude a priori certain individuals or classes of individuals from membership. The postbellum South, for example, sought to exclude the Negro from community life in spite of his legal rights and any desire that he may have had to participate in the affairs of the community. And Heinrich Himmler's Gestapo, in the service of Adolf Hitler and the Third Reich, did not hesitate to exclude even the most nationalistic German Jews from the community life.

The territorial base of the political community must at least be definable in its major parts, if not always in terms of precise boundaries. The exact borders of such a community may indeed be undefined, or may even be the subject of dispute between two or more rival political communities. The territorial limits of Virginia, for instance, were not clearly established until that state ceded its western land claims to the Union in 1783. And the boundaries of such countries as

Integrative Processes

Germany or India, and some of the Latin American states, are still open and, occasionally, burning questions.

More significant than the outer limits or boundaries of a political community is its core area (or core areas).[1] Thus the political community of colonial Virginia comprised that part of America that looked to Williamsburg as its capital city, the source of its laws and procedures for the legal settlement of disputes, and the place setting "the standards of taste and elegance."[2] Similarly, the pioneers and settlers who streamed westward out of the original thirteen states in the decades after the War of Independence continued in most cases to direct their allegiance toward and to identify their interests with the core area of the American political community on the Atlantic seaboard.[3]

A political community must have some structures or processes —whether pluralistic or amalgamated—to perform political functions in the community interest. For convenience, it might be said that the major political functions in a community are the familiar legislative, judicial, and executive aspects of government.[4] In the case of a military alliance, which may involve intense distrust among the individual units, the structures and processes might not be of a unified nature at all: the success of the alliance would rest upon the coordination of the individual governments' structures and processes acting in a parallel manner. If the alliance were so successful over a long period of time that the idea of a war among the units came

1. Deutsch et al., *Political Community and the North Atlantic Area*, pp. 72, 137–39.
2. The phrase is Karl W. Deutsch's, in *Nationalism and Social Communication*, p. 88.
3. For a case-study of this process, see Justin H. Smith, *The Annexation of Texas* (New York, Barnes and Noble, 1941).
4. Cf., for a different classification, Almond's introductory chapter in Gabriel A. Almond and James S. Coleman, eds., *The Politics of the Developing Areas* (Princeton, Princeton University Press, 1960), pp. 3–64.

to be considered repugnant or even illegitimate, it would be possible to speak of a pluralistic but integrated political community. Amalgamation could be said to take place if the individual units were to adopt and submit to common governmental structures and processes. Since the eventual outcome of the American case was amalgamated integration (or union), the present study will concern itself primarily with that type of political community.

The minimum degree of popular consensus on political values required for an amalgamated political community comprises, first, the expectation by those forming the community that a common government would meet their needs—those of self-expression, internal peace, and so forth—better or at least not worse than a plurality of governments, and, second, the willingness of the members to comply with the demands of the common government, at least in most cases most of the time. Voluntary compliance is particularly important as a balance to the feature of enforcement mentioned in the previous paragraph: the necessity to restrain or to punish those who violate the values of the community as codified in the laws of the common government. It is, after all, a mixture of compulsion and voluntary compliance that makes politics and facilitates the working of a political community. If, however, the fringe percentage of violators grows too strong for the community structures to handle properly, or if the community itself allows the structures to become so weak that they are incapable of coping with the slightest degree of noncompliance, then it is questionable whether there is any consensus at all on political values within the community. Disagreement on the content of the political arena, a philosophy of government, a division of power within the community and within the government, the rules of political decision-making, the enforcement of decisions in the political arena, and similar topics is subordinated to the desire to remain under a common government rather than join other governments or set up separate governments. Thus even such opposed groups as the Communists and Monarchists of modern France, or the Federalists and the Jeffersonians of early America, could be in agreement on the need for a national form of government.[5]

A political community, then, is a marriage of both love and convenience. Essentially, it is a more or less exclusive social group, within a territory definable in its major parts or at least in terms of its core area, with a common desire to have pluralistic or amalgamated structures and processes for making and enforcing political decisions, and with a willingness to comply with those decisions voluntarily. Each of the requirements is flexible enough to allow a given community to follow a number of paths of possible development. It would be difficult, if not entirely impossible, to describe in advance the scope and limitations of the "ideal" political community. What matters is that the basic elements be present in a proportion that will maintain the community's continued existence and a rule of law within the community.

In the case of the amalgamated political community, a sense of community consists in the willingness of a social group, living in a particular territory, to create common structures and processes of government and to comply with their injunc-

5. There could be, of course, individual exceptions. In 1774, for instance, Patrick Henry declaimed: "The distinctions between Virginians, Pennsylvanians, New Yorkers, and New Englanders, are no more. . . . I am not a Virginian but an American." He nonetheless opposed the adoption of the federal Constitution as finally drafted in 1787, since it encroached too much, he felt, on the rights of the individual states. Henry, then, perceived American integration as a pluralistic concept, as did many fellow Southerners down through the Civil War. Cf., David Potter, "The Historian's Concern with the Problem of Large-Scale Community Formation," in Social Science Research Council, *A Conference on the Social Sciences in Historical Study, June 20–22, 1957* (Stanford, Hoover Institution on War, Revolution, and Peace, 1957, multigraphed), Appendix IV.

tions. Thus it is a broad form of political consensus, in which the participants are themselves conscious of this consensus. Implicit in this definition is a considerable amount of intercommunication, producing not only a group awareness within the community but also an internalization or active sharing of interests among its members strong enough to encourage them to coordinate their behavior in the pursuit of common interests.

When an amalgamated political community has a sense of community and a set of political structures sufficient to enable the achievement or at least the satisfactory pursuit of the community interests, it may be said to be integrated.[6] It is a territorially based group possessing all of the half dozen group attributes discussed above. But how do we know when an aggregate of individuals or countries or colonies is integrated to such an extent that it comprises, or is capable of forming, a political community? There are several signs of successful integration, some or all of which may be present in an enduring political community: when there is a common name for the community used not only by outsiders but also by members of the community in reference to themselves; when there are political parties or leadership groups that transcend purely regional boundaries; when there are common symbols of community (such as flags and anthems), and a common stock of historic memories and myths together with common attitudes toward them; when there is a substantial division of labor within the community in a political or economic sense; when there are common verbal and sign languages; when the term "we" is or may be used to refer to most or all of the members of the community (as, for example, in the phrase, "We, the people of the United States, . . ."); when the members of a

6. Cf. Deutsch et al., *Political Community and the North Atlantic Area*, p. 5 and Caryl P. Haskins, *Of Societies and Men* (New York, Norton, 1951), pp. 30, 155, 161–64.

community communicate more effectively among themselves than with outsiders, and can predict each other's behavior to some degree through introspection; when some or all of the most important institutions of government of the various aggregates have been amalgamated.

Integrative processes, then, are those patterns of activity or thinking that tend to increase a community's sense of community and to create or to balance community structures with community interests. This is not to say that such processes will inevitably produce integration, for it is quite conceivable that some of them might affect the degree of integration between two groups adversely, particularly if used prematurely.

What were the integrative processes that led to a unified American political community? How important to the emergence of a sense of American community were long-run communication transactions, such dramatic events as the Stamp Act crisis, and the creation of common political structures? Two types of evidence are needed to evaluate the relative significance of such processes.

The first sort of evidence, readily available in the basic textbooks and chronologies of American history, comprises a list of the more important formative events of the pre-Revolutionary period as well as an indication of when the colonists created unified community structures. We are not so much interested here in determining when the first intercolonial political structure appeared in the New World, or even the point at which it could be said that the colonists possessed a comprehensive set of governmental structures and processes. More to the point is the question of when the colonists crossed the threshold of amalgamation, when common political structures were performing the most important functions of a national government.

The second sort of evidence is more difficult to secure. The need to find some means to measure or at least to indicate the development of community consciousness in the American colonies is nonetheless of signal importance. It is not simply a question of precedence: who was the first to refer to the colonists as "Americans" rather than as "British subjects," and at what point in time did this occur? Of more interest are the frequency patterns of group awareness, and changes in these patterns: How often did the colonists identify themselves as "Americans" in 1735 in contrast to the number of times they termed themselves "British subjects"? How did the relative frequency of such identifications change by 1775? What were the most important shifts in the degree of similarity and symmetry in colonial attention patterns during the pre-Revolutionary years? How did the amount of attention devoted to American events change relative to that focused on the mother country? In its most useful form, this type of evidence would comprise quantitative indicators of changes in the level of group awareness prevailing among the colonists.

With such evidence, the development of an American sense of community could be depicted graphically. The horizontal axis of the graph would represent the time dimension. The individual years from 1735 to 1775 would be spaced along this axis at regular intervals; notations would indicate the dates of the most important formative events of the colonial period as well as the point at which the colonists crossed the threshold of functional amalgamation. The vertical axis would represent the level of American group awareness. For each year during the four decades it would be possible to state in terms of percentages the level of American group awareness, that is, an indication of the extent to which the colonists perceived themselves as a group. A line connecting the changing yearly percentages, then, would be a curve representing the development of an American group awareness. Correlating this curve with the formative events and the transition to functional amalgamation would give us some important clues about the integration of the eighteenth-century American political community.

What results might we anticipate from such a correlation? If the school of thought that emphasizes formal integrative processes is correct, the curved lines on the graph indicating American community awareness would remain relatively low and relatively stable until after the threshold of functional amalgamation was crossed and substantive institutions of community had been created. Thereafter it would rise at a markedly steeper angle. If, however, the curves were unstable in the years before the colonists crossed the threshold of functional amalgamation, or if they rose either gradually or sharply before that point in time, we might conclude that, on the basis of the evidence, the growth of a sense of American community awareness preceded the creation of amalgamated community structures.

If the theory emphasizing formative events is correct, there would be a rise in the curves representing American community awareness after, for example, the enactment of the Sugar and Stamp Acts in 1764 and 1765. But if changes in the curves of American community awareness preceded in time or were otherwise not related to the formative events of the pre-Revolutionary period, we might question the validity of the thesis stressing the importance of events over other integrative processes.

If it is true that a sense of American community grew along with intercolonial habits of and facilities for communication and that both preceded (and perhaps even accounted for) the formative events and the willingness of the colonists to create and to accept unified community structures, then the curves of American group awareness would be on the rise well before these events occurred. The curves might even rise particularly sharply just before the occurrence of such an event. In the latter case increasing community awareness may have made the colonists especially sensitive to perceived threats from the outside, made them ready to magnify the importance of subsequent events to an extent undreamed of in an earlier era when the colonists were not so conscious of their ties of community. Should the degree of American community awareness be negligible or diminishing prior to these events, however, and should it rise markedly only after their occurrence, then the evidence would seem to cast doubt upon this third theory of political integration.

One final possibility should be noted. The analysis of these data may show that, in its purest form, none of the alternative theories about political integration adequately explains the emergence of the American political community. It may turn out that this community resulted from a combination of integrative processes and that it was the point in time at which each came into play, rather than the presence or absence of any given factor, that was significant in its origin and development. In such a case, we should be able to learn a great deal about the timing of integrative processes from the mutual confrontation of evidence on patterns of group awareness, dramatic or formative events, and the creation of unified governmental institutions.

CHAPTER THREE

The Search for Evidence: Formative Events and Institutions

Among the questions important in evaluating the roles of the various integrative processes in the development of political communities are two that find a prominent, if generally only implicit, place in the standard histories of the eighteenth-century American colonies. First, what were the most significant formative events in the period prior to the outbreak of revolution? And, second, when did the colonists cross the threshold of political or functional amalgamation? It would be helpful to reexamine the oft-analyzed material of American history to seek explicit answers to these questions.

Formative events, it will be recalled, may be of four types: those making strong ties of community even firmer; those strengthening newly formed ties of community, or ties that the passage of time had weakened; those jolting a population (or part of it) into an awareness of significant differences between it and another population (or segment of the population); and those leading separate groups to an awareness of their need for a greater degree of integration. The outstanding characteristic of such events is that they vividly impress themselves upon the consciousness of the populations experiencing them.

At present we are concerned solely with those formative events in the last colonial decades that seemed to work toward the formation of an American political community. That some of these events may also have stimulated pride in or otherwise furthered the integration of an Anglo-American or even purely British political community is clear. Events of this latter sort —perhaps the royal suppression of the Second Jacobite Rebellion at the Battle of Culloden (April 1746), which contemporary colonial newspapers reported extensively and in glowing terms; or the joint British–American conquest of Canada during the French and Indian War—will for the most part be ignored.

An event that clearly encouraged closer cooperation among the colonists was the Stamp Act crisis, which began with the parliamentary enactment of the Sugar Act in March 1764 and ended with the repeal of the Stamp Act two years later. Not only did this crisis emphasize the difference between English and American conceptions of colonial rights, but it drew the colonists together, a movement formally symbolized by the convention of the Stamp Act Congress in New York City and by the adoption of a set of resolutions by that Congress. As Edmund S. Morgan and Helen M. Morgan have written, "Hitherto the colonies had never been able to unite for any purpose, not even for their own defense against the French and Indians. The Stamp Act, much to their own surprise, enabled them to act together."[1] For the colonists, overjoyed that their resistance had forced the British parliament to retreat, such an event doubtless spurred a sense of pride in their unique achievements.

As the events tending most to increase colonial integration

1. Edmund S. and Helen M. Morgan, *The Stamp Act Crisis: Prologue to Revolution* (Chapel Hill, University of North Carolina Press, 1953), p. 294.

in the four decades prior to the Revolutionary War, I would suggest the following:

1739–48 The War of Jenkins' Ear, which turned into the War of the Austrian Succession (or, in colonial parlance, "King George's War").

    1739–41 Caribbean phase: Admiral Vernon's capture of Porto Bello (1739), and defeats at Cartagena (1740) and Cuba (1741); many colonists participated in the last two battles.

    1740–42 Southern American phase: the successful Spanish defense of St. Augustine against an attack led by James Oglethorpe (1740); the Battle of Bloody Marsh (1742), which ended the Spanish threat to Georgia and South Carolina.

    1745 Northern American phase: the capture of the French base at Louisburg by New England troops; Saratoga in New York burned by the French and Indians in retaliation.

    1748 Treaty of Aix-la-Chapelle: the return of Louisburg to the French caused some resentment of British policy among New Englanders.

1754 The Albany Conference, symbolized by the snake cut into eight pieces and the motto "Join or Die."

1754–63 The French and Indian War (later, the Seven Years' War, declared between England and France in 1756).

    1754–57 Predominantly American phase: the

construction of Fort Necessity by George Washington, and its loss to the French (1754); General Braddock's defeat on the banks of the Monongahela (1755), which aroused considerable criticism in the colonies; important but generally indecisive skirmishes near the border between New York and Canada (1755–57).

1758–60 Predominantly Canadian phase: the capture of Louisburg, with the assistance of provincial troops and the "Royal American" regiment (1758); the Battle of Abraham Plains and the capture of Quebec under General James Wolfe (1759); and the capture of Montreal (1760), which ended French resistance in North America.

1763 Treaty of Paris: the formal cession of Canada to Britain.

1763–65 Pontiac's Conspiracy, crushed after extensive Indian attacks on the northwestern frontier.

1763 Imperial reorganization: the Royal Proclamation of 7 October organized the newly conquered territory in America, erased the western land claims of the colonies, restricted the activity of the colonists on the northwestern frontier, provided for the stationing of British troops in the colonies, and asserted the colonial obligation to pay for such measures of defense.

1764–66 The Stamp Act crisis: the enactment of the Sugar Act (March 1764), which presaged further taxation and enforcement; the enactment of the Stamp

Act (March 1765) led to the convention of the Stamp Act Congress (October 1765); intense opposition forced parliament to repeal the acts (March 1766).

1767–70   The Townshend Revenue Acts (passed by parliament in January 1767) met with extensive colonial hostility; all duties, except those on tea, were removed in 1770.

1770   The Boston Massacre (5 March).

1773   The Tea Act was put into effect in April; colonial opposition was epitomized in the Boston Tea Party (16 December).

1774   The first of the so-called "Intolerable Acts" closed the port of Boston (31 March).

1774   The Quebec Act, passed by parliament in June, restated the right of Canadians to practice the Roman Catholic religion.

1774   The first Continental Congress convened (5 September).

1775   The Battle of Lexington (19 April).

1775   The second Continental Congress convened (10 May).

Present-day historians might argue about the relative importance of one or another of these events, but it seems very likely that they would not differ substantially about the list as a whole. Considerably more problematical is the question of when the colonists crossed the threshold of political or functional amalgamation.

In theory, obedience to the Crown and the British parliament united the colonies politically, while the supervision, after 1696, of the Board of Trade united them administratively. With the passage of time, however, royal and parliamentary politics reduced the Board's importance as a decision-making body. It was retained primarily as an agency to investigate and channel colonial problems to the fragmented but authoritative decision-makers, and to provide a gloss of administrative uniformity to all decisions affecting the colonies.

> Actually the lower houses of the [colonial] assemblies prevented the English Government from reaping full results from this relative uniformity in colonial administration, because they controlled both the purse and the patronage; and colonial politics are largely the story of struggles between the assemblies and the royal or proprietary governors. In such a conflict between colonists with a lively sense of their rights and interests, and the representatives of a central government with not so keen a sense of imperial needs or English interests, and which did not wish to be bothered, the colonists generally won. The system worked well enough, for the British Government by veto or disallowance was able to prevent things, such as abuse of paper money, that it did not like; but it was unable to get positive things done, such as full co-operation in time of war.[2]

Although it is true that some cooperation did result from instructions issued to colonial governors, the effect of this system of imperial control in the New World was political decentralization.

This is not to say that no effort was made to unite the po-

2. Samuel Eliot Morison and Henry Steele Commager, *The Growth of the American Republic* (4th ed. New York, Oxford University Press, 1950), 1, 116. Cf. ibid., pp. 84–85, and Leonard W. Labaree, *Royal Government in America* (New Haven, Yale University Press, 1930).

litical structures of the colonies. The Stuart King James II, between 1685 and his downfall in 1689, sought to combine the New England colonies, New York, and New Jersey into a single New England Confederation. The Confederation collapsed, however, when the American version of the Glorious Revolution overthrew the royally appointed governor, Sir Edmund Andres, and the colonies revived their traditional governments.

An intercolonial congress met in New York City during the following year to coordinate policy in the War of the League of Augsburg or, as the Americans called it, "King William's War." The congress, comprising the colonies of Massachusetts Bay, Plymouth, Connecticut, and New York, planned a land attack on Montreal and a sea attack on Quebec. Both ventures ended in failure. Later appeals from individual colonies or their governors for assistance or for a coordinated war effort against the French went for the most part unanswered.[3]

The next major attempt to secure a measure of unity among the colonies did not come until two thirds of a century later when, in June of 1754, delegates from several colonies met at Albany in the colony of New York. The Philadelphia printer Benjamin Franklin, whose *Pennsylvania Gazette* of that year carried a drawing of a snake cut into eight pieces and exhorted the colonists to "Join or Die," drafted a plan of union that embodied many of the ideas later incorporated into the federal Constitution of 1787. But the Albany Plan of Union, accepted by the congress, met speedy defeat at the hands of both the Crown and the colonial assemblies.

Finally, 11 years later, representatives of several colonies met together again, this time, however, to raise their voices in

3. Daniel J. Boorstin, *The Americans: The Colonial Experience* (New York, Random House, 1958), pp. 358–59.

a united protest against the Stamp Act rather than to plan long-term common policies or to create common political structures.

Throughout the colonial period, in the midst of political, military, and economic disunity, there were but two structures that performed governmental functions on an intercolonial basis. The first of these was the post office, which dated from 1692, when William and Mary gave Thomas Neale a patent to establish colonial post offices for a period of twenty-one years. After 19 of those years had passed, a parliamentary Post Office Act reorganized the postal system of the British Empire, placing a Deputy Postmaster for America in New York City. But it was not until 1753, when Benjamin Franklin and his fellow publisher, William Hunter of Virginia, assumed the posts of Joint Deputy Postmasters General for North America, that the colonial post office system became an effective means for intercolonial communication.[4] In considering the post office as an intercolonial structure, therefore, it could be argued that the date of its revival under Franklin and Hunter is the crucial one for our study.

The second intercolonial organization, neither as formal nor as closely coordinated as the post office system, was a network of committees of correspondence. The idea of such committees, linking town, county, and colonial assemblies throughout the continent, emerged in 1764 during the early stages of the Stamp Act crisis. They fell into disuse, however, after the colonists' victory and the repeal of the odious Stamp Act in 1766. The idea did not remain dormant for long. The Massachusetts House of Representatives revived it in its essential

4. William E. Rich, *History of the United States Post Office to the Year 1829* (Cambridge, Harvard University Press, 1924), pp. 31–41. Some pertinent comments on the interlocking roles of the post and the press are made by Kraus, *Intercolonial Aspects of American Culture,* pp. 102–03, and by Boorstin, *The Americans,* pp. 337–40.

34

Formative Events and Institutions

form when, on 11 February 1768, it addressed a "Circular Letter" to the other colonial assemblies. Drafted by the fiery Samuel Adams, the letter protested against the Townshend Acts, claiming that they violated the principle of "no taxation without representation." Within a short period of time the assemblies of seven other colonies endorsed the "Circular Letter" either formally or informally. It was the same Sam Adams who, almost five years later, badgered the Selectmen of Boston until they called a town meeting to protest a rumor that local judges were henceforward to be paid out of customs receipts. On the third evening of the meeting (2 November 1772), he introduced a motion to create a standing committee of correspondence that would "state the Rights of the Colonists and of this Province in particular . . . communicate and publish the same to the several Towns in this Province and to the World as the sense of this Town, with the Infringements and violations thereof that have been or from time to time may be made; also requesting of each Town a free Communication of their Sentiments." [5] The Boston town meeting adopted the motion without a dissenting voice.

Scarcely four months had gone by when, on 12 March 1773, the Virginia House of Burgesses created a committee of correspondence with a much broader scope "to obtain the most early and authentic intelligence of all such acts and resolutions of the British Parliament or proceedings of the Administration, as may relate to or effect [sic] the British colonies in America, and to keep up and maintain a correspondence and communication with our sister colonies, respecting these important considerations." [6] The idea struck a responsive chord

5. Cited in Arthur Meier Schlesinger, *The Colonial Merchants and the American Revolution, 1763–1776* (New York, Columbia University Press, 1918), p. 257.
6. Cited in Lawrence Henry Gipson, *The Coming of the Revolution, 1763–1775* (New York, Harper, 1954), p. 209.

in other colonies. Before long committees of correspondence linked the legislatures of all the American colonies in a single if loosely organized communication network. It was through these committees, slightly over a year later, that the appeal for the convention of the first Continental Congress was sounded throughout America.

The existence of an effective post office system after 1753 and a communication net among the colonial assemblies two decades later hardly denotes an extensive amalgamation of colonial political structures. Together the two agencies performed only minor governmental functions. They did not constitute an attempt at overall amalgamation, at a comprehensive set of structures to carry on such major functions as the distribution of power and income, the establishment of legitimacy principles, the allocation of resources, and the use of force on an intercolonial basis.

Even the first Continental Congress, which met at Carpenter's Hall in Philadelphia on 5 September 1774, was not originally intended to be a permanent structure to legislate for all of the colonies. Much as the Stamp Act Congress had met almost nine years earlier to present a united front of opposition to specific parliamentary measures, so, too, did the delegates of 12 colonies gather in the City of Brotherly Love to coordinate colonial opposition to the so-called Intolerable Acts.

It was this conference, however, that broke the commitment of the colonies to independent and uncoordinated (if often parallel) courses of action. In lieu of accepting Joseph Galloway's plan of union, which called for the creation of an intercolonial legislature that would have coequal control over colonial affairs with parliament, the first Continental Congress drafted petitions of rights to be sent to the people of Great Britain and to the king, and passed a series of resolutions enjoining colonial merchants to refrain from trading with the mother country. These resolves, which the delegates termed an "Association,"

> provided for a system of committees of inspection in every town or county, in order to supervise the non-importation, non-exportation, and non-consumption agreements. The Association was charged to inspect customs entries, to publish the names of merchants who violated the agreements and to confiscate their importations, and even to "encourage frugality, economy, and industry . . . and discountenance every species of extravagance and dissipation, especially all horse-racing, and all kinds of gaming, cockfighting, exhibitions of shews, plays, and other expensive diversions and entertainments." [7]

Thus, based on a claim to legitimacy that was intercolonial in extent, the Association was in fact an effort to exercise amalgamated enforcement functions based on local but parallel activity throughout the continent.

The rush of events in the next half year prevented the colonists from testing the operation of their Association fully in practice; and much of the fury that fell upon Loyalists and merchants who refused to subscribe to the principles of the congressional resolutions during this period stemmed not from the embryo investigative, administrative, judicative, and enforcement agencies created under the terms of this agreement, but from an aroused citizenry or from local committees of

---

7. Morison and Commager, *The Growth of the American Republic, 1,* 188. Cf. Jensen, *The Articles of Confederation,* p. 56. The text of the Association may be found in Henry Steele Commager, ed., *Documents of American History* (6th ed. New York, Appleton-Century-Crofts, 1958), pp. 84–87.

enthusiastic Sons of Liberty. This first major breakthrough in the formation of intercolonial structures was nonetheless of great significance for later political unification.[8]

The ensuing months saw the proliferation of structures seeking to perform intercolonial functions. The second Continental Congress, which met some three weeks after Major Pitcairn's skirmish with the Minutemen at Lexington, began to assume more than mere consultative powers. On 15 June 1775, two days before the Battle of Bunker Hill, the Congress elected George Washington commander-in-chief of a unified "Continental Army," and a week later it began to issue paper currency. On 26 July Congress established a national post office system, with the venerable Benjamin Franklin as Postmaster General. And, before the year was out, not only had Congress created a navy (with one ship) and marine corps, but it had undertaken to open diplomatic relations with France and other European powers through its Committee of Secret Correspondence.

During the course of a single year, the net of intercolonial structures had developed from the level of marginal importance to that of far-reaching functional amalgamation. By the end of 1775, these institutions were performing a significant number of the wartime and peacetime functions of a national government.

That the degree of integration was not perfect is less important than the fact that an intercolonial form of central government, albeit temporary, had been established. It is indeed true that the first few years of the Revolutionary War found a group of pluralistically organized colonies carrying on cer-

8. Indeed, Henry Leffmann concluded that the Association was the first real act of separation from the mother country by the colonists, in "The Real Declaration of Independence: A Study of Colonial History under a Modern Theory," *The Pennsylvania Magazine of History and Biography*, 47 (1923), 281–97.

tain functions in a manner not unlike the operation of a military alliance. A Continental Army with a commander-in-chief existed, to be sure, but George Washington's influence in the decision-making circles of the individual colonies with respect to such matters as recruitment and war-financing seems to have been less than that exerted on alliance partners by the two Supreme Allied Commanders in both world wars of our century, Marshal Foch and General Eisenhower; nor did the Continental Congress of 1775 have any more power to lay and collect taxes than does the NATO Council today. In fact, it could be argued that the colonists, in amalgamating certain functions during the year before the Declaration of Independence, took only the first step along the road that led, by 1791, to overall amalgamation. But it was an important first step. From both a functional and a psychological point of view, the colonists crossed the threshold of political amalgamation in that year of decision, 1775.

CHAPTER FOUR

The Search for Evidence:
Indicators of American Community Awareness

Evidence on the growth and scope of intercolonial communication habits and facilities is at best scanty and far from complete. To be sure, some aspects of these patterns are subject to fairly accurate analysis. Reconstructing the intercolonial commercial and shipping patterns, for example, is possible in many instances through a careful examination of such documents as customs house reports. And an analysis of existing data may reveal the extent to which colonial elites, through ties of family, friendship, or business, formed clustering and overlapping patterns across colonial boundaries.

The problem facing the student of the American political community, however, is to find empirical means to reconstruct or to indicate the informal communication patterns of the politically relevant strata of the colonial population. He must ascertain when the colonists began to think or at least to speak of themselves as "Americans" rather than as transplanted Englishmen. He must determine the extent to which ties of communication existed among the colonies prior to the outbreak of revolution, or whether, as such historians as Greene and Ranney have suggested, the colonies were separated by barriers of indifference and mutual ignorance, interested only in their British connections or in local affairs.

Such a concept as community awareness cannot be measured directly. But, then, neither is the state of a patient's health nor the condition of a national economy subject to direct measurement. The physician or the economist may nonetheless find quantitative measures of aspects of the event he studies—body temperature and blood pressure, for example, or levels of unemployment and capital investment. As the techniques used to measure these aspects become more refined, they may better serve as indicators of the true state of a person's health or of a nation's economy. Is it possible for the student interested in the developing American political community to find adequate means to indicate the degree and growth of community consciousness among the colonists?

One aspect of community awareness is the attachment of symbols of identification, referring to the community, to such events as persons ("an American farmer"), the land inhabited by the community ("the American continent," "America"), an actual or attributed quality ("American ingenuity"), a concept ("the American way of life"), and so forth. Such symbols are two-sided coins. On the one side is the recognition of the community's existence, and its distinctiveness from other such communities, by people who are not a part of the community; and, on the other, a similar acknowledgment of that fact—whether the acknowledgment be consciously or unconsciously made—by members of the community itself.

The idea of symbolic identification raises a number of significant, quantitative questions about the colonists' changing identification patterns. When, for example, did the perception of "Americans" as a group arise? When did the colonists stop referring to themselves as "His Majesty's subjects" or as

Symbols of American Community

"British colonists"—perceptions compatible with membership in a British (or, possibly, Anglo-American) political community—and start more often calling themselves "Americans"? When did their brethren in the mother country begin to make this verbal distinction? If there was in fact a shift in the use of the symbol "Americans," did colonists with explicit Tory sympathies adopt the same patterns as colonial "Sons of Liberty" did? When did the colonists begin to look at the land they inhabited as "America" rather than as "the British colonies" or even "British America"? Did they recognize the land as "American" before or after perceiving its population to be "American"? Or did these symbolic distinctions emerge at the same time?

Finding a suitable source of data for studying such changes in the attitudes and perceptions of the politically relevant portion of the colonial population poses a serious research problem. One requirement or test of suitability is that the source of data be important for a significant share of that population. It must provide a degree of continuity over a good part of the colonial years or at least those crucial decades immediately prior to the outbreak of the Revolution. It must enable us to examine differences between the modes of Tory and Patriot attitudes, between the modal attitudes of different colonies.

In spite of their shortcomings, the newspapers in colonial America fulfill these requirements most satisfactorily.[1] Their continuous publication at regular weekly intervals enabled the printers to expose the colonists to a certain body of news and opinion, as well as to certain patterns of symbol usage, over a long period of time. That the colonists were willing to accept, or at least to read, the news and opinions offered by these

1. See Richard L. Merritt, "Public Opinion in Colonial America: Content Analyzing the Colonial Press," *Public Opinion Quarterly*, 27 (1963), 356–71.

poorly printed and often dingy journals is indicated indirectly by the life span that some of them enjoyed. While individual pamphlets, such as Thomas Paine's *Common Sense,* might attract immediate attention, possibly even leading to direct action, the newspapers reflected and helped to shape colonial perceptions, attitudes, and interests more persistently and over a much longer period of time. An analysis of the colonial press, looking for the changing frequency of symbols used to refer to the colonists collectively and to the land they inhabited, would tell us much about the changing identification patterns of the eighteenth-century Americans.

Moreover, information about the distribution of news space in these newspapers would provide us with evidence about a second aspect of community awareness: the extent to which the colonists focused their attention upon each other and upon the American community as a whole. Of prime importance is the direction toward which the colonists looked in their search for news. How much space did the newspapers devote to local, intercolonial, British, and foreign news? To what extent were they aware of and interested in events and problems of colonies other than their own? When did they become more interested in the news and gossip of other colonies than they were in news from the mother country? If and when colonial events began to crowd other news out of the colonial span of attention, was British news or that of European courts and wars more likely to lose its saliency for the American newspaper editors? How great, relative to that reserved for purely local news, was the news space devoted to events affecting the American community as a whole?

By comparing the attention patterns of several of the main population centers in the colonies, it would be possible to discover the extent to which intercolonial communication was symmetrical and balanced. Were shifts in their patterns of attention parallel, or did some colonies cling longer than others to traditional patterns? Which colonies were the leaders in promoting intercolonial communication ties and in giving a greater share of their attention to colonial events? Were there any colonies whose affairs and problems were more likely to be noticed and reported in the newspapers of the other colonies?

In attempting to answer such questions, I analyzed the frequency and distribution of place-name symbols used in the colonial press from 1735 to 1775. I systematically examined the news columns of four randomly selected issues per year of newspapers from each of five colonial population centers— Boston, New York, Philadelphia, Williamsburg, and Charleston in South Carolina—including journals from Boston of both Tory and Patriot persuasion.[2] Using standardized coding procedures and a pretested symbol list, I counted each appearance of the name of an actual political unit, whether it was a continent ("Europe"), a country ("Italy"), a region ("the Carolinas" or "the northern colonies"), a province or colony ("Virginia"), a county or other unit of local government ("Warwickshire" or "Suffolk County"), or a city or town ("London" or "Boston"). In a search for useful indicators of colonial attention and identification patterns, I then analyzed three different aspects of these place-name symbols.

First of all, the place-name symbols were categorized into the broadest sets possible: American symbols, comprising references to the area that later became the United States of Amer-

2. The newspapers were: *The Massachusetts Gazette. And Boston News-Letter* (issues from 1735 to 1775) and *The Boston Gazette and Country Journal* (1762–1775); *The New-York Weekly Journal* (1735–1751) and *The New-York Mercury* (1752–1775); *The Pennsylvania Gazette* (1735–1775); the various *Virginia Gazettes* (under William Parks from 1736 to 1750, and under William Hunter and his successors from 1751 to 1775); and *The South-Carolina Gazette* (1735–1775). Appendix I discusses the research design in greater detail.

ica; British symbols, including the British possessions of Minorca and Gibraltar in Europe as well as the British Isles; and other symbols, consisting in Canadian, Caribbean, South American, European, Asian, and African place-names. Such a tabulation may serve as an indicator of the global focus of attention of the colonial press. It would show, for example, changes in the importance of news about American events relative to that of the mother country and elsewhere.

Second, American place-name symbols were then broken down further into four subcategories: symbols referring to the American continent as a whole and to its inhabitants (or "continental symbols"); symbols referring to places in the region (that is, the northern, middle, or southern colonies) in which the newspaper using them was published; symbols referring to places in the newspaper's own home colony; and symbols referring to places in colonies other than those of the home region. A graphic distribution of these symbols would pinpoint the areas in America upon which the newspapers focused their attention during the colonial years. Such a tabulation would also suggest the extent to which the newspapers' attention patterns were parallel and symmetrical, as well as the importance of the community as a whole in their news columns.

Third, the continental symbols—those referring to the colonies as a whole and to their inhabitants—were then categorized in three ways: according to whether they appeared in news items of American, British, or foreign origin; according to whether they referred to the land itself or to the inhabitants; and according to whether they identified the land or its inhabitants as part of a British or American political community. In the last instance the spectrum of identifications of the land might run from "British America" or "His Majesty's colonies" to "the colonies" or "the provinces" to "America." An analysis of such symbols would indicate whether outsiders or members of the community itself first recognized a distinctly American political community. It would also indicate whether eighteenth-century writers first perceived the American land or its population to be separate from the British political community (or whether these symbolic distinctions came at the same time). Most important, such an analysis would indicate the colonists' changing patterns of self-identification.

These three sets of data may serve as indicators of the growth of community awareness in colonial America. Their correlation with evidence about formative events and the colonial transition to unified political structures would provide a useful test of the alternative theories of political integration discussed above.

In another sense, the attention patterns of the colonists can be used to indicate intercolonial communication patterns as well as the growth of community awareness. The focus of a group's attention—those events to which its members give heed—reflects, above all, the volume of messages (or communication transactions) received by the group from all sources, and the group's priority ratings for incoming messages competing for its attention. When a group alters its focus of attention in favor of another group (when, for example, colonial Massachusetts devotes a greater share of its attention span to messages stemming from New York) it may be the result of one factor or a combination of them: the source has more messages to communicate (skirmishes are taking place in New York); the source is interested in directing its messages to a particular receiving group (New York is trying to enlist Massachusetts' assistance in the war); the communication channels between the source and the receiver have improved (through the creation of new post roads or the construction of more ships to ply between New York and Massachusetts);

the receiver is predisposed to accept messages from the particular source (many inhabitants of Massachusetts have friends or relatives who have recently moved to New York); or the receiver, with expanded reception facilities, is able to accept more messages from all sources (the arrival of new printing presses and more newsprint in Massachusetts enables that colony's newspapers to circulate more news about events throughout the world, including those of New York).[3] Whatever the reason, however, the result is the same: an increased volume of communication between the source and the receiver.

The volume of attention to intercolonial affairs indicates the saliency of such news in the minds of the readers (or, at least in the minds of the colonial newspaper editors). The saliency of this news, however, is but one dimension of the relationship between the growth of intercolonial communication transactions and integrative processes in colonial America. An increase in the communication links between two groups does not automatically lead to an enhanced sense of common destiny. That modern American newspapers and politicians devote a great deal of attention to the affairs of the Soviet Union by no means indicates that the two countries are nearing the threshold of integration. And the mind of Adolf Hitler, preoccupied with the Jews, saw extermination rather than integration as the final solution.

The second dimension lies in what might be termed the quality of the communication transactions, in the ratio of rewarding or mutually beneficial transactions to the total num-

3. These factors may be mutually self-reinforcing. An increased number of messages coming from New York may whet the New Englanders' appetites for more news from their sister colony; and if improved channels of communication may lead to an increase in their communication loads or number of messages, it is also true that an increase of communication between the two colonies may necessitate the expansion of the communication channels.

ber of transactions. When the individual colonies threw their spotlights of attention upon the other colonies, what did they see? Did the Southerners see the New Englanders as "the Goths and Vandals of America," as did the Loyalist Jonathan Boucher? Or were they more captivated by the view of Northerners as brethren oppressed by the Redcoats stationed in Boston? Did the image that the colonists had of each other become more or less friendly as the colonial years passed? Was the attention paid to events occurring in Great Britain—parliamentary proceedings, for example, or incidents at the Court of St. James's—more or less favorable in the decade prior to the Declaration of Independence than in the 1730s or 1740s?

The present study will deal with only the first dimension of the intercolonial communication transactions: the volume of attention paid by the colonists to their own colonies and to others in the North American continent, to the mother country and to other parts of the globe. This necessitates the assumption that the quality of attention paid by the colonies to each other rose (or at least did not decline) in the period before the outbreak of revolution. A concomitant assumption is that the quality of colonial attention given to England declined during these years, that is, that the colonists' comments about the mother country appeared in ever less favorable contexts.

These two assumptions are not unrealistic. It is a commonplace that, on the whole, the quality of communication transactions among the colonies improved during the decades prior to 1775, particularly in contrast to the deteriorating transactions between the colonies and England. Those who argue that the colonists had no sense of community awareness before that date most often base their case on indifference rather than fear and mutual distrust, on parochialism rather than hate. And even such historians as Evarts Boutell Greene have suggested that, in spite of "prevalent and extended ignorance" as well as "mutual prejudice and clashing interests" separating the colonies, the "intercolonial barriers" became "less formidable" during the colonial period.[4] Greene also recognized that "an increasingly detached and critical attitude toward British society" was a "factor in the rise of Americanism." [5]

A brief test applied to place-name symbols appearing in samples of colonial newspapers for 1738 and 1768 tends to bear out this commonplace. Following the general sampling procedure outlined above and a standard means for indicating the quality of symbol usage, I examined the contexts in which symbols referring to American and British place-names occurred. It seems to have been characteristic of the colonial press that few such symbols appeared in contexts clearly approving or disapproving of the place-name represented by the symbol. According to the sample, however, American symbols appeared in more favorable contexts in 1768 than in 1738, while the reverse was the case for British symbols.[6]

4. Greene, *The Revolutionary Generation*, p. 185; Evarts Boutell Greene, *The Foundations of American Nationality* (rev. ed. New York, American Book Company, 1935), p. 340.
5. Greene, *The Revolutionary Generation*, p. 187.
6. Using the method described by Ithiel de Sola Pool (with the collaboration of Harold D. Lasswell, Daniel Lerner, et al., *Symbols of Democracy*, Hoover Institute Studies, Series C, No. 4 [Stanford, Stanford University Press, 1952], p. 14), I subtracted the number of American symbols appearing in unfavorable contexts from the number of such symbols appearing in favorable contexts, and divided the remainder by the sum of all American symbols appearing in the sample of newspapers for each year. The formula for this is $\frac{F-U}{F+U+N}$, where F is the number of symbols appearing in favorable contexts, U the number appearing in unfavorable contexts, and N the number appearing in neutral contexts. I then performed the same test for British symbols during these two years. For American symbols in 1738, the quality of symbol usage was $-.013$; by 1768 it had gone up to $\pm.000$. The change in the quality of British symbol usage was from $+.079$ in 1738 to $+.004$ in 1768. The low scores result primarily from the high number of symbols appearing in neutral contexts.

So far we have discussed changing symbol usage in the colonial press solely as an indicator of intercolonial communication patterns and the development of an American community awareness. But what about the other facet of community consciousness—the internalization of group interests? It is, of course, possible to ask when the colonists shared interests and coordinated their actions to a degree high enough to permit them to increase their capabilities, to prevent the revival of objectionable acts of trade and navigation, to prevent the royal foreclosure of future colonial expansion, to form a common government. The answers to these questions, however, would not indicate completely the extent to which the colonists shared expectations and demands, or when they shared such expectations and demands beyond the minimum level required for the success of a political community. Through a careful investigation of existing source data, such as public records, diaries, newspapers, letters, and other documents, the analyst could make some shrewd judgments on these points. But should the judgments of independent scholars differ—and, as I have suggested, they certainly do differ—how can we determine which of them are valid?

The internalization of group interests seems to be a natural concomitant of the development of group awareness. The indicators of American group awareness discussed above give us information about the volume and salience of intercolonial communication transactions and about the degree to which the colonists identified themselves collectively as a group separate and distinct from the British political community. Let us assume that the level of American group awareness, as suggested by these indicators, was low in the 1730s. (This assumption, by the way, is not only intuitively reasonable but is also validated by the data presented in later chapters.) Proceeding from this assumption we may imagine four alternative developments in the ensuing four decades. (1) Both the intercolonial communication transactions and level of American self-identification may have remained constant or declined. An earlier chapter discussed the difficulty that individuals with low rates of intercommunication have in determining what interests they in fact have in common, let alone deciding upon appropriate strategies to achieve these interests. Their points of commonness are likely to be few in number and poorly articulated. If the level of communication within the group does not rise with the passage of time, then it seems unlikely that the individuals would broaden the scope of their shared interests and increase the extent of their active cooperation. Moreover, in this first case, the constant or declining level of group identification would give us no reason to believe that such efforts, if made, were successful. In short, if this situation had prevailed in eighteenth-century America, then we would anticipate that the result would have been the stagnation of any American community consciousness at the level of the 1730s. (2) But suppose that intercolonial communication remained constant or declined while the level of American self-identification rose. This situation may have had one or both of two effects. First of all, the colonists might have internalized to a high degree a limited number of (vague and perhaps poorly understood) interests, that is, those shared by colonists in the 1730s. Second, the colonists might have developed a false sense of consciousness, projecting their own disparate interests upon the "group" as a whole. Either would have been unstable: the former would have made new alignments (such as regional groupings) based on immediate and concrete interests highly likely; the latter would have ended in disillusion and dissolution with the emergence of any real or perceived conflict among the colonies. (3) There may have been increasing communication together with a constant or declining level of collective American self-identification. This development is no less the story of some potential political communities than it is of many marriages and other social groupings. It suggests the classic instance of increasing awareness of the real obligations of membership in a group resulting in disputes about or even a rejection of these obligations. In such instances the use of collective symbols of identification normally would not increase but would, in all probability, decline.[7] (4) Both intercolonial communication transactions and American self-identification may have increased. In such a situation, we would anticipate that the individual who continues to assert his group identity, or who asserts it increasingly more strongly, is becoming more and more conscious of the demands and expectations of membership in the group.

In all these cases the level of community awareness can be used to indicate roughly the extent to which the colonists internalized community interests and, hence, in a broad sense, to indicate the development of American community consciousness. This may be stated somewhat more formally: the scope and direction of community consciousness vary directly with simultaneous changes in the scope and direction of both intergroup communication and group identification patterns. I must, however, stress the fact that this hypothesis rests on

7. It is possible that Virginians and New Yorkers of the 1820s may firmly have believed themselves to be Americans, and yet may have held differing views of the (pluralistic vs. amalgamated) constitutional nature of the American republic; by the 1850s, however, differences in perspectives may have led to differing group identities, as Virginians increasingly more often called themselves "Southerners," while New Yorkers termed themselves "Northerners" or "Unionists." Professor Potter has suggested that there was a "shift from primary American loyalties accompanied by secondary Southern loyalties to primary Southern loyalties accompanied by secondary American loyalties," in his discussion, "The Historian's Concern with the Problem of Large-Scale Community Formation," *Social Sciences in Historical Study,* p. 7.

rational postulates and logic rather than upon empirical foundations discussed in any detail.

Thus the proposed measures of attention and identification patterns in the colonial press serve a variety of purposes. Most directly these measures (of the global focus of attention in the newspapers, of the focus of attention on places within the American continent, of the symbols used to identify the American land and people) may serve to indicate the colonists' changing sense of community awareness. They may also serve as indicators of intercolonial communication patterns and, if in a less direct sense, of the colonists' changing community consciousness. Moreover, their correlation with evidence about formative events in colonial society and the colonists' adoption of unified political institutions would provide a useful test of the alternative theories of political integration discussed earlier.

Symbols of American Community: An Overview

The following three chapters analyze different aspects of symbol usage in the colonial press: the overall focus of attention; the attention paid to place-names within America itself; and the terms used in the colonial press to refer to the American land and people. This chapter provides a brief summary of the findings. Since any summary must reduce a maze of complexities to a general characterization that highlights the most salient points, the reader interested in more detailed information will want to refer to specific sections of the data chapters. In any event a careful perusal of the charts in these chapters will add greatly to the reader's understanding of the data presented and analyzed.

THE OVERALL FOCUS OF ATTENTION
OF THE COLONIAL PRESS

From 1735 to 1775 the newspapers sharply increased their attention to symbols of American place-names, while maintaining a fairly steady interest in Britain and paying ever less attention to European and other place-name symbols (Figure 5-1). The American share grew from 13.2 per cent in the decade 1735–44 to 34.3 per cent in 1765–75—an increase of

160 per cent—and, in the last two pre-Revolutionary years, consumed well over half (54.2%) of the newspapers' total symbol space. For the period as a whole, the press devoted roughly one fifth of its symbol space to British place-names. The space occupied by the Anglo-American community in 1735–44, by the way, was given over to America alone by 1765–75.

Generally speaking, all the newspapers followed the same patterns of symbol usage. While the patterns were the same, however, the levels of symbol usage varied widely: the *Massachusetts Gazette* paid more than average attention to American events in 38 of the 41 years (93%); and the *Pennsylvania Gazette* paid less than average attention to symbols of American place-names in 32 of these years (78%). Divergencies among the individual newspapers nonetheless decreased with the passage of the years. By the end of the colonial era their foci of attention were remarkably congruent.

The process by which American place-names came to play an important role in the colonial focus of attention was essentially cyclical. Each of the cycles was shorter and at a higher level than the previous one. And while their peaks coincide with years of significant events in colonial history (such as 1766, the year in which the Stamp Act was repealed), the more important points in the cycles are the years when downward trends were reversed (such as 1763). What occurred during those years, we must ask, that arrested a declining interest in events taking place in America?

Collectively and individually, the newspapers began to shift their attention dramatically to American place-name symbols in 1763. Intensive analysis of the *Boston Gazette* and the *New-York Mercury* reveals that the upsurge began in July 1763—months after news about the Treaty of Paris had died down in the journals, but well before reports of pending parliamentary legislation on taxation and restrictions on the westward movement of the colonists became current.

Among the American place-name symbols, collective self-referent symbols, that is, those referring to the colonies or the colonists as a single unit (e.g. "His Majesty's colonies," "Americans"), increased most markedly. From 1735 to 1761 the average newspaper devoted about 6.5 per cent of its American symbol space to such symbols; this average quadrupled to 25.8 per cent in the fourteen years from 1762 to 1775. The evidence, not so clear as in the overall distribution of symbols, because of the smaller number of symbols, suggests that here, too, the most significant upward swing began in the summer of 1763. Of the individual colonies, Virginia gave almost twice as much space as the average newspaper to collective self-referent symbols; New York, Pennsylvania, and South Carolina were about average; and Massachusetts was somewhat less than average.

Symbols referring to places in the home colonies of the individual newspapers consumed about three tenths of the total American symbol space during the 41 years. It should be added, however, that the percentage share decreased from 40.4 per cent in 1735–44 to 26.3 per cent in 1765–75. Massachusetts and South Carolina newspapers seemed most preoccupied with local events, while those of New York and Pennsylvania were least self-preoccupied; Virginia's emphasis on local events was about average.

The analysis of the patterns of attention to one another among the five colonies was done by the Alker computer program for transaction flows. The balance of intercolonial attention was not symmetrical, although these patterns became increasingly congruent during the 41 years. No relationship was found between the distance separating colonies and their mutual flow of attention. Of the five colonies considered, Pennsylvania was most in balance with the others, followed by Massachusetts and New York, with South Carolina and Virginia trailing behind.

These results, viewed as a whole, reveal three distinct perceptual patterns in colonial America. The middle colonies (Pennsylvania and to a lesser extent New York) had a pluralistic outlook, concentrating their attention on other colonies rather than on themselves or on a collective concept identifying all the colonies as a single political community. The southern colonies (and Virginia more so than South Carolina) were nationalistic. They led in paying attention to the collective concept, while they were not overly concerned with either themselves or other colonies individually. Massachusetts was relatively self-centered. It was not particularly prone to be attentive to other colonies and was the least interested of the five in the collective concept.

SELF-PERCEPTIONS: VIEWS OF THE AMERICAN
LAND AND PEOPLE

To get at changing group identities among the colonists, a separate analysis of collective self-referent symbols was undertaken. These include symbols referring to both the land ("the British colonies," "America") and the people inhabiting that land ("His Majesty's colonists," "Americans"). Of primary interest is the implicit or explicit identification content of the symbols—whether they refer to the land or people as part of a British (or possibly Anglo-American) political community or as part of a distinctly American political community. Since it seemed likely that the identification patterns of colonial journalists would differ from those of their colleagues in the mother country or elsewhere, the symbols of common identity were also categorized according to whether they appear in articles with American, British, or foreign datelines.

English writers (at least those whose articles and letters appeared in the colonial newspapers) preceded American writers in identifying both the land and its people as "American." Throughout the whole of the 41 years, articles with British datelines more often than not associated the territory with an American community. The transition for American writers did not come until about 1763. Symbols referring to the population were far fewer in the newspapers, for not until the 1760s did the reference to Americans as a collective unit become popular in the colonial press. Available evidence indicates that Englishmen began to identify the colonial population as "Americans" persistently after 1763—a decade before Americans themselves did so.

Accompanying these changes was a subtler but equally interesting shift in the use of self-referent symbols. If we subdivide these symbols according to whether they explicitly or implicitly identify the colonies as "British" or "American," then we have a spectrum of four categories: "explicit British," "implicit British," "implicit American," and "explicit American." Among articles with British datelines, the ratio of "implicit British" to "explicit British" symbols mushroomed from 0.4 to 1 in 1735–44 to 3.3 to 1 in 1765–75; although the share of "implicit American" symbols stayed the same during this span of time, the ratio of "explicit American" to "explicit" and "implicit British" grew from 0.9 to 1 in 1735–44 to 1.5 to 1 in 1765–75 (Tables 7-1 and 7-2). Meanwhile, among articles with American datelines, the share of "implicit British" and "implicit American" symbols was expanding at the expense of "explicit British" symbols, with the share of "explicit American" symbols declining only somewhat (Tables 7-3 and 7-4). These findings suggest two points. First, as the colonial years rolled by, English no less than American writers were increasingly reluctant to assert strong imperial ties between colonies and mother country. Very few symbols indeed identified the colonial territory explicitly as British during the last pre-Revolutionary decade. Second, while the colonists were consciously or unconsciously substituting ambiguity (albeit a somewhat "pro-American" ambiguity) for precision in their use of symbols, their brethren in England were symbolically asserting the separation of America from Britain.

The shifts in attention and symbolic identification came neither overnight nor as a result of slow, steady, and virtually automatic processes. Judging from the use of symbols in their newspapers, the colonists had to learn to think in a purely American rather than in an imperial context. The learning process seemed to progress rapidly at some stages, to hold relatively steady in others, and in some cases even to decline. It moved more rapidly in New England, slowly in the middle and southern colonies until the 1760s. During the last colonial decade the individual newspapers presented quite similar patterns of symbol usage. In all cases the secular trend of the learning curve, despite cyclical fluctuations, was upward throughout the years from 1735 to 1775.

CHAPTER FIVE

The Colonists Discover America

The overall focus of the colonists' attention shifted dramatically during the four decades before the War of Independence. The nature and extent of this shift may best be seen by categorizing into three broad groups all place-name symbols appearing in the colonial press: American symbols, comprising references to the area that later became the United States of America; British symbols; and other symbols, consisting in Canadian, Caribbean, South American, European, Asian, and African place-names. The next task is to find a composite picture of the colonial focus of attention as a whole. This may be done by averaging the attention patterns of newspapers from the five colonial towns of Boston, New York, Philadelphia, Williamsburg, and Charleston in South Carolina.[1] We

1. This is found by dividing the total number of symbols in each category by the total number of symbols in all categories appearing each year in all of the newspapers together. Thus the composite is the mean of the actual occurrence of symbols rather than the mean of the percentage distributions for each newspaper. The symbol distribution of the *Boston Gazette* will not be included in the composite picture, since the analysis of that newspaper covered only the 14 years from 1762 to 1775; its symbol distribution is sufficiently different from the others that its inclusion for 14 of the 41 years would distort the composite picture of the colonial newspapers.

may then consider the five sets of newspapers individually, to see how they differed from the average or composite attention patterns. Of particular interest is the question of which colonies led in focusing attention upon American events.

THE COLONISTS VIEW THE WORLD'S NEWS: A COMPOSITE PICTURE

At a first glance a curve representing the composite percentage distribution of place-name symbols in the colonial press (Figure 5-1) seems to show a high degree of correlation between levels of interest in America on the one hand and, on the other, some of the more spectacular events of the colonial era. Except for two peak years in 1738 and 1740 (the latter of which corresponds to a critical year in the War of Jenkins' Ear), the curve remained low until the outbreak of the French and Indian War in 1754. The highest point of the ensuing cycle occurred in the year of Braddock's defeat, 1755. In the next years, as the scene of battle in North America began to shift from American to Canadian fields, the percentage share of American symbols dropped off by more than 60 per cent. The period from 1764 to 1766, which encompassed the announcement, enactment, and repeal of the Stamp Act, was one of heightened attention paid by the newspapers to colonial events; for the first time they devoted more than one third of their symbol space to American symbols. The next decade saw three more peak years in the curve representing interest in colonial events: 1768, when opposition to the Townshend Acts was mounting; 1770, the year of the Boston Massacre; and 1774–75, the tension-filled years of the Intolerable Acts, the first Continental Congress, the Association, and the second Continental Congress. In these latter two years the newspapers devoted over one half of their symbol space to American events.

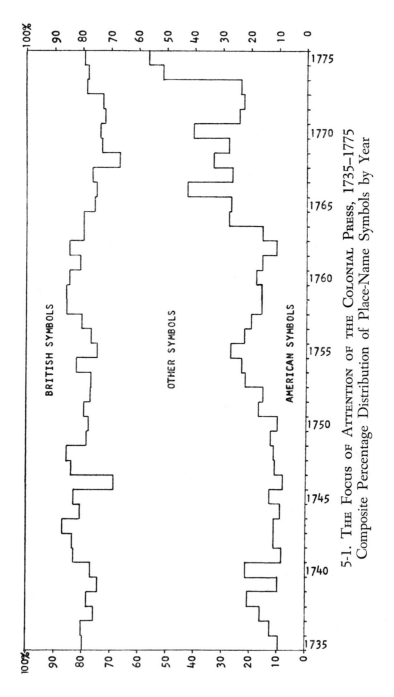

5-1. The Focus of Attention of the Colonial Press, 1735–1775
Composite Percentage Distribution of Place-Name Symbols by Year

A similar if not so marked pattern occurred in the distribution of British symbols. The high points of the two rather shallow cycles of the 25 years prior to 1760 appeared in 1739 and 1755—the early years of the War of Jenkins' Ear and the French and Indian War respectively—while the troughs, from 1743 to 1748 (with the exception of the year 1746) and from 1758 to 1760, were time periods coincidental with the intensively European phases of the War of the Austrian Succession and the Seven Years' War. In the year 1746 (the most noticeable aberration from the trend of shallow cycles), the Royal Army defeated the Pretender's forces at Culloden, ending the Second Jacobite Rebellion. In 1759 began another cycle that reached its peak in 1768 before dropping off to a level not too different from that of the 1730s and 1740s.

There is another aspect of the total picture, however, one tempering the conclusion that the focus of attention in the colonial press changed solely in response to single, spectacular events. Considering first of all just the American share of the total symbol count, three interesting points emerge.

First, the essentially cyclical pattern representing the emphasis upon American symbols in the colonial press—with its low points in 1735 (or earlier), 1744–46, 1762, and 1772, and its peaks in 1740, 1755, 1766, and 1775 (or possibly later)—appears in sharp relief. I have already noted that the peaks in the curves were years of important and dramatic events in colonial history. It is probably not accidental, nor is it particularly surprising, that the newspapers gave heavy emphasis to American symbols during those years. More significant are the first years of increasing attention to America—1747, 1763, and 1773—following troughs in the cycles. What was it during those years that arrested a declining interest in American events, sending the curve upward? We might also ask why the curves dropped off sharply immediately after the spectacular events of the peak years.

Second, the cycles of attention to American symbols became progressively shorter. A time span of fifteen years divided the first two peaks, eleven years passed between 1755 and 1766, and nine years between the latter date and 1775. A similar pattern marked the cycles' visibly low points of 1744–46, 1762, and 1772.

Third, and related to the ever shorter cycles, the general trend of the curve was upward. This can be seen by drawing a line connecting the peaks of the cycles, or even their low points. The low year of 1762 was on a plane higher than the previous low period of 1744–46, while the lowest point of the next cycle, 1772, was on an even higher level. In the period from 1764 to 1775 there were but three years in which the American share of the symbol distribution dropped to a plane slightly below the 1755 peak. During only six of the 29 years from 1735 to 1763 did American self-awareness reach the 20 per cent level; afterwards it never fell below that level.[2] In a metaphorical sense, the trend toward shorter and higher cycles is similar to an automobile's motor being started on a cold day: with each new contact the motor is more responsive and turns over more quickly, until finally it begins to run smoothly. The data found in the present inquiry suggest that the cycles of increasing and decreasing interest in American events had turned into a smooth pattern of self-awareness and self-interest by 1774.

2. On the basis of these data, some interesting (although a posteriori) parabolic curves could be constructed, showing the progressively shorter and steadily rising cycles. For future studies of the pre-Revolutionary era in America, such curves showing the rise of American community senti-ments might be projected and tested. These data, if verified through addi-tional empirical tests, would seem to contradict the theory of revolution proposed by James C. Davies, "Toward a Theory of Revolution," *American Sociological Review*, 27 (1962), 5–19.

There is still another point of importance in the distribution of the broad categories of symbols: the ratio of American to British symbols. As may be seen in Figure 5-1, attention to British symbols fluctuated around the 20 per cent level during the entire 41 years. From 1735 to 1753 there was not a single year in which the number of American symbols was greater than the number of British symbols. The ten years of the French and Indian War (1754–63) comprised a transitional period, during which American symbols appeared more often in the colonial press than did British symbols one half of the time. Only three times during the next twelve years did British symbols take precedence over American symbols, and by 1775 there were almost three American symbols for each British. British and American symbols combined accounted for roughly one out of every three (34.7%) symbols in the colonial newspapers from 1735 to 1763. In the twelve years after 1764 one out of three (34.0%) was American. Thus, by the decade prior to the Revolution, it might be said that the American political community alone had taken over the space in the colonial press previously allocated to the entire Anglo-American community.

THE INDIVIDUAL NEWSPAPERS
AND THE WORLD'S NEWS

The curves representing the American share of the total symbol count, as shown in Figure 5-2, are roughly similar for each of the newspapers included in the analysis. This is not to say that the curves are identical in all respects, or even that they are on the same level. The American share of symbols in the *Massachusetts Gazette,* for example, was above the average or composite distribution curve 90 per cent of the time—in 26 of the first 29 years, and in each of the last twelve years of the period. The *South-Carolina Gazette* paid a greater than average amount of attention to America about one half (51.7%)

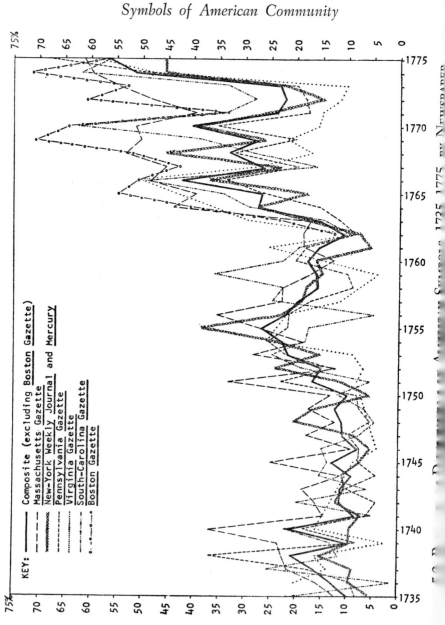

of the time between 1735 and 1763, and in ten of the twelve years from 1764 to 1775 (an overall average of 61.0%). For the 28 years for which the *Virginia Gazette* is currently available, the percentage of space devoted to American symbols was below the average in 21 (or 75.0%) of them; the curve for the *Pennsylvania Gazette* was below the composite curve almost four times in five (78.0%); while the New York newspapers gave a greater than average share of attention to American events only 34.1 per cent of the time. The *Boston Gazette's* curve was higher than the composite in each of the 14 years analyzed. In spite of these variations, however, it is significant that, in terms of the share of symbol space devoted to American symbols, the degree of difference among the newspapers declined during the course of the 41-year period.[3]

The basic similarity as well as the marginal dissimilarities of the distribution curves for the various newspapers can be shown most clearly and simply by linear regressions or trend lines. Such trend lines smooth out all fluctuations into single, straight lines, the slopes of which, that is, the average yearly percentage change for the period as a whole, provide means for accurate comparisons.[4] Figures 5-3A and 5-3B reveal that for both the entire 41-year period (1735–75) and the crucial 14

3. In terms of the share of symbol space devoted to American symbols, the degree of correlation among the ten pairs of newspapers in the period 1764–75 was more than twice as high as in the 1735–63 period. Using the nonparametric "Spearman Rank Order Correlation Coefficient r_s," the average coefficient of correlation for the ten pairs of newspapers for the earlier period was $\bar{r}_s = .24$. The coefficient of correlation was significant at the .05 level (using a one-tailed test) for only three of the ten pairs, and was not significant at that level for the average or mean coefficient. For the twelve years from 1764 to 1775, the average coefficient of correlation was $\bar{r}_s = .57$. The mean coefficient as well as those for seven of the ten pairs were significant at the .05 level. For a more extensive discussion of this test, see Sidney Siegel, *Nonparametric Statistics for the Behavioral Sciences* (New York, McGraw-Hill, 1956), pp. 202–13.

4. For a discussion of this technique, see Harold T. Davis, *Political Statistics* (Evanston, The Principia Press of Illinois, 1954), pp. 168–69.

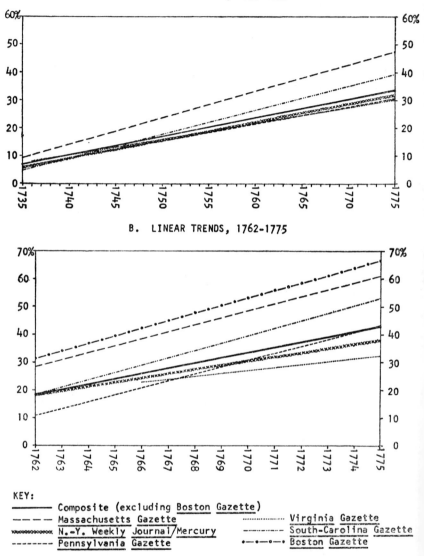

A. LINEAR TRENDS, 1735-1775

B. LINEAR TRENDS, 1762-1775

KEY:

———— Composite (excluding Boston Gazette)
— — — Massachusetts Gazette
xxxxxxxxxxxxx N.-Y. Weekly Journal/Mercury
- - - - - - - Pennsylvania Gazette

················ Virginia Gazette
—··—··— South-Carolina Gazette
•—•—•—• Boston Gazette

5-3. Trends in American Symbol Usage, by Newspaper

years leading up to the outbreak of the Revolution (1762–75) the secular trend of attention to American events rose. In no newspaper did the share of American symbols decrease generally from 1735 or 1762 to 1775. The differences in the slopes of the individual trend lines are shown in Table 5-1. Figures

TABLE 5-1. Slopes of Trend Lines Showing Attention to American Symbols, by Newspaper, 1735–1775 and 1762–1775

Newspaper	1735–1775	1762–1775
Massachusetts Gazette	.95	2.51
South-Carolina Gazette	.86	2.60
Virginia Gazette	.82	1.00
New-York Weekly Journal/Mercury	.66	1.53
Pennsylvania Gazette	.60	2.49
Boston Gazette		2.74
Composite[1]	.67	1.90

1. Excludes *Boston Gazette*.

5-3A and 5-3B indicate that for both the longer and the shorter time periods the New England newspapers not only started at a point well above the average but, with one exception, also rose at a steeper angle than did the others. The *South-Carolina Gazette* did not lag far behind: for the 41-year period the slope of its trend line, which crossed the composite trend line in the late 1740s, was nine tenths as great as that of the *Massachusetts Gazette*; from 1762 to 1775 its annual percentage increase in attention to American events was second only to that of the *Boston Gazette*. While the trend lines from 1735 to 1775 for the Virginia, New York, and Pennsylvania newspapers were all below the composite trend line, only that of the New York journals rose more sharply than the composite. Perhaps most surprising of all was the rapid increase in the amount of attention that the *Pennsylvania Gazette* paid to

American symbols from 1762 to 1775. Although still less steep than the slopes of the trend lines for the Massachusetts and South Carolina newspapers, the trend line for the *Pennsylvania Gazette* for the 1762–75 period was more than four times as steep as its slope for the 1735–75 period as a whole.

If the colonial newspapers became increasingly unified as to the amount of attention that they paid to American symbols, their patterns of attention to British symbols diverged increasingly.[5] Their general congruence is nonetheless remarkable. With the single exception of the *Pennsylvania Gazette,* all of them presented a greater than average amount of news about the mother country between one half and two thirds of the time. The Philadelphia journal did so in only nine of the 41 years (22.0%). It was the *Virginia Gazette,* however, that deviated most significantly from the composite curve—once, in 1753, by more than 25 percentage points.[6] It is also interesting to note that, as a general rule, again with the exception of the Virginia newspaper, the journals that devoted a greater than average amount of symbol space to American events tended also to pay a greater than average amount of attention to Britain.

Particularly important in assessing the interests of the individual newspapers are the varying ratios of American to British symbols. In the 29-year period from 1735 to 1763, the *Massachusetts Gazette* had more American than British sym-

5. In terms of the share of symbol space devoted to British symbols, using the "Spearman Rank Order Correlation Coefficient" discussed in n. 3 above, the mean coefficient for the 1735–63 period was $\bar{r}_s = .29$, significant at the .10 level (using a one-tailed test), while the correlation coefficients for four of the ten pairs were significant at the .05 level. The mean coefficient for the 1764–75 period was $\bar{r}_s = .27$, which is not significant even at the .10 level. None of the ten pairs was significant at the .05 level (using a one-tailed test).

6. The apparently erratic curves of the Virginia newspapers may in part be due to the incompleteness of the files of these journals—and hence of the sample used in this study—for the middle years of the 41-year period.

bols in twelve different years (41.4%), the New York and South Carolina newspapers seven years (24.1%), the *Pennsylvania Gazette* six years (20.7%), and the *Virginia Gazette* only four years of the eighteen (22.2%) of that period for which Virginia newspapers are extant. For the twelve years from 1764 to 1775, the *Massachusetts Gazette* printed more American than British symbols every single year, the *South-Carolina Gazette* in ten of the twelve years (83.3%), the *New-York Mercury* in seven years (58.3%), the *Pennsylvania Gazette* one half of the time, and the *Virginia Gazette* in four of the ten years available. Each of the fourteen years from 1762 to 1775 saw the *Boston Gazette* devoting more space to American symbols than to British symbols. Over the entire 41-year period, as may be seen in Table 5-2, only the Virginia

TABLE 5-2. Total Symbol Distribution, by Newspaper, over Entire Period, 1735–1775

Newspaper	American Symbols	British Symbols	Other Symbols	Total Symbols
Massachusetts Gazette	28.8%	22.4%	48.8%	100.0%
South-Carolina Gazette	25.4	21.5	53.1	100.0
N.-Y. Weekly Journal/Mercury	21.2	21.1	57.7	100.0
Virginia Gazette	19.9	26.4	53.7	100.0
Pennsylvania Gazette	18.2	19.2	62.5	99.9
Boston Gazette[1]	48.8	25.4	25.7	99.9
Composite[2]	22.3	21.5	56.3	100.1

1. Figures include fourteen years (1762–75) only.
2. Excludes *Boston Gazette*.

and Pennsylvania newspapers gave more prominence to British than to colonial events.

What do all of these figures tell us about variations among the colonial newspapers in the distribution of their news space? The first and most obvious point is that the two Boston newspapers, the *Massachusetts Gazette* and the *Boston Gazette*, were far and away the leaders in reporting both colonial and British events, and more inclined to give precedence to the former. This was particularly true during the dozen years immediately prior to the outbreak of revolution, when both prints devoted about one quarter of their news space to British symbols and almost twice as much to occurrences in the colonies.

The second point is related to the first: although the Whiggish *Boston Gazette* devoted more space to American symbols and presented a higher ratio of American to British symbols for the fourteen years from 1762 to 1775 than did the Tory-oriented *Massachusetts Gazette,* the two New England newspapers differed from one another in these respects to a far lesser extent than either of them differed from the New York, Pennsylvania, Virginia, or South Carolina journals. This fact argues for the case that, whatever the political biases of the newspapers, there was a common shift of attention toward the discussion of American news and problems in their columns.

Third, the newspapers of the middle colonies—the *Pennsylvania Gazette,* the *New-York Weekly Journal,* and the *New-York Mercury*—presented a fairly congruent picture of interest in American news. Their growing tendency to print American symbols was not essentially dissimilar from, although a bit below, the composite trend line (Figure 5-3A); and while the New York prints had a higher ratio of American to British symbols in 14 of the 41 years (34.1%), those of Philadelphia had a higher ratio in only nine (22.0%). As Table 5-2 indicates, over the entire period each of them printed roughly as many American as British symbols. The major difference between them, and the difference that sets the *Pennsylvania Gazette* off from all of the colonial newspapers included in this study, is that the Pennsylvania newspaper was generally much more preoccupied with European (and to a lesser extent Caribbean and Canadian) events than any of the others. Why this was so poses an interesting problem. Was it, for example, in response to the reading wishes of the colony's population, one third of which was German or of German origin?

If any laggard in terms of interest in American news and symbols existed, it was the *Virginia Gazette*. In only eight of the 28 years (28.6%) for which that newspaper is available did it print more American than British symbols; it was above average in giving symbol space to Britain about two thirds of the time, and below average in its share of American symbols three years in four. Over the entire 41-year period, as may be seen in Table 5-2, the Virginia newspapers devoted a third again as many symbols to the mother country as to the colonies. It would seem that, from the point of view of its communications and focus of attention, the Old Dominion retained closer ties to England throughout the last four decades of the colonial period than did the other provinces in America.[7]

Finally, in spite of some fairly extreme fluctuations, the *South-Carolina Gazette* was second only to the Massachusetts newspapers in giving space to American symbols. Its slope of rising interest in colonial news was even steeper during the last 14 years of the colonial era than was that of the *Massachusetts Gazette*. Thus, in an era when its geographic core area was more concerned with British than with American events, the population centers at either end of the chain of American colonies were focusing their attention more upon American than upon British events. It was the geographic periphery rather than the core area of eighteenth-century America that led in the symbolic revolution of shifting images and foci of attention.

7. On the ties of Virginia to Great Britain during the later colonial years, see Carl Bridenbaugh, *Seat of Empire: The Political Role of Eighteenth-Century Williamsburg* (Williamsburg, Virginia, Colonial Williamsburg, Inc., 1950), pp. 7-10.

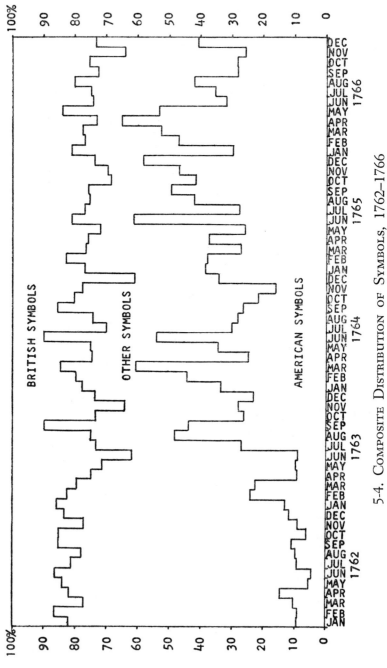

5-4. Composite Distribution of Symbols, 1762–1766

The Colonists Discover America

The analysis of the 41-year period from 1735 to 1775 revealed that the sharpest incline in the percentage of symbol space devoted to American symbols occurred during the five-year period from 1762 to 1766. As shown in Figure 5-1, the American share of the total composite symbol count rose from 10.7 per cent in 1762 to 42.2 per cent in 1766, an increase of 300 per cent. A glance at Figure 5-2 assures us that the sharp rise in the American percentage occurred during this time period for all of the newspapers analyzed, with the most marked change in the *Boston Gazette,* which rose from 12.6 per cent in 1762 to 54.7 per cent in 1765 and fell off slightly in the following year. A similar, though not quite so dramatic, trend occurred in the distribution curve of British symbols: the most sustained period of incline during the years from 1759 to 1768 came during these same five years.

The more intensive analysis followed the methodology outlined above, except for the size of the sample and the newspapers selected. Using a standard technique for random sampling, an independent sample of one issue per month for each of the five years (or 60 issues in all) was drawn from each of two newspapers, the *Boston Gazette* and the *New-York Mercury.* These journals were selected as representative of newspapers paying, respectively, more and less than average attention to American events. As for the manner of presenting the data, the extreme fluctuations in the symbol distributions from month to month (Figure 5-4) become more readable and perhaps more meaningful through the use of trend lines (Figure 5-5) produced by the method of "moving averages." [8] Such

8. A "moving averages" curve smooths out extreme fluctuations in a year-by-year curve (such as Figure 5-1) and presents a curved line that may serve to indicate the trend of symbol usage. To find the "moving average" for any single year, it is necessary merely to find the mean average

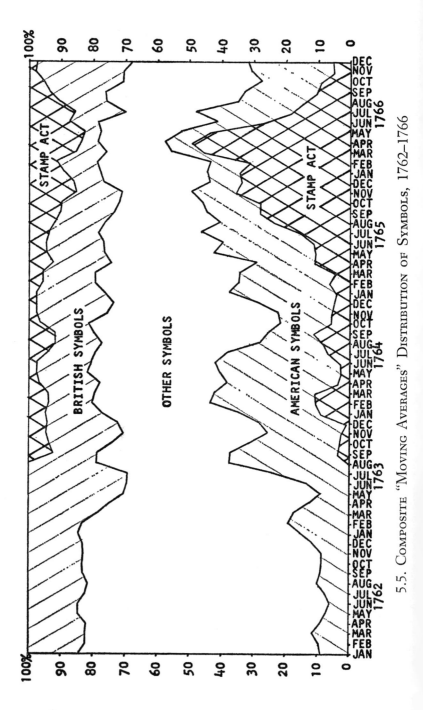

5.5. Composite "Moving Averages" Distribution of Symbols, 1762–1766

trend lines also enable the clear presentation of another aspect of the data, the role of the Stamp Act crisis in changing colonial attention patterns.

Generally speaking, the results of the intensive analysis were rather close to those of the general study, as may be seen in Table 5-3. In both analyses, the American share of the total

TABLE 5-3. Comparison of Composite Symbol Distributions, 1762–1766, for Quarterly-Sample and Monthly-Sample Analyses

Symbol Categories	1762	1763	1764	1765	1766
Quarterly Sample[1]					
American symbols	10.7%	15.4%	27.5%	26.7%	42.2%
British symbols	15.4	20.5	20.5	24.4	24.9
Other symbols	73.9	64.1	52.0	48.9	32.9
Total	100.0	100.0	100.0	100.0	100.0
Monthly Sample[2]					
American symbols	8.8%	20.3%	33.7%	41.1%	40.5%
British symbols	17.0	24.4	21.3	23.8	24.2
Other symbols	74.2	55.3	45.0	35.1	35.3
Total	100.0	100.0	100.0	100.0	100.0

1. Mean average annual distribution of symbols in four issues per year of the *Massachusetts Gazette*, the *New-York Mercury*, the *Pennsylvania Gazette*, the *Virginia Gazette*, and the *South-Carolina Gazette*.

2. Mean average annual distribution of symbols in twelve issues per year (one per month) of the *Boston Gazette* and the *New-York Mercury*.

symbol count rose from about ten per cent to 40 per cent over the five years, while the British share rose from approximately 16 per cent to about 25 per cent. The most important differences in the year-by-year comparison of the two samples lay

---

of the symbol usage for the year itself, the year preceding, and the year following. While a "moving averages" curve is quite useful for showing trends, it cannot be used to show the precise symbol distribution for any single year.

in the patterns of the growth of American symbol usage: the monthly sample revealed a steady rise culminating in a peak in 1765, and dropping off slightly in the following year; while the quarterly sample showed a slower rise until 1764, a decline in 1765, and a very sharp rise in 1766. Statistical tests designed to determine the extent to which two independent samples of the same body of data differ suggest that there was no significant difference between the sample of four issues per year and the sample of twelve issues per year 90 per cent of the time.[9] The monthly analysis, however, presents a picture more sensitive to the changes in the colonial newspapers' foci of attention.

Looking at the composite monthly distribution of symbols as a whole (Figure 5-5), it may be seen that there were two major cycles in the curve representing the American share of the total symbol count. The first of these started in May of 1763 and ended in October of the following year, while the second started at the latter date and continued for two years. The structure and composition of these two cycles are of considerable importance in our discussion and evaluation of the development of self-awareness processes in colonial America.

The most significant revolution in symbol usage during these five years, the most crucial period of the 41 years prior to the outbreak of the Revolution, occurred during the summer of 1763. From June until August of that year the share of American symbols rose almost fivefold (Figure 5-4) and, after a decline during the autumn, rose to new heights in the following

9. Statistically speaking, in nine of ten cases (that is, two different sets of newspapers, each for five separate years), nonparametric tests did not reject a null hypothesis asserting that there was no significant difference between the sample of four and the independent sample of twelve issues. For the *New-York Mercury* in 1765, the test rejected the null hypothesis at a significance level of .05 for a two-tailed test. For a discussion of this test—the "Mann-Whitney U Test"—see Siegel, *Nonparametric Statistics for the Behavioral Sciences*, pp. 116–27.

spring and early summer. A similar pattern appeared in the curves of American symbol usage for both the *New-York Mercury* and the *Boston Gazette*. Indeed, the curve of the latter suggests that for Bostonians the height of American self-interest came during this period, for between January and July of 1764 the *Gazette* devoted more than seven out of ten place-name symbols to American affairs.

While the second cycle in the composite curve reached a higher point (in the spring of 1766, when it rose above the 50 per cent level) it is perhaps not quite so dramatic in that it seems merely to have been a continuation of the previous cycle. Considered as a unity, the two cycles present a picture of increasing interest in American affairs, building to a climax in the months when the joyous colonists received word from the mother country that their opposition had forced parliament to repeal the Stamp Act, probably the most spectacular and important event of the 1760s for the Americans.

But how important was the Stamp Act crisis in these cycles of increased American self-awareness? To ascertain this it was necessary to divide the content of the American share of symbols into two categories: one category comprising news directly or indirectly related to the Stamp and Sugar Acts—their announcement, enactment, and repeal—as well as all forms of colonial opposition, such as trade associations, decisions to simplify funeral clothing, colonial versions of the "buy American" principle, and the Stamp Act Congress; the other category consisting in news not in the least pertaining to these acts. The cross-hatched portion of Figure 5-5 shows the trend in the share of symbols in the first category.

Such an analysis reveals that, although the climax of the Stamp Act crisis coincided with the culminating point of interest in American events, it was not the news of the trade restrictions that touched off the aroused interest. The trend toward increased interest in American events and news was well under way before information about trade restrictions began to appear regularly in the colonial press. Prior to the fall of 1764 the only news items pertaining to the Sugar and Stamp Acts were scattered bits in the *New-York Mercury* echoing colonial disgruntlement at trade restrictions already existing, and reporting rumors about parliamentary intentions vis-à-vis colonial trade. And it was not until a year later that symbols found in news of the Stamp Act crisis consistently began to outnumber symbols relating to other events. In the issues that reported the repeal of the Stamp Act, about nine in ten symbols referring to America pertained more or less directly to the parliamentary tax measures.

As a triggering event of American self-awareness, if we may judge from symbol usage in the *Boston Gazette,* the Stamp Act crisis was particularly irrelevant in Boston. The American share of the total symbol count reached its climax months before the *Gazette* began to discuss the trade restrictions. As the crisis mounted, to be sure, Bostonian interest in it grew rapidly, until by the spring of 1766 the *Gazette's* focus of attention upon American events and news was absorbed almost totally by items on the Stamp Act and its repeal.

There is another point to be mentioned before leaving the discussion of the intensive analysis of the *New-York Mercury* and the *Boston Gazette:* the relative unimportance of the Stamp Act crisis as an influence on the distribution of British symbols. It is of course true that the period from January of 1762 to December of 1766 saw the British share of the total symbol count gradually increasing (Figure 5-5); and during the height of the crisis itself most of the British symbols appearing in the two newspapers were related to the trade measures. But the peak months shown by the trend lines occurred either before or after the bulk of the news pertaining to the Stamp Act crisis. And the British share of the symbols was higher during the summer of 1763 than at any point prior to the fall of 1766, when the Stamp Act crisis itself was no longer of great moment.

The dramatic shifts of attention in the early summer months of 1763 should not eclipse the dynamic context of symbol usage in which they occurred. Even before that time, as was pointed out earlier, the colonists were increasingly substituting a self-awareness for their absorption in European wars and other events outside the Anglo-American political community. And, although British news generally occupied about one fifth of the newspapers' columns throughout the entire period from 1735 to 1775, its share was declining sharply relative to the space given over to American symbols. The evidence of the newspapers nonetheless suggests that the "takeoff" point of increased interest in America came during the early summer of 1763—before news of Pontiac's uprising reached the inhabitants of the towns along the Atlantic seaboard, before the announcement of the Royal Proclamation restricting the settling and trading patterns of the colonists, and before the beginning of agitation about British mercantile policies.

That attention to America increased tremendously during these four decades is in itself interesting, but it leaves a number of important questions unanswered. After all, even in the middle of the eighteenth century America was a big country. It is, therefore, necessary to analyze somewhat more closely the attention that was paid to American symbols, to see what it was in this vast continent that colonial publicists thought important enough to substitute for European news in their journals.

CHAPTER SIX

The Balance of Intercolonial Communication

From 1735, when America was little more than a string of dependent colonies scattered along the Atlantic seaboard, until 1775, when these same colonies were practically an independent political community, the colonial press took increasing interest in things and events American. At the same time they shifted their foci of attention within that part of the North American continent that later became the United States of America. The nature of these latter shifts throws considerable light upon the growth of an American sense of political community. When, for example, did a collective concept—one that referred to all of the colonies as a single unit—become salient for the provincial press? How important was purely local news, relative to news and reports from other colonies, in the individual newspapers? Which colonies were the more important and which less important as foci of attention for newspapers printed in other colonies? Which colonies were more and which less preoccupied with themselves?

By dividing the American place-name symbols appearing in the colonial press into several categories it is possible to trace significant changes in the colonial focus of attention. The most relevant categories are four in number: symbols referring to the American colonies as a whole or, as they will be termed here, *continental symbols*[1] (or, alternatively, "symbols of common identity"); *home colony symbols,* or those referring to the colony in which the newspaper using the symbols was published; *home region symbols,* referring to areas outside the home colony but within the region (southern, middle, or northern colonies) in which the newspaper using the symbol was published; and *symbols of other colonies,* that is, those outside the region in which the newspaper using the symbol appeared. The third category, home region symbols, overlaps the second and the fourth, and will not be considered in too much detail here.

Two methodological points must be noted before proceeding to an analysis of American place-name symbols. First, this chapter will discuss only symbols referring to American place-names. Thus, while the percentages discussed in the previous chapter were in terms of the *total* symbol count (that is, the sum of American, British, and other symbols), the percentages in this chapter will be expressed as a share of the total number of *American* symbols. Second, in contrast to the preceding chapter, which dealt only with direct place-name symbols (such as "London" or "South Carolina"), this and the following chapter will consider indirect place-name symbols as well. Indirect place-name symbols are those that replace the specific name of a place with such terms as "here," "that place," "this

1. The term is perhaps slightly misleading, but in this study it is used exclusively to denote the area comprising the American colonies (and neither the North American continent as a whole nor the European continent). This is the same sense in which the colonists themselves used the term in convening the Continental Congress and creating the Continental Army. The content of the category—that is, whether the symbols identified the land or its inhabitants as a part of the British political community (e.g. "British colonies," "English colonists") or as members of an embryo American political community (e.g. "America," "Americans")—is a topic that will be left for more complete analysis in the following chapter.

city," and so forth. I include indirect symbols in the analysis for two reasons. First, the total number of direct references to American places in the sample of newspapers was too small to produce interesting and illuminating results; the inclusion of indirect symbols enlarged the total number of American place-name symbols without making the category so large as to be unmanageable. Second, a close reading of the colonial newspapers uncovered a tendency of editors and correspondents to refer at some length to local occurrences without mentioning the name of their particular locality. I felt that a refusal to take this tendency into account, especially since the newspapers devoted an increasing amount of their space to the letters of correspondents and to news items from other colonies, would in the long run distort the actual changes in the journals' focus of attention.[2]

THE COLLECTIVE CONCEPT: THE COLONIES LOOK AT THE CONTINENT

For a major portion of the 41 years 1735–75, attention to the colonies as a whole was negligible. Not until 1755 did the continental share of the American symbols rise above the ten per cent level (Figure 6-1), and not until eight years later did it go above that level and remain there. From 1735 to 1761 the average newspaper devoted about one American symbol in 16 (6.5%) to continental events. Although this average quadrupled to 25.8 per cent in the 14 years from 1762 to 1775, for the entire 41 years slightly over one in six American symbols (17.9%) referred to the colonies as a whole. And in only six

2. The number of direct and indirect references to American place names is to be found in the Appendix. It is my impression—an impression that was not checked empirically—that the inclusion of indirect references to British and other place-names would not have altered significantly the analysis presented in the preceding chapter.

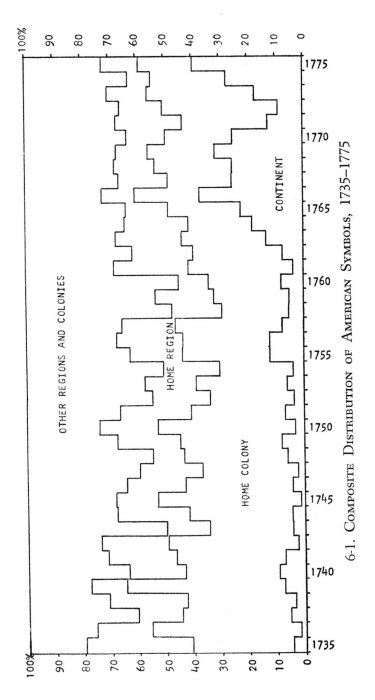

6-1. Composite Distribution of American Symbols, 1735–1775

of these years did the continent overshadow the home colonies in the colonial press.[3]

The trend in the usage of continental symbols was essentially cyclical. The first two upward cycles in the curve were gentle, both culminating in years of significant formative events: the one, from 1736 to 1740, in the outbreak and initial stages of the War of Jenkins' Ear; and the other, between 1754 and 1756, in the outbreak and intensively American period of the French and Indian War. But the importance of the collective concept as a newspaper symbol declined to very low levels after each of these gentle upward swings of the curve.

The first significant break in the pattern of slight interest in the colonies as a whole occurred in 1762, when the share of continental symbols more than doubled over the previous year; and the level in 1763 was almost four times that of 1761. By 1766, the year in which the colonists rejoiced that their resistance had effected the repeal of the odious Stamp Act, the continental share of the total American symbol count had risen to 37.3 per cent—an increase of almost 1,000 per cent over the level of 1761. Although the curve declined to the nine per cent level in 1772, it rose to a new height three years later. Even so, in 1775, as the colonies' representatives were meeting in Philadelphia to consider matters of great moment for the budding American political community, slightly less than two in five American symbols referred to the entire country or to its inhabitants.

The trend of rising interest in continental events and news, beginning in the 1760s, was not only the case for the composite or average colonial newspaper, but in general true for each of

3. For the sake of comparison, a survey of 51 American newspapers in 1953 revealed that 23.4 per cent of the nonforeign news pertained to national events or to news about Washington, D. C., that did not bear international implications. Cf. The International Press Institute, *The Flow of the News* (Zurich, 1953), p. 63.

the individual journals as well.[4] The most marked exception to this generality was the *Virginia Gazette*. During the course of the 41 years from 1735 to 1775, the sample of the *Virginia Gazette* included in the study gave almost twice as much space to continental symbols as the average colonial print did (Table 6-1); and, as may be seen in Figure 6-2, the Virginia curve

TABLE 6-1. Comparative Share of American Symbols Devoted to the Continent, 1735–1775

Newspaper	Continental Share of American Symbols			Change from 1735–61 to 1762–75
	1735–61	*1762–75*	*1735–75*	*1762–75*
South-Carolina Gazette	8.4%	34.3%	23.9%	+410.5%
N.-Y. Weekly Journal/Mercury	5.3	21.2	15.9	+400.0
Massachusetts Gazette	5.1	20.1	13.8	+393.9
Virginia Gazette	9.8	36.9	29.0	+376.7
Pennsylvania Gazette	7.0	23.7	16.2	+338.6
Boston Gazette	—	23.8	—	—
Composite[1]	6.5	25.8	17.9	+399.7%

1. Excludes *Boston Gazette*.

was much more erratic than the others for years when the files of the Old Dominion's newspapers were both complete and incomplete. The other four sets of newspapers—the *South-Carolina Gazette*, the *Pennsylvania Gazette*, the *New-York Weekly Journal* and the *New-York Mercury*, and the *Massachusetts Gazette*—varied to a lesser degree from the composite curve, with the *Massachusetts Gazette* the least responsive of all to continental symbols. For the entire 14-year period for which the *Boston Gazette* was included, the difference be-

4. A computation of Spearman Rank Order Correlation Coefficients for attention to continental symbols indicates that the newspapers became more congruent from 1735–61 ($\bar{r}_s = .33$, with five of ten pairs significant at the .05 level using a one-tailed test) to 1762–75 ($\bar{r}_s = .39$, with six of ten pairs significant at the .05 level using a one-tailed test).

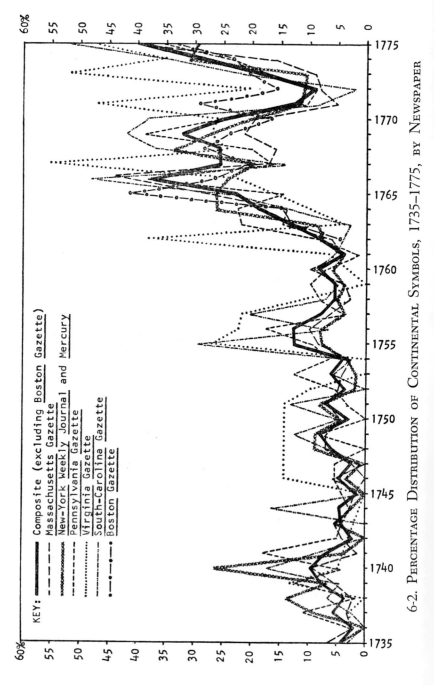

KEY:

— Composite (excluding Boston Gazette)
- - - Massachusetts Gazette
×× New-York Weekly Journal and Mercury
-·- Pennsylvania Gazette
···· Virginia Gazette
-··- South-Carolina Gazette
•—•— Boston Gazette

6-2. PERCENTAGE DISTRIBUTION OF CONTINENTAL SYMBOLS, 1735–1775, BY NEWSPAPER

tween it and the composite was insignificant; and it devoted a greater than average amount of space to continental symbols for five of the 14 years.

In the composite distribution of continental symbols, and in the symbol distributions of the individual newspapers as well, the most significant period of rising interest in continental events came in the six years after the low year 1761. What does the intensive analysis, encompassing twelve issues per year for the *New-York Mercury* and the *Boston Gazette* from 1762 to 1766, tell us about these crucial years?

The continental share of American symbols fluctuated considerably during the months from January of 1762 to December of 1766. After three previous high points—in the early winter of 1763–64, the following autumn, and the spring of 1765—around the 30 per cent level, the trend reached a peak in the spring of 1766 (Figure 6-3). In April and May of that year, more than seven in ten American symbols appearing in the two newspapers referred to the collective concept.

The intensive analysis does not clarify the role of the Stamp Act crisis in the series of ascending cycles. On the one hand, after the first mention in the monthly sample of existing or proposed trade restrictions and until the end of 1766, almost nine in ten of the continental symbols appeared in articles related to the restrictions. For the *New-York Mercury* this was true 86.3 per cent of the time, while the *Boston Gazette* was even more consistent (92.2%). Further, the fact that the most important peaks in the curve came after the first discussions of the existing and proposed measures seems to argue that the increased interest in the continent was associated rather closely with the progress of the Stamp Act crisis.

On the other hand, as suggested previously, more important than the climaxes in analyzing trends in symbol usage are the points at which the downward cycles of trends are reversed.

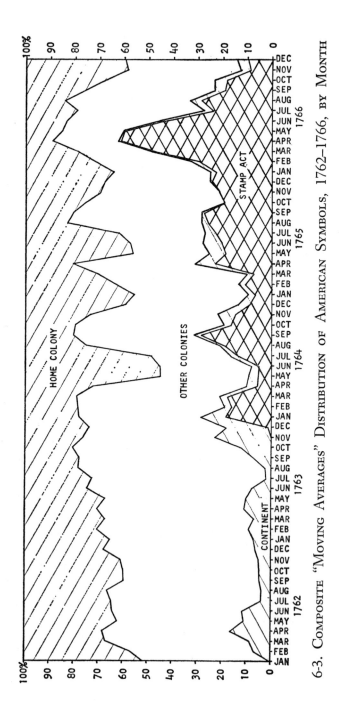

6-3. Composite "Moving Averages" Distribution of American Symbols, 1762–1766, by Month

For the *New-York Mercury* the first important increase in the share of American symbols devoted to the continent came from the summer to the late fall of 1763, when the percentage share rose from less than one per cent in July and August to 37.7 per cent in November and December. In the next two months, before the passage of the Sugar Act, the first two articles which might be considered a part of the Stamp Act crisis appeared, the first grumbling about existing trade restrictions and the second reporting rumors of parliamentary intentions. While, to be sure, there was a similar pattern of increased interest in continental events taking place during the summer and fall of 1763 in the news columns of the *Boston Gazette,* it was not significant in that newspaper's long-run distribution of symbols. Rather, a line connecting the peaks of the *Gazette's* trend-line from 1762 to 1766 would reveal a steadily rising curve.

If the analysis of the intensive sample does not point conclusively to the cause of the upsurge in continental interest, it nonetheless indicates that the trend was well under way by the winter of 1763–64. It is, of course, impossible to tell whether the cyclical fluctuations in the newspapers' trend-lines, and particularly those of the New England print, would have continued to rise in the absence of the Stamp Act crisis. It is interesting to note in this connection that the trends for both of the newspapers (one of which, according to the sample, reported news of trade restrictions in January and February of 1764 and the other of which did not do so until the following summer) acted similarly in the spring of 1764 in decreasing the relative number of continental symbols after the peak months of the late fall and early winter of 1763–64.

The evidence of the newspapers suggests, then, that the continent of America was not itself an important concept in colonial thinking until the early 1760s. In spite of mild cyclical fluctuations prior to that time, with the climaxes of the upward swings occurring at the same time as some of the more important formative events of the two and one-half decades from 1735 to 1761, it was not really until 1763 that emphasis on the continent approached any degree of significance. And even in the last third of the 41-year period, only one in four American symbols in the colonial press referred to the continent as a whole. The intensive analysis of the crucial five years from 1762 to 1766 does not reveal any clearcut evidence demonstrating the importance or unimportance of the Stamp Act crisis as a factor producing increased interest in that part of the North American continent that was later to become the United States of America. It would seem that Stamp Act news was more important in the rise of interest in the collective concept than it was in shifting the focus of colonial attention from Europe and Britain to America; but it is also true that the latter half of 1763 saw increases in the amount of space devoted to continental symbols that were unrelated to the Stamp Act crisis.

LOCAL INTEREST IN THE COLONIAL PRESS

In contrast to the often sporadic, if growing, use of continental symbols in the colonial press, those of the home colony appeared prominently throughout the 41 years. In only one of these years did the newspapers on an average devote less than one fifth of their symbol space to home colony news, while the average for the entire period was almost three in ten (29.7%).[5] The exceptional year, 1775, was one in which the colonists paid unprecedented attention to the continent as a whole.

The share of American symbols devoted to the home colony

5. The modern American newspaper devotes 42.8 per cent of its domestic news space to local and state news; in addition, 33.8 per cent of the non-foreign news concerns sports or society events. International Press Institute, *Flow of the News*, p. 63.

nonetheless decreased during the four decades from 1735 to 1775. This diminished interest in local news may be seen graphically in Figure 6-1, where the lines delineating the home colony share of American symbols come closer together. In the first decade, from 1735 to 1744, the newspapers devoted 40.4 per cent of their American symbol space to local events; by the last decade, from 1766 to 1775, this percentage share had dropped by more than one third to 26.3 per cent.

The relative decrease in the share of home colony symbols may be seen most dramatically in the changing ratio of these symbols to continental symbols. And, as Figure 6-4 suggests, the most significant decline in home colony symbols relative to those referring to the continent came between the years from 1761 to 1766—the period already mentioned as crucial in the American symbol revolution. Between 1735 and 1761 the ratio fluctuated at a rather low level, between .05 (that is, one continental symbol for every twenty home colony symbols) and .25 (or one continental symbol for every four home colony symbols), with few exceptions. By 1766, however, 1.6 continental symbols appeared in the colonial press for every local symbol. After a sharp drop in the ratio during the years from 1771 to 1773, the curve returned to an even higher plane immediately prior to the outbreak of the Revolution.

The intensive analysis of the years from 1762 to 1766 re-emphasizes the importance of the summer and fall of 1763 as the takeoff point in the revolution in colonial symbol usage. It was at the end of this half year of increased interest in events affecting all of the colonies that the number of symbols in the colonial press referring to the home colony of the newspapers fell for the first time below the number discussing continental events (Figure 6-5). After several steep cycles, the ratio of continental to home colony symbols reached a climax in the spring of 1766, when six continental symbols appeared

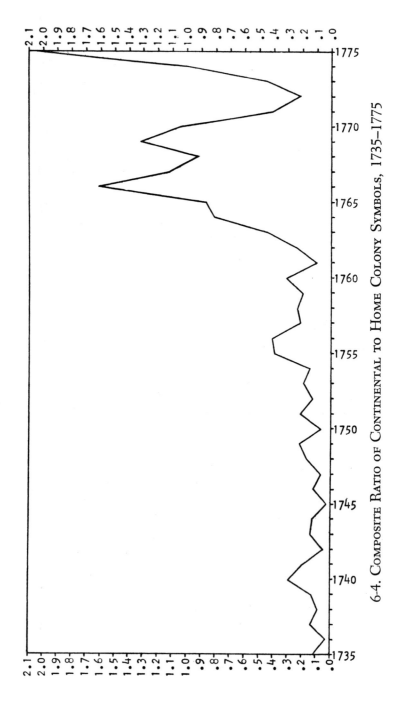

6-4. Composite Ratio of Continental to Home Colony Symbols, 1735–1775

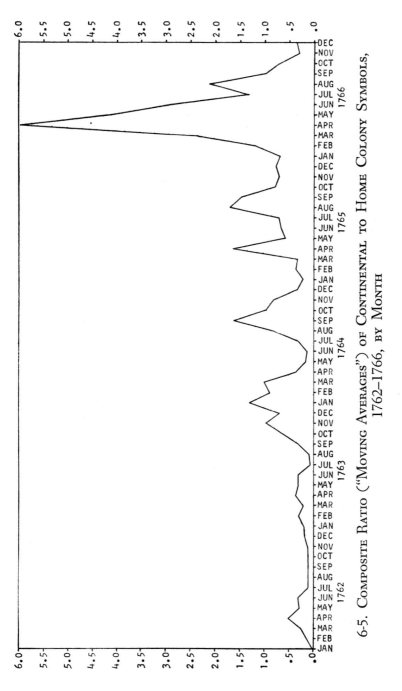

6-5. Composite Ratio ("Moving Averages") of Continental to Home Colony Symbols, 1762–1766, by Month

95

in the newspapers for each place name in the home colony.

Considering the individual newspapers separately, there was less congruence in the amount of space they devoted to their home colonies than in any aspect of the symbol distributions previously discussed. Certain patterns are nonetheless discernible. The New England and South Carolina prints, for example, were relatively more preoccupied with local events than were the other newspapers. In each of the 14 years included in the study the whiggish *Boston Gazette* was above average in reporting local news, devoting more than one half of its total American symbol space during this period to home colony symbols. As may be seen in Table 6-2, in only two of 41 years

TABLE 6-2. Local Interest in the Colonial Press, 1735–1775

Newspaper	Home colony share of American symbols	Years home colony share above composite share		Years continental symbols outnumber home colony symbols	
		No.	%	No.	%
Pennsylvania Gazette	24.1%	11/41	26.8%	6/41	14.6%
N.-Y. Weekly Journal/ Mercury	26.0	16/41	39.0	7/41	17.1
Virginia Gazette	28.2	17/28	60.7	6/28	21.4
South-Carolina Gazette	33.5	33/41	80.5	6/41	14.6
Massachusetts Gazette	36.2	29/41	70.7	2/41	4.9
Boston Gazette	51.7	14/14	100.0	1/14	7.1
Composite[1]	29.7	—	—	6/41	14.6

1. Excludes *Boston Gazette*.

did the *Massachusetts Gazette* give more space to continental than to home colony symbols, and more than 70 per cent of the time that newspaper was above average in reporting purely local events. For the period as a whole, the *Massachusetts Gazette* devoted more than one fifth more than average symbol space to its home colony news. The major exception to this pattern of self-preoccupation came during the years from 1754 to 1764, encompassing the whole of the French and Indian War: in nine of these eleven years the *Massachusetts Gazette* was under par in presenting local news, and in nine years it reported more news from the middle colonies than from Massachusetts. The *South-Carolina Gazette* was second only to the Boston journals in its emphasis upon local news. Fully a third of its American symbol space was devoted to place names in South Carolina—a greater than average interest in four out of five years.

If New England and South Carolina newspapers seem to have been preoccupied with events in their own colonies, those newspapers from the middle colonies included in the study tended to be much less concerned with local news. Each devoted approximately one quarter of its American news space to the home colony over the entire 41-year period; both of their home colony news curves were under the average or composite curve much more often than they were above it; and each had a higher than average ratio of continental to home colony symbols. It is not surprising, however, that local interest in these journals was above average in six of the 11 years between 1754 and 1764, for an important part of the French and Indian War took place either on or near territories claimed by these two colonies.

The *Virginia Gazette* was about average in its emphasis on local news, exceeding the composite share of home colony symbols in 17 of 28 years (60.7%). Where the Virginia print differed from the others, however, was in the amount of interest it took in continental news relative to its emphasis on local news. It has been previously noted that the *Virginia Gazette* gave almost twice as much space to continental events as the average newspaper did; it is also true that the Old Dominion had a higher ratio of continental to home colony symbols one and one half times as often as the average newspaper.

Emphasis on events taking place within the home region but outside the home colony also decreased with the passage of time (Figure 6-1). In the decade from 1735 to 1744 the average newspaper devoted more than one fifth of its total American symbol space to home region news; by the end of the colonial period, however, in the years from 1765 to 1775, it was giving less than one seventh of its space to that end. For the 41 years as a whole, in addition to discussions of home colony news, 17.1 per cent of the newspapers' American symbol space concerned the home region.

THE COLONIES LOOK AT EACH OTHER

News of other colonies appeared prominently in the columns of the colonial press throughout the years from 1735 to 1775. During this period the average newspaper devoted roughly one sixth of its American symbol space to continental symbols, about three tenths to news of the home colony, and the remainder (52.4%) to place-name symbols of colonies other than the one in which the newspaper appeared. It goes almost without saying that the mutual flow of attention was not even. Each colony paid more attention to some of its sister colonies and less to others. This is not to say, however, that interesting patterns of imbalance were not present.

To determine the nature and direction of these imbalances I submitted to computer analysis data about the mutual flow of attention among the five colonies emphasized in this study. In brief, the computer routine analyzes transaction flows of all types (labor migration, for instance, or international trade or attention patterns) in terms of the divergence of actual transaction flows from those that might be expected in the absence of any offsetting factors or relationships.[6] The information

6. I am indebted to Hayward R. Alker, Jr., of Yale University not only for suggesting the possibility of computer analysis but also for assistance in

used in this analysis was the average number of symbols that each newspaper devoted to the other four colonies during each of the decades from 1735 to 1775. Table 6-3 indicates that from 1735 to 1744 1.45 names of places in Massachusetts appeared in the average issue of the *New-York Weekly Journal*, 1.18 such symbols in the average issue of the *Pennsylvania Gazette*, and so forth.

The computer program analyzed these data first of all in terms of the propensity of each colony to pay attention to news from other colonies and in turn to have its own messages heeded by those other colonies. The hypothetical propensity of a newspaper to pay attention to a set of colonies for any period is the actual ratio (adjusted to take into account the fact that the model excludes any references in a newspaper to that newspaper's home colony) of the number of symbols from other colonies it printed to the total number of symbols from all of the colonies printed by each other's newspapers. Similarly, the hypothetical propensity of a colony to have attention paid to it is the adjusted ratio of the number of its place-name symbols appearing in the columns of newspapers from other colonies to the total number of symbols from all of the colonies printed by each other's newspapers.

The five sets of colonial newspapers differed markedly in their attentiveness to symbols of place-names in other colonies (Table 6-4). For the four decades as a whole, the *Pennsylvania Gazette* led in this respect, with the New York newspapers a close second. The *Gazette* was clearly the leader during the decades when Benjamin Franklin was active as its editor. Thereafter it declined in the rankings, although main-

---

technical matters and interpretation of the results. For details, see I. Richard Savage and Karl W. Deutsch, "A Statistical Model of the Gross Analysis of Transaction Flows," *Econometrica*, 28 (1960), 551–72, and Hayward R. Alker, Jr., "An IBM 709 Program for the Gross Analysis of Transaction Flows," *Behavioral Science*, 7 (1962), 498–99.

TABLE 6-3. The Intercolonial Flow of News: Symbols
per Issue, by Decades, 1735–1775

1735–1744: Symbols in newspapers of

Symbols about	Mass.	N. Y.	Penn.	Va.	S. C.
Massachusetts		1.45	1.18	1.65	.35
New York	1.85		3.05	2.20	.15
Pennsylvania	.98	.58		1.40	.18
Virginia	.75	.43	.58		.28
South Carolina	1.60	.63	2.58	1.20	

1745–1754: Symbols in newspapers of

Symbols about	Mass.	N. Y.	Penn.	Va.	S. C.
Massachusetts		4.44	4.48	.16	1.60
New York	3.83		4.70	1.16	.78
Pennsylvania	2.18	3.33		1.00	1.08
Virginia	.63	1.23	2.75		1.13
South Carolina	1.33	3.26	1.85	.26	

1755–1764: Symbols in newspapers of

Symbols about	Mass.	N. Y.	Penn.	Va.	S. C.
Massachusetts		5.85	5.15	.58	2.00
New York	13.05		9.10	5.17	5.38
Pennsylvania	6.23	9.50		2.58	3.85
Virginia	3.23	2.35	2.75		1.35
South Carolina	3.10	4.58	3.88	2.92	

1765–1775: Symbols in newspapers of

Symbols about	Mass.	N. Y.	Penn.	Va.	S. C.
Massachusetts		12.64	12.86	8.40	6.34
New York	9.41		9.30	2.70	3.09
Pennsylvania	6.91	9.95		2.35	2.00
Virginia	3.52	2.73	6.05		2.16
South Carolina	3.27	3.68	1.75	1.03	

taining a consistently high score. Meanwhile Hugh Gaine's *New-York Mercury* replaced the Philadelphia journal as the leader. For three of the four decades the *Massachusetts Gazette* ranked third. Its attentiveness to other colonies nonethe-

TABLE 6-4. Attentiveness to Intercolonial News (Hypothetical Propensities to Pay Attention to Other Colonies), by Decades, 1735–1775

Newspaper	1735–44	1745–54	1755–64	1765–75	Average
Pennsylvania Gazette	.312	.326	.227	.261	.282
N.-Y. Weekly Journal/					
Mercury	.157	.322	.301	.263	.261
Massachusetts Gazette	.233	.198	.249	.259	.235
Virginia Gazette	.253	.054	.102	.114	.131
South-Carolina Gazette	.044	.100	.121	.102	.092
Total	.999	1.000	1.000	.999	1.001

less increased and, by the last pre-Revolutionary decade, it differed in this respect only insignificantly from the newspapers of the middle colonies. Place-name symbols from other colonies made the slightest impact in the southern newspapers, the *Virginia Gazette* and the *South-Carolina Gazette*.

A close look at Table 6-4 reveals still another aspect of the colonies' attention patterns. The difference between the first-ranked and the fifth-ranked newspapers, which in 1735–44 was .268, declined by almost one half to .141 in the decade from 1765 to 1775. This decreasing discrepancy suggests increasing congruence in the attention patterns of the five colonies, at least in regard to one another.

Turning to the colonies' newsworthiness, that is, the propensities to have their own place-name symbols printed in the newspapers of other colonies (Table 6-5), it comes as no surprise that the colonies that were the scene of battle also tended to have attention focused upon them. South Carolina, for example, was never more salient for other colonial newspapers than in the decade when the Carolinians, under the leadership of General Oglethorpe, fought the Spaniards in St. Augustine and Bloody Marsh. Pennsylvania reached its pinnacle as a

TABLE 6-5. The Newsworthiness of Colonies
(Hypothetical Propensities for News from Each
Colony to Be Reported in Newspapers of
Other Colonies), by Decades, 1735–1775

Colony	1735–44	1745–54	1755–64	1765–75	Average
New York	.305	.288	.387	.232	.303
Massachusetts	.214	.249	.150	.379	.248
Pennsylvania	.162	.210	.237	.200	.202
South Carolina	.223	.139	.136	.076	.144
Virginia	.097	.113	.089	.114	.103
Total	1.001	.999	.999	1.001	100.0

focus of colonial attention from 1755 to 1764 when the western reaches of its territory witnessed numerous skirmishes against the French and their Indian allies. News from Massachusetts was important for the newspapers of other colonies from 1745 to 1754, a decade that began with the conquest of Louisburg by the New Englanders.

In none of these three cases, however, was the embattled colony able to break through New York's position as the colony whose news was most likely to be cited in the journals of other colonies. That colony's hold on first place doubtless rested in part upon its involvement in conflict, particularly in 1745 when the French burned Saratoga in retaliation for the capture of Louisburg, but also during the whole of the French and Indian War. Not until the last colonial decade, from 1765 to 1775, did another colony replace New York as the primary focus of attention. The colony that did so, Massachusetts, was embroiled in a different kind of battle, this time against the English parliament rather than the French and the Indians. Again, as in the colonies' tendency to cite news from others, the high ranking of New York in newsworthiness is in marked contrast to the generally low position of both Virginia and South Carolina.

Although the colonies converged in their attentiveness to others, the opposite was the case with their propensities to attract attention, that is, their newsworthiness. The difference between the first-ranked and the fifth-ranked colonies increased by one half, from .208 in 1735–44 to .303 in 1765–75. In fact, during this last decade, news of Massachusetts was five times as likely to be printed as was news of South Carolina. Table 6-5 suggests that this shift was due more to the declining importance of the southern colonies than to increasing convergence upon any single northern or middle colony as a focus of attention.

The second major portion of the computer program determined the amount of attention that, in the absence of any offsetting factors, each colony would be expected to pay to each of the other colonies. This step necessitated the assumption (the "null-model" assumption) that the total number of symbols would be distributed randomly for each decade solely according to the attentiveness and newsworthiness of each colony.[7] From 1735 to 1744, for instance, the model would

7. The expected value is computed by multiplying the adjusted actual total number of symbols for a time period by the product of colony i's propensity to give attention and colony j's propensity to receive attention. Hence, the expected number of symbols of place names in New York appearing in an average issue of the *Massachusetts Gazette* from 1735 to 1744 would be the total number of symbols devoted to each other in one average issue of each newspaper ($T = 23.07$) multiplied by an adjustment factor ($S = 1.22355$) multiplied by the product of Massachusetts' propensity to give attention to other colonies ($P_i = .233$) and New York's propensity to receive attention from other colonies ($Q_j = .305$). In this case the expected value is 2.01, that is, from 1735 to 1744 the average issue of the *Massachusetts Gazette* would be expected under the "null-model" assumption to contain 2.01 symbols of place-names in New York.

predict that .95 symbols of place-names in Massachusetts would appear in the *New-York Weekly Journal,* 1.89 symbols in the *Pennsylvania Gazette,* 1.53 symbols in the *Virginia Gazette,* and .26 symbols in the *South-Carolina Gazette.*

By comparing the actual distribution of symbols during a given time period with the expected distribution, the computer program produced a measure of the *relative attention* (RA) of a colony to each of the others. This measure of relative attention provides information about the direction and extent of the divergence between the actual and the expected distributions. Table 6-6 shows that the *New-York Weekly Journal* paid 52.4 per cent more attention to news from Massachusetts than one would expect solely on the basis of the Bay Colony's newsworthiness (that is, the propensity for place-name symbols in Massachusetts to be printed in the newspapers of other colonies) and New York's general attentiveness to intercolonial news. Relatively speaking, Pennsylvania paid about 37.5 per cent less attention to Massachusetts news than might be expected, while Virginia and South Carolina, even though farther away, were more attentive than expected. South Carolina, for instance, paid 32.4 per cent more of its attention to Massachusetts than would be expected on the basis of the null model; and Virginia was slightly more attentive (8.0%) than the relevant propensities would have indicated. A simple calculation then indicated whether or not the measure of relative attention for each pair of colonies was statistically significant. Those that are statistically significant are in italics in Table 6-6. By way of a caveat for the reader, it must be remembered in examining these measures of relative attention that their bases—the propensities of the colonies to be attentive to other colonies and to be newsworthy for other colonies —changed from decade to decade. Hence if the measure of relative attention paid by one colony to another was positive

TABLE 6-6. Indices of Relative Attention
by Decades, 1735–1775
(Statistically significant indices of relative attention are in italics)

To symbols from	Mass.	N. Y.	Penn.	Va.	S. C.
			1735–1744		
			Relative attention by		
Massachusett		*.524*	*−.375*	.080	*.324*
New York	−.079		*.135*	.011	*−.602*
Pennsylvania	−.081	*−.193*		.212	−.099
Virginia	.176	−.0001	*−.320*		*1.344*
South Carolina	.090	*−.363*	*.314*	−.245	

To symbols from	Mass.	N. Y.	Penn.	Va.	S. C.
			1745–1754		
			Relative attention by		
Massachusetts		.036	.032	*−.779*	.206
New York	.252		−.066	*.382*	*−.493*
Pennsylvania	−.023	−.081		*.634*	−.037
Virginia	−.476	*−.370*	*.390*		*.869*
South Carolina	−.098	*.361*	*−.237*	*−.357*	

To symbols from	Mass.	N. Y.	Penn.	Va.	S. C.
			1755–1764		
			Relative attention by		
Massachusetts		.074	*.256*	*−.687*	−.083
New York	*.118*		*−.142*	.080	−.046
Pennsylvania	*−.128*	*.101*		−.120	.114
Virginia	*.201*	*−.276*	.125		.038
South Carolina	*−.245*	−.076	.040	*.734*	

To symbols from	Mass.	N. Y.	Penn.	Va.	S. C.
			1765–1775		
			Relative attention by		
Massachusetts		*−.116*	*−.093*	*.357*	*.139*
New York	*.091*		.071	*−.287*	−.093
Pennsylvania	−.072	*.317*		*−.281*	*−.320*
Virginia	*−.168*	*−.364*	*.420*		*.292*
South Carolina	*.163*	*.290*	*−.382*	−.166	

in one decade and negative in the next, it is not necessarily true that the flow of news between the two colonies in fact decreased. A comparison of the individual cells in Table 6-6 over time must also take into account the colonies' changing propensities to be attentive and to be newsworthy.

Some of the general patterns in Table 6-6 are nonetheless of interest. Consider, for example, the direction and persistence of the statistically significant entries. Table 6-7 summarizes such patterns by indicating whether news from each colony was always or generally given more or less attention than expected in the journals of each other colony or whether such news received less attention as often as it received more attention. At one extreme, news from Virginia appeared more often than expected in the *South-Carolina Gazette* in each of the three decades in which the actual and the expected flows of news diverged significantly. (The measures of relative attention in Table 6-6, by the way, were in no case statistically significant in any single cell for all four decades.) The average of the significant measures of attention paid to Virginia in the Charleston journal was 83.5 per cent above the expected level. At the other extreme, news of New York always appeared less often than expected in the *South-Carolina Gazette*: the average of the measures of attention to New York in the *Gazette* was 54.8 per cent less than the expected level in the two decades in which the divergence was statistically significant.

Table 6-7 also suggests two aspects of the balance of intercolonial attention. First of all, of ten possible pairs of colonies, only two pairs (Virginia and Pennsylvania, Virginia and Massachusetts) are classified in the same category in this chart. Others, such as New York and South Carolina or South Carolina and Virginia, are in categories separated by as many as two intervening categories. Second, in such a context of imbalance, news from neighboring rather than nonneighboring colonies tended to appear more prominently than expected in the newspapers. Of the eight possible ways in which news could flow from one of the five colonies to its nearest neighbor, five such patterns are to be found in the first two categories of Table 6-7. Generally less attention than expected was paid

TABLE 6-7. The Direction and Persistence
of Attention Patterns

(Averages of the statistically significant measures of relative attention are in parentheses)

Always more attention than expected (in 3 of 3 decades) paid to:
    Virginia by South Carolina ($\overline{RA}$ = .835)
    Massachusetts by South Carolina ($\overline{RA}$ = .223)
    New York by Massachusetts ($\overline{RA}$ = .154)

Generally more attention than expected (in 2 of 3 decades) paid to:
    Pennsylvania by Virginia ($\overline{RA}$ = .188)
    Virginia by Pennsylvania ($\overline{RA}$ = .163)
    South Carolina by New York ($\overline{RA}$ = .096)
    Pennsylvania by New York ($\overline{RA}$ = .075)

Equally more and less attention than expected (1 decade in each direction) paid to:
    Massachusetts by New York ($\overline{RA}$ = .204)
    New York by Virginia ($\overline{RA}$ = .048)
    New York by Pennsylvania ($\overline{RA}$ = −.003)
    South Carolina by Massachusetts ($\overline{RA}$ = −.041)

Generally less attention than expected (in 2 of 3 decades) paid to:
    South Carolina by Virginia ($\overline{RA}$ = .044)
    Massachusetts by Pennsylvania ($\overline{RA}$ = −.071)
    South Carolina by Pennsylvania ($\overline{RA}$ = −.102)
    Virginia by Massachusetts ($\overline{RA}$ = −.148)
    Massachusetts by Virginia ($\overline{RA}$ = −.370)

Always less attention than expected paid to:
    Virginia by New York in 3 of 3 decades ($\overline{RA}$ = −.337)
    New York by South Carolina in 2 of 2 decades ($\overline{RA}$ = −.548)
    Pennsylvania by Massachusetts in 1 of 1 decades ($\overline{RA}$ = −.128)
    Pennsylvania by South Carolina in 1 of 1 decades ($\overline{RA}$ = −.320)

in only one instance, Virginia's relative attention to news from South Carolina, but even in this instance the average of the significant measures of relative attention was 4.4 per cent above the expected level.

The extent to which attention patterns among pairs of colonies were imbalanced is shown even more dramatically by computing from the data in Table 6-6 a crude index of the "attention balance" within each pair. Specifically, this index of attention balance is the difference between two colonies' scores of relative attention to each other. From 1735 to 1744, for example, the relative attention paid to symbols from Massachusetts in the *New-York Weekly Journal* was .524, or 52.4 per cent greater than a "null model" of symbol distribution would have led us to expect. Since the relative attention to symbols from New York in the *Massachusetts Gazette* for this decade was —0.079 (that is, 7.9% less than expected), the index of attention balance between Massachusetts and New York was .603. And, of course, the closer that the index of attention balance between two colonies approached the zero level, the more balanced their relative attention to each other might be said to be. If two colonies, in focusing attention upon each other, actually diverged from the expected by the same degree and in the same direction (that is, if their indices of relative attention to each other were identical), then their index of attention balance would be at the zero level.

Mutual flows of attention were not highly balanced in colonial America. For some pairs of colonies, notably Virginia and South Carolina, the indices of attention balance ranged very high indeed (Table 6-8). In 1735–44, when South Carolina's relative attention to news from Virginia was +1.344 and Virginia's relative attention to news from South Carolina was —0.245, their index of attention balance was 1.589. The colonies most closely balanced in their mutual flow of news were New York and Virginia (attention balance = .011) during the same decade. The average index of attention balance for all pairs of colonies for all decades was .359, that is, the average pair's mutual measures of relative attention to each other differed by a factor equal to 35.9 per cent of the expected flow of news between the two colonies.

TABLE 6-8. Indices of Attention Balance among
Five Colonies, by Decades, 1735–1775

Pairs of Colonies	1735–44	1745–54	1755–64	1765–75	Average
Massachusetts and South Carolina	.234	.304	.162	.024	.181
Pennsylvania and South Carolina	.413	.200	.074	.062	.187
Massachusetts and Pennsylvania	.294	.055	.384	.021	.189
New York and Pennsylvania	.328	.015	.243	.246	.208
Massachusetts and New York	.603	.216	.044	.207	.268
New York and Virginia	.011	.752	.356	.077	.299
New York and South Carolina	.239	.854	.030	.383	.377
Pennsylvania and Virginia	.532	.244	.245	.701	.431
Massachusetts and Virginia	.096	.303	.888	.525	.453
Virginia and South Carolina	1.589	1.226	.696	.458	.992
Average	.434	.417	.312	.270	.359

Certain patterns nonetheless characterize the overall imbalance of attention. First of all, the average index of attention balance for the ten pairs of colonies as a whole declined from decade to decade. By 1765–75 the imbalance was less than two thirds as great as in 1735–44, a finding suggesting increasing congruence of intercolonial attention patterns. Second, attention imbalance did not decrease with decreasing distances among colonies. The average of all indices of attention balance in Table 6-8 for pairs of colonies that were neighbors (that is, Massachusetts and New York, New York and Pennsylvania, Pennsylvania and Virginia, and Virginia and South Carolina) was .475, whereas the average for all nonneighboring pairs of colonies was .281, only three fifths as great. Third, the colony most in attention balance with its sister colonies was Pennsylvania. For all pairs of colonies in Table 6-8, the average index of attention balance for those in which Pennsylvania is a partner is .254. Massachusetts (.273) and New York (.288) follow closely behind Pennsylvania and, some distance back, South Carolina (.435) and Virginia (.544) trail.

These imbalances, together with the earlier findings about the importance to the newspapers of the home colony and of the colonies as a collective unit, produce a composite picture suggesting three modes of intercolonial attention patterns. The outlook of the middle colonies was essentially pluralistic. Relative to the other colonies, Pennsylvania was least preoccupied with local affairs, somewhat below average in the amount of attention it paid to the colonies as a collective whole, and foremost in the propensity to devote attention to sister colonies. Moreover, in terms of the mutual flow of attention, Pennsylvania was most in harmony with the other colonies. New York, too, exhibited such characteristics, although not to such a marked degree. Furthermore, until the middle 1760s at least, New York was the colony most likely to be in the primary focus of attention of its sisters.

In contrast the views of the southern colonies—and Virginia more so than South Carolina—were nationalistic. These two colonies led in paying attention to the colonies as a whole, in considering events that affected all of the colonies as a single unit. At the same time they lagged well behind the others in paying attention to individual colonies, besides being most out of kilter with the others in terms of the mutual flow of attention. Nor were they overly self-concerned. Virginia was slightly below and South Carolina somewhat above average in paying attention to the home colony. And, it must be added, judging from the propensities of these southern colonies to have attention paid to them, other colonies shared their relative lack of concern with events taking place at home.

If the middle colonies emphasized the other colonies as individuals and the southern colonies stressed the collective character of colonial society, Massachusetts was comparatively self-centered. It was not particularly prone to be attentive to other colonies, and was the least interested of the colonies in the collective concept. In a metaphorical sense Massachusetts was an exporter of information that sought to rally the other colonies to its side in the struggle against colonial rule. By the last colonial decade at least, other colonies were quite likely to look to the Bay Colony as a primary source of news.

It is worth noting that these different attention patterns, which formed a significant part of the context of emerging American nationalism, were characteristic of other aspects of colonial behavior that cropped up time and again as late as 1787 in the Constitutional Convention. It was in this context that the colonists formed their perceptions of and attitudes toward their community as a whole and toward themselves as a people.

CHAPTER SEVEN

Americanism: Symbols of Common Identity

The symbolism of names plays a significant role, not only in the magic of primitive people and the games of children, but in the process of group development as well. The designation of a group by a name—a specific name that serves as a symbol under which all would-be members of the group can unite, no less than as a means to differentiate the group from other such groups—is indicative that the group has come of age. In a situation where people are beginning to shift their primary group loyalties, the symbolism of names is of signal importance.

The conditions under which changes in group identity take place may range, at least theoretically, from a state of complete consciousness to complete unconsciousness of group identity. At the one extreme, typified by a revolutionary situation, the individual faces a decision on group membership, on the basis of which he must act and perhaps die. The immediate, if not always long-range, consequences of membership in a revolutionary or antirevolutionary group may appear for the most part evident—or at least some of them are vividly imagined— and play an important part in the individual's decision. Pictured graphically, a curve denoting the degree of his identification with the new group would remain at the zero level until a particular point in time—the point of decision—at which it would rise instantly to the 100 per cent level. To consider a case at the other extreme, it is conceivable that the members of a group may drift apart so gradually that the rift between them is virtually imperceptible until it is a gaping chasm. In this latter example, the curved line would rise steadily and gradually, if slowly, throughout the entire period of drift.

While it is possible to think of cases to fit into both of these extreme patterns, we might anticipate that most changes in group identity would fall somewhere between them. The immigrant, however well assimilated into his new culture, is generally unable to cut all ties of loyalty to his native land; nostalgic memories of and loyalties to the old country often endure through generations. Even the revolutionist, unless acting from motives of pure opportunism, probably goes through a period when he does not know or cannot say with which of two groups he would identify himself if called upon to make an immediate decision. This is one of the types of phenomena that Harold Guetzkow has described as a "multiple loyalty": "an array of loyalties [coexisting] in the same person toward different objects at the same time." [1]

The presence of multiple loyalty patterns may pose no problem for the individual, provided that his membership in two or more groups is not in fact incompatible, or that he does not perceive his obligations to the different groups to be incompatible. Thus Benjamin Franklin was able to write in 1760: "No one can more sincerely rejoice than I do, on the reduc-

1. Harold Guetzkow, *Multiple Loyalties: Theoretical Approach to a Problem in International Organization,* Publication No. 4, Center for Research on World Political Institutions, Woodrow Wilson School of Public and International Affairs (Princeton, Princeton University Press, 1955), p. 39.

tion of Canada; and this is not merely as I am a Colonist, but as I am a Briton." [2] Where multiple loyalties make conflicting demands upon the individual, however, the result might be hesitation, distortion, inaction, or some other form of breakdown. As Guetzkow has written, "multiple loyalties are quite admissible, *provided* the different objects are furnishing compatible solutions to different needs." [3] In the case of incompatible multiple loyalties, we might anticipate that a curved line depicting changing group identities would be irregular or even jerky, rising neither instantly nor steadily and smoothly.

An analysis of symbols of common identity in the colonial press—the "continental symbols" discussed in the previous chapter—would tell us much about group identification patterns in eighteenth-century America. First of all, by categorizing these symbols according to their origin, that is, whether they appear in articles with British, American, or foreign (that is, outside the Anglo-American sphere) datelines, it will be possible to tell how different areas viewed the colonial scene. Did the London journals refer to the colonists as "British Americans" or as "Americans"? With what political community did the colonists identify themselves, that is, what symbols of common group identity did they use in reference to themselves? Since foreign-datelined symbols comprised an insignificant share (about 2%) of the total number of symbols of common identity, they will not be discussed in any detail here. A second means of categorization is the primary identification content of the symbols: do they denote the geographic area that later became the United States, or its population? Third, these symbols of common identity may be categorized according to the specific label—a so-called secondary

2. Cited in Greene, *The Revolutionary Generation*, p. 181.
3. Guetzkow, *Multiple Loyalties*, p. 39.

symbol—that they attach when identifying the primary content. Do the symbols associate the land or its population with the British political community or with a distinctly American community? In this respect we may differentiate five groups of such symbols: (1) Symbols of explicit British common identity: "British North America," "the English colonies," "British America," or "British colonists," "British Americans," "English provincials"; (2) Symbols of identification with the British Crown: "His Majesty's colonies," "royal colonies" or "crown colonies," "His Majesty's subjects in America," "Royal Americans"; (3) Symbols of implicit British common identity: the "colonies" or "provinces," "our colonies in America" (only when used in the British press), "colonists," or "provincials"; (4) Symbols of implicit American common identity: the "continent" or "country," the "American colonies" or the "colonies in America," the "United Colonies," the "continentals," "American colonists"; and (5) Symbols of explicit American common identity: "America" or "North America," "Americans" or "North Americans." It must be emphasized again at this point that the following discussion will consider both explicit or direct ("the colonies") and indirect ("here" or "they") symbols of common identity.

THE LAND: BRITISH COLONIES OR AMERICA?

The British Look at the Land   To the extent that newspapers were important in helping to shape the colonists' image of common identity, the symbol usage of British news items reprinted in the colonial press was almost as important as the use of symbols in articles written by the colonists themselves. Of the total number of symbols of common identity referring to the land in the sets of newspapers surveyed, 45.6 per cent appeared in items with British datelines or in letters written from Great Britain to correspondents in the colonies.[4]

The high percentage of symbols with British datelines by no means suggests that our sample of newspapers adequately reflects the British image of the colonies. It is entirely possible that one or more of the colonial printers, who presumably geared the content of their newspapers to the interests of their own readers, systematically or unwittingly reproduced items from British journals that mirrored a certain point of view or symbol usage. The data gathered for this inquiry do not pretend to be an accurate sample of the news presented by English editors to their readers. More important for our purposes is the fact that the colonial printers presented to the colonists a British image of the American colonies. It is this image that will be discussed in the following pages. Whether or not the image that the colonial printers presented corresponds to the real image found in the British press, however interesting and significant that question might be, is a subject that must be left for further studies of the emerging American political community; the present study can deal only with the images or messages that actually appeared in the newspapers of eighteenth-century America.

In each of the eight five-year periods from 1735 to 1775, the British image appearing in the colonial newspapers as

4. From 1735 to 1763, 42.2 per cent of such symbols appeared in items with British datelines, while 48.9 per cent were of American origin. In terms of linage, as discussed above, 52.6 per cent of the average newspaper's news space in 1738 was devoted to news reprinted from English journals, and 43.7 per cent had originally appeared in colonial newspapers. From 1764 to 1775, 46.3 per cent of the symbols of common identity bore British datelines, as compared to 52.8 per cent of American origin. The source of linage in the average colonial newspaper of 1768 was: 27.6 per cent from Britain; 25.1 per cent reprinted from other colonial prints; and 44.2 per cent original reports. To some measure these figures reflect the degree to which colonial printers relied upon British sources to fill their own journals.

often or more often identified the land as American than as British (Figure 7-1). Almost from the outset the term "America" was more popular in articles with British datelines than "His Majesty's colonies," "British America," or, more simply, "the colonies." As shown in Figure 7-1, the percentage of symbols of American common identity rose from 50.0 per cent in 1735–39 to 76.2 per cent in 1755–59; and, although the percentage dropped off to less than 60 per cent during the next decade, by 1770–75 it was again 67.5 per cent. A linear trend line, smoothing out the fluctuations in the curve over the entire time span, shows a rise from 52.8 per cent in 1735–39 to 67.7 per cent in 1770–75.

The yearly averages of the British use of symbols of common identity present a slightly different and somewhat more complex picture. To be sure, considering the 22 years from the outbreak of the French and Indian War to the year of the skirmishes at Lexington and Concord, there were only three years in which the percentage of symbols identifying the colonies as American rather than British dropped below the 50 per cent level (Figure 7-2). More interesting, however, are the fluctuations in the curve. After a five-year period during the height of the French and Indian War (1757–61), in which British symbol usage was almost unanimous in referring to the colonies as American, came a decline that reached its low point in 1764—the year in which the Sugar Act was passed in England and the colonial press began to express dissatisfaction with parliamentary taxation policies. The average for the four years from 1764 to 1767 was 54.0 per cent, that is, lower than any of the five-year periods shown in Figure 7-1 after 1740. In 1768 the curve swung upward and for the remaining eight years (1768–75) remained relatively stable around the 70 per cent level. The major fluctuations occurred in the year of the Boston Massacre, 1770, when the

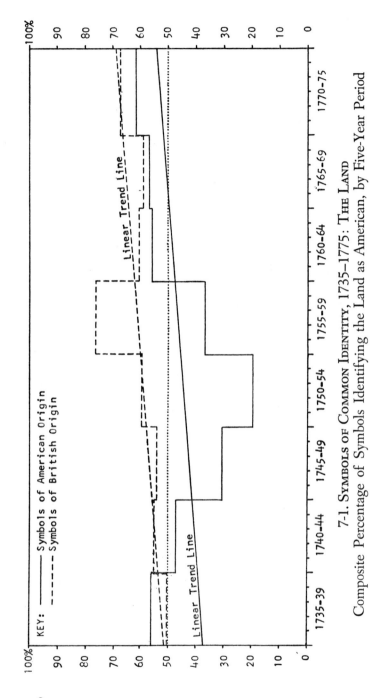

7-1. Symbols of Common Identity, 1735–1775: The Land

Composite Percentage of Symbols Identifying the Land as American, by Five-Year Period

curve dropped to 58.6 per cent, in 1773 when it rose sharply, and in 1775, the year of the outbreak of the Revolution, when it sank to 66.8 per cent. In general, as the linear trend line indicates, a declining proportion of symbols with British datelines over the 22-year time span identified the land as American rather than British.

The data gathered for this study, although indicating the general patterns of symbol usage in news items of British origin in the years after 1754, cannot account conclusively for minor changes in these patterns. The data do, however, suggest an interesting hypothesis that could be tested further: as tension between the colonies and the mother country increased, the image of the colonies presented in the newspapers of the mother country increasingly sought to tie the colonies to the mother country. Thus, during periods of Anglo-American unity, such as during the war against the French and their Indian allies, there was no need to assert the colonial tie. And it is indeed true that, during the years from 1757 to 1761, the reprinted English items included in this survey seldom referred to "His Majesty's colonies" or to "the colonies," preferring to term them "America" or "North America." When the period of unity ended, however, and crises of one sort or another threatened to estrange the colonies from the mother country, the English press again began to speak of "British America" and "His Majesty's colonies"—emphasizing the colonial tie.[5] It should be added that all of these fluctuations occurred in the context of an overall secular trend from 1735 to 1775 that increasingly referred to the land as American.

The use of the individual symbols of common identity

5. To test this hypothesis it would be necessary to turn to an analysis of the British press itself, for the image presented in the American prints, as suggested above, might not be accurate.

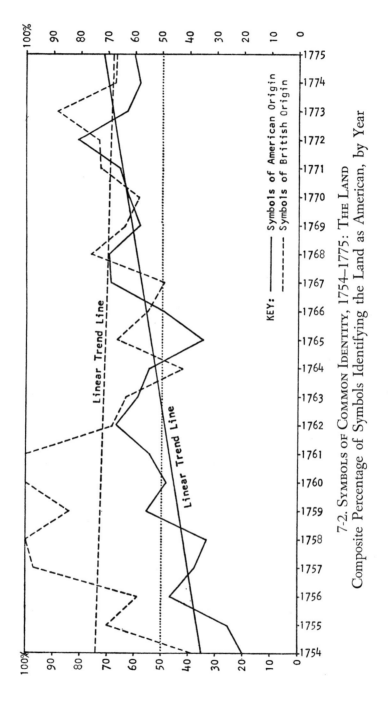

7-2. Symbols of Common Identity, 1754–1775: The Land

Composite Percentage of Symbols Identifying the Land as American, by Year

KEY: ——— Symbols of American Origin
‑ ‑ ‑ ‑ Symbols of British Origin

themselves in the British-datelined articles presents another set of interesting patterns. Relative to the total number of symbols of common identity, for example, symbols of identification with the British Crown decreased sharply over the 41 years, as did symbols of explicit British common identity ("British America" or "the British colonies"), if not to such a great degree (Table 7-1). As the use of symbols clearly and

TABLE 7-1. Distribution of British-Datelined Symbols of
Common Identity Referring to the Land,
by Decades, 1735–1775

Period	Explicit British	Royal British	Implicit British	Implicit American	Explicit American	Total	Total Symbols
1735–44	9.1%	25.0%	13.6%	6.8%	45.5%	100.0%	44
1745–54	14.8	14.8	13.1	9.8	47.5	100.0	61
1755–64	12.7	7.3	12.7	4.2	63.0	99.9	354
1765–75[1]	6.2	2.3	28.4	6.9	56.2	100.0	1,829
1735–75	7.5	3.8	25.3	6.6	56.8	100.0	2,288

1. Includes eleven years.

strongly identifying the American colonies with the British Empire declined, terms of a more neutral shading—that is, symbols of implicit British common identity, such as "the provinces" or "the colonies"—became more popular. Bar graphs may present somewhat more dramatically the qualitative shifts shown by the data in Table 7-1. Table 7-2 shows the percentage distribution of the British-datelined symbols of common identity for the first and last decades of our 41-year period. At the left end of each of these bar graphs is the percentage of the total number of symbols strongly identifying the land as a part of either the British or royal domain; and proceeding from left to right are symbols of implicit British common identity, symbols of implicit American common identity, and, finally, symbols explicitly identifying the land as "American." On the one hand, of course, it is possible that these data merely indicate that the reprinting habits of the colonial printers changed over the course of the last four pre-Revolutionary decades. But, on the other hand, it seems more

TABLE 7-2. Shifts in the British Image of the American Land

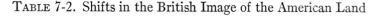

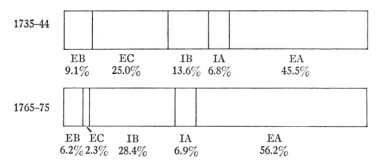

1735–44					
	EB	EC	IB	IA	EA
	9.1%	25.0%	13.6%	6.8%	45.5%

1765–75					
	EB	EC	IB	IA	EA
	6.2%	2.3%	28.4%	6.9%	56.2%

EB: Explicit British ("the English colonies," "British America").
EC: Explicit Crown ("His Majesty's colonies," "the royal provinces").
IB: Implicit British ("colonies," "provinces").
IA: Implicit American ("continent," "country," "American colonies").
EA: Explicit American ("America," "North America").

likely that, from the first to the last decade of this 41-year period, the British press became less sure that the colonies were a part of the British realm. This is indicated by the decrease in strong British symbols and the increase in ambiguous or implicit British symbols. At the same time the British press gave relatively more room to strong American symbols, suggesting a firmer belief that the colonies constituted a distinctly separate American territory.

The Americans Look at the Land The changing colonial image of America presents an interesting contrast to the British image. Considered by five-year periods, articles in the colonial press with British datelines, it will be recalled, more often viewed the land as American rather than British after 1740 (Figure 7-1). The American image, however, viewed the land as a part of an emerging American political community slightly over one half of the time. The ratio of American identifying symbols to all symbols of common identity with American datelines during the first half-decade (1735–39) was 56.0 per cent; but this ratio dropped steadily throughout the next 15 years. By 1750–54 less than one in five symbols identified the land as American. The British-datelined ratio, discussed in the previous section, started at roughly the same level, but rose constantly throughout the next two decades. Thus, at a time when the British were increasingly often identifying the colonies as an entity distinct from the British realm, the colonists were viewing their land more and more as a part of that British community. Viewed in terms of integrative and disintegrative processes, the British image during the twenty years from 1735 to 1754 reflected a slight weakening of Anglo-American ties of community, while at the same time the colonial image reflected substantial decreases in sentiments of separate identity and, by implication, an increased readiness to accept symbolic ties to the mother country.

The next two decades saw a reversal of these trends. The data summarized in both Figures 7-1 and 7-2 reveal that the British-datelined symbols identifying the colonies as American reached a peak during the French and Indian War years. After a decline in the early 1760s, the distribution curves for symbols of British origin never regained their former height. For the period as a whole from 1754 to 1775, expressed by the linear trend line in Figure 7-2, a declining proportion of symbols with British datelines recognized the continent as American. The curves showing the distribution of American-datelined symbols, however, moved sharply upward during these years. Indeed, the linear trend line (Figure

7-2) rose 36 percentage points—or 1.7 per cent per year—from 1754 to 1775, crossing the trend line for British-date-lined symbols in 1773. In short, while the British image was seeking to slow up the disintegrative processes during this period, the colonists were more often viewing Britain and America as separate entities.

The distribution curves for the last two decades of the colonial period point to an interesting interaction of symbol usage with stresses in the eighteenth-century Anglo-American community. Figure 7-1, for example, reveals a parallel and yet differential response to the outbreak of the French and Indian War in colonial and British symbol usage. The share of symbols identifying the colonies as American rose by about 17 percentage points from 1750–54 to 1755–59 in the distribution of symbols of both colonial and British origin. But in spite of this parallel shift in symbol usage during a period of stress imposed by the hostility of a common enemy, a very important difference remained: about 76 per cent of the symbols of British origin identified the colonies as American in 1755–59, while only 37 per cent—less than one half as many—of the symbols of American origin made this distinction.

The end of the French danger to America in about 1760 brought with it cross-pressures creating strains in the mutual relations of the colonies and the mother country. While the British, as reflected in the colonial press, began to reassert the colonial ties, the colonists emphasized their separate identity to an ever greater degree (Figure 7-2). In 1759 the colonists termed their land American more often than British for the first time; and by 1763 their curve showing the distribution of symbols of American common identity rose above the curve of British origin.

After 1763, however, the curves of the two sets of symbols moved together to a remarkably high degree (Figure 7-2). In spite of cross-pressures in the Anglo-American community during the last colonial decade, in spite of stresses and strains in their mutual relations, the images that British and American journalists held of the embryo American political community proceeded in a fairly parallel fashion, with periods of decline in the curve during the height of the Stamp Act crisis and the colonial agitation following the passage of the Tea Act in 1773, and with inclines in the late 1760s and early 1770s.

By 1763 the colonists had crossed an important threshold in symbol usage and in their perceptions of the American community. The linear trend line in Figure 7-2 indicates that it was in 1763 that the trend in colonial symbol usage crossed the 50 per cent line; after that date symbols of American origin more often identified the colonies as American than British in every year save two, 1765 and 1766. Since, except for 1764 and 1767, this was also true for symbols of British origin, this means that the colonists who read newspapers after 1763 were more likely to see their country described in terms of an American political community than in terms of the imperial connection with the mother country. If this symbol usage actually reflected the changing perceptions of the colonists or at least of their politically relevant strata—an assumption that is basic to the present study—then it is extremely likely that these colonists also perceived their own interests to be apart from, if not actually incompatible with, those of Great Britain.

Looking at the distribution of symbols with American datelines (Figure 7-2) in terms of integrative processes, it can be seen that the colonial image of an emerging separate identity conformed to neither of the extreme patterns discussed at the outset of this chapter. There was no single point at which the curve rose dramatically from a low to a high level of American common identity, nor did the curve rise smoothly and steadily. Rather, it resembled what might be termed a typical learning curve.[6] When a small child learns a new skill, such as standing, it is most often a matter of trial and error. His first successful attempt may be nothing more than an accidental patterning of his otherwise random motions and actions (behavior). The proud parents are, however, quite often dismayed when the child seems to have forgotten how to stand up—that is, when he is unable to repeat his earlier, random pattern—for a matter of several days or even weeks. After his second successful attempt the child is able to put together the winning combination of behavior increasingly more often until he crosses what might be termed the threshold of achievement, when more than 50 per cent of his attempts are successful. But even after he has reached that point, as every parent knows, he will have occasional relapses and garner his share of bumps and bruises. Pictured graphically, a learning curve is one that rises gradually and fitfully rather than smoothly: the peaks of achievement follow more closely upon each other, and depressions in the curve are ever more infrequent.

In this manner the colonists "learned" to call their homeland "America," as they haltingly replaced one pattern of symbol usage with another. And the crucial point—that at which the colonists crossed the threshold of American common identity—came, as the trend lines in Figures 7-1 and 7-2 suggest, during the course of 1763.

6. The variables underlying this phenomenon, as well as the means of describing it, are subjects of hot dispute in the field of educational psychology, particularly since the publication of Edward L. Thorndike's *Animal Intelligence* in 1898, in which he identified the most characteristic form of learning of both lower animals and man as "trial-and-error" (or selecting and connecting) learning. Cf., Ernest R. Hilgard, *Theories of Learning* (2d ed. New York, Appleton-Century-Crofts, 1956), p. 16. For other examples of such curves and mathematical models of learning, see Robert N. Bush and Frederick Mosteller, *Stochastic Models for Learning* (New York, Wiley, 1955).

Common Identity

Considered qualitatively, American news items did not differ very significantly from British news items in the use of individual symbols. Using the data in Table 7-3 to construct another pair of bar graphs, and comparing the two sets

TABLE 7-3. Distribution of American-Datelined Symbols of Common Identity Referring to the Land, by Decades, 1735–1775

Period	Explicit British	Royal British	Implicit British	Implicit American	Explicit American	Total	Total Symbols
1735–44	7.7%	19.2%	23.1%	3.8%	46.2%	100.0%	78
1745–54	10.6	27.1	37.6	4.7	20.0	100.0	85
1755–64	6.3	13.6	35.4	13.0	31.6	99.9	316
1765–75[1]	5.1	1.2	34.2	16.7	42.8	100.0	2,135
1735–75	5.5	4.1	34.2	15.5	40.8	100.1	2,614

1. Includes eleven years.

of bar graphs, the points of similarity and difference between British-datelined symbols and symbols of American origin may easily be seen. The use of symbols strongly identifying the colonies with the British Empire (e.g. "His Majesty's colonies," "the British colonies," "British America") dropped off slightly more sharply in American-datelined items than in those of British origin; while the rise in the use of symbols of implicit British common identity was more marked in items with British rather than American datelines.

More significant, however, is the distribution of symbols of implicit and explicit American common identity. From the first to the fourth decade of our period, the relative number of explicit American symbols remained practically unchanged, dropping somewhat from 46.2 per cent in 1735–44 to 42.8 per cent in 1765–75. Meanwhile, the percentage of implicit American symbols increased from less than one out of 25 to more than one out of six, quadrupling the share of implicit

American symbols with colonial datelines relative to all symbols of common identity of colonial origin. British-datelined implicit American symbols, it will be recalled, increased but slightly, while the relative share of explicit ones rose more than ten percentage points.

But what do these shifting images mean? On the one hand, it would seem that the colonists, like the British, became in time less convinced that the colonies were essentially British, but that they were less willing than their English brethren to commit themselves definitely and strongly to the existence of an American community. On the other hand, however, the colonists' behavior, as indicated by their patterns of symbol usage, suggests that they were following a more or less definite policy, substituting ambiguous symbols oriented toward an American political community in the place of symbols clearly asserting the ties of the colonies to the mother country. Whether it stemmed from hesitation or design, the effect was that explicit and royal British symbols all but disappeared from the language of the colonial press in the decade prior to the outbreak of the Revolution.

The bar graphs shown in Table 7-4 also point to another qualitative change in the colonial use of symbols of common identity. We may look at these graphs as scales of attitudes and perceptions, with strong pro-British attitudes on the one side and strong patriotic or anti-British sentiments at the opposite end. In the decade from 1735 to 1744, when the share of implicit American symbols was quite small, the implicit British symbols stood midway between the strongly phrased perceptions. In a figurative sense, this sizable group of implicit British symbols resembles a middle-of-the-road political party, flanked by major parties of a more extreme character. A person wishing to express a neutral sentiment in the 1735–44 period would probably have used such implicit British symbols as "the colonies" or "the provinces."

By the last decade of the colonial period, however, the common meeting ground of symbol usage had shifted from im-

TABLE 7-4. Shifts in the Colonial Image of the American Land

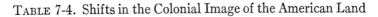

1735–44

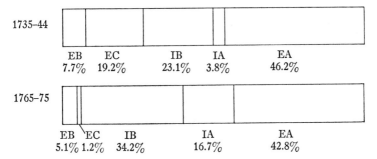

EB	EC	IB	IA	EA
7.7%	19.2%	23.1%	3.8%	46.2%

1765–75

EB	EC	IB	IA	EA
5.1%	1.2%	34.2%	16.7%	42.8%

EB: Explicit British ("the English colonies," "British America").
EC: Explicit Crown ("His Majesty's colonies," "the royal provinces").
IB: Implicit British ("colonies," "provinces").
IA: Implicit American ("continent," "country," "American colonies").
EA: Explicit American ("America," "North America").

plicit British to implicit American symbols. To extend the comparison used above, if one of two flanking parties disappears (or almost disappears), the party in the center finds itself in a relatively more extreme position. In the years from 1765 to 1775 the use of explicit or royal British symbols had paled into insignificance. The use of implicit British symbols became virtually an extreme position (even though the relative share of these symbols had grown). If, without stretching our fantasy too far, we can imagine the Tory and the Patriot finding a common means of communication in the 1735–44 period by using ambiguous symbols implying their identity with the mother country but not explicitly asserting it, it would seem that by the 1765–75 period this symbol usage no longer served a mediating function in colonial communication. The middle position, the symbol usage expressing a mean or average sentiment or perception, had become the category of implicit American symbols. The person wishing to express a neutral attitude in the last decade of the colonial era would probably have used such terms as "the continent" or, in the immediate pre-Revolutionary years, the "United Colonies."

THE POPULATION: BRITISH COLONISTS OR AMERICANS?

Prior to 1763 the colonial press was all but unanimous in identifying the colonists with the British political community: not one of the twelve symbols of British origin referred to them as "Americans"; and only three of 124 items with American datelines did so.[7] In 1740 articles in both the *New-York Weekly Journal* and the *Massachusetts Gazette* used the term "Americans," but the next instance of its use in our sample did not come until 1756, in an item in the *Virginia Gazette*. By far the most popular terms during these 29 years were those identifying the colonists as subjects of the British Crown —"His Majesty's subjects," "His Majesty's colonists," and, after 1756, the regimental name "Royal Americans"—which together comprised 108 (or 79.4 per cent) of the total of 136 symbols of both British and American origin.

It was not until the years after 1764 that the distinction between "His Majesty's subjects" or "British colonists" and "Americans" became a real one in the colonial newspapers.

7. The total number of symbols of common identity referring to the colonial population—908 symbols in all—is small compared to the 5020 referring to the land, and is rather poorly distributed over the 41-year period. Less than one sixth (138) of them occurred during the twenty-nine years from 1735 to 1763; and 348, or almost two fifths, of them are to be found in the newspapers after 1773.

But even during this period the relative paucity of symbols resulted in wide fluctuations in the distribution of the symbols from year to year (as may be seen in Figure 7-3A). These data become considerably more meaningful when expressed in terms of trends, either a "moving averages" curve that smooths out the extreme fluctuations or a trend line that reduces the fluctuations to a straight line (Figure 7-3B).

Throughout these twelve years, from 1764 to 1775, articles of British origin were more apt to portray the inhabitants of the American continent as Americans than were items with colonial datelines. In fact, as Figure 7-3A shows, in only four years of the twelve did the American dateline curve rise above that derived from British sources. It is also interesting to note that the trend line for the usage of American symbols of common identity rose more sharply for symbols appearing in British items: while the American press increased its use of American identification symbols on an average of 1.4 per cent per year, the growth rate of the recognition of the colonists as Americans in the British-datelined articles was 2.9 per cent.

Again it appears that the changeover in the colonial view of the American population was neither revolutionary nor so gradual as to be almost unnoticeable. Rather, it seems to have been a process resembling a learning curve, taking place over a period probably longer than the twelve years shown in Figures 7-3A and 7-3B. The data available suggest that, as far as symbol usage in the colonial press is concerned, the colonists' own threshold of self-conscious or explicit "Americanism"—that imaginary 50 per cent line—was crossed at the latest in 1773, although it is true that there were some three years before that date when the curve was above the 50 per cent level, and at least one year after 1773 when it was below the halfway mark.

As in the case of symbols of common identity referring to

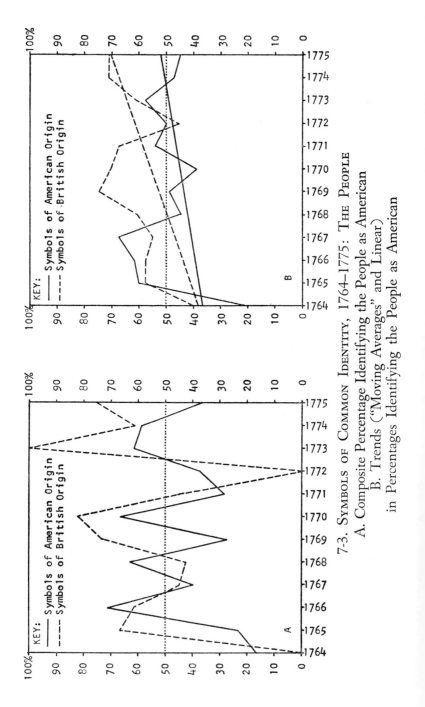

7-3. Symbols of Common Identity, 1764-1775: The People
A. Composite Percentage Identifying the People as American
B. Trends ("Moving Averages" and Linear)
in Percentages Identifying the People as American

the land, British-datelined symbols distinguished the colonists from the British political community before symbols of American origin did so. The linear trend line in Figure 7-3B for British symbols crossed the 50 per cent line as early as 1768 —five years before the curve representing the distribution of symbols of American origin crossed that level.

COLONIAL VARIATIONS ON THE PATTERN
OF AMERICAN IDENTIFICATION

The relative scarcity of symbols of common identity in the colonial press for the earlier years—the average issue during the first half of the 41-year period had less than one such symbol—sharply limits the usefulness of a breakdown of the analysis for individual newspapers. By considering these data by five-year periods, however, and looking at the total image of common identity (consisting of items of American, British, and foreign origin referring both to the American land and population) presented in the press of the different colonies, the resulting set of "moving averages" trend lines illustrate some interesting points (Figure 7-4). While not as satisfactory an analysis as we might wish, it does have one important justification: the trend lines show the total image of the American community presented to the inhabitants of the various colonies. This does away with the assumption that the readers either consciously or unconsciously differentiated items stemming from the pens of colonial journalists from those reprinted from English prints or excerpted from letters sent from the mother country.

The composite image of group identification patterns presented to the colonists by the press was one of stability from 1735 to 1749, followed by 26 years of steadily increasing Americanism. Figure 7-4 suggests that the threshold of at least implicit Americanism was crossed in the late 1750s. It is none-

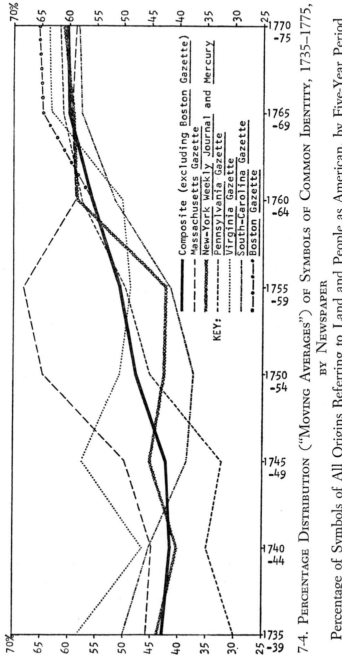

KEY:
Composite (excluding Boston Gazette)
Massachusetts Gazette
New-York Weekly Journal and Mercury
Pennsylvania Gazette
Virginia Gazette
South-Carolina Gazette
Boston Gazette

7-4. Percentage Distribution ("Moving Averages") of Symbols of Common Identity, 1735–1775, by Newspaper

Percentage of Symbols of All Origins Referring to Land and People as American, by Five-Year Period

theless clear that, even by 1775, editorial opinion in the colonial press was far from crystallized in its choice of symbols: the average newspaper that labeled the colonies and colonists "American" two times in five during the first fifteen years of our period was doing so only on three of five occasions during the course of the last decade.[8]

The trend lines for the individual newspapers present some interesting contrasts to the composite pattern. While, for example, the *Virginia Gazette*[9] was far above average in its Americanism during the first part of the 41 years, the *Pennsylvania Gazette* was far below average. The trend lines of the Virginia and Pennsylvania journals crossed in 1755–59, reversed their relative positions, and recrossed in the middle of the 1760s. The New York and Massachusetts newspapers' degree of Americanism hovered around the 45 per cent level from 1735 to 1749: somewhat more than two fifths of the symbols referring to the colonies or the colonists during those years identified them as "American." The Bay Colony's newspaper increased its percentage of American identification symbols to about the 60 per cent level after 1750. The attitude of the New York prints, however, remained constant for another decade before rising to the higher level. The pattern for the *South-Carolina Gazette,* meanwhile, started at a relatively high level, declined steadily to a very low level, and then rose again.

8. We might anticipate, however, that an extension of the present study into the years after the outbreak of revolution would reveal that, by the early 1780s, it was the rare newspaper indeed that used the terms "British subjects" or "British America" in reference to the newly confederated country.

9. It must be remembered that the curve for the *Virginia Gazette* from 1735 to 1749 is doubtless the least reliable of all of them, due primarily to the incompleteness of that journal's files for this early period. Only fifteen symbols of common identity appeared in our sample of this print during these fifteen years.

But what do these patterns tell us about colonial variations in the use of American symbols of common identity? The first, and perhaps the most important, point is that, with the passage of time, and as the newspapers began to include more symbols of common identity in their columns, their choice of symbols tended to become more congruent. Although the degree of Americanism in the four sets of newspapers ranged over almost 30 percentage points at the outset of our period, the difference in the decade from 1765 to 1775 was (except for the *Boston Gazette*) only five percentage points. Thus, while the curve of the *Virginia Gazette* varied as much as 15.4 percentage points from the average or composite curve in 1735–39, by the last five-year period the most dissident newspaper, again the *Virginia Gazette,* varied no more than 3.2 percentage points from the composite curve. (Even the *Boston Gazette,* whose symbols were not included in the computation of the composite curve, varied only 4.9 percentage points from the average in these last six years.)

In the first three decades of the 41 years, the most advanced in presenting an image of Americanism to its reading public was the *Massachusetts Gazette.* Not only did this journal contain more symbols of common identity, but, except for the *Virginia Gazette* from 1735 to 1749, it also consistently identified the colonies and colonists as American more often than did the other newspapers. The *Massachusetts Gazette's* curve of Americanism slipped downward after 1765, and in the fourth decade was below that of the other prints.

As the *Massachusetts Gazette's* trend line was dropping, however, that of the *Boston Gazette* rose—from 55.7 per cent in 1762–66 to 65.4 per cent in 1770–75—and assumed the position of leadership.[10] What is the explanation for such a

10. A linear trend line based on the ratio of *Boston Gazette* American symbols of common identity to those in the *Massachusetts Gazette* reveals

phenomenon? Was it, perhaps, the political orientation of the two newspapers? The data gathered for the present study cannot explain this swing in leadership conclusively, but it does seem quite possible that the editors of the Tory *Massachusetts Gazette,* after the disturbances of the Stamp Act period, were anxious to reassert the ties of the colonies to the mother country, while the *Boston Gazette's* editors became increasingly committed to a course of independence.

If the New England prints were the leaders in recognizing the "Americanness" of the colonies and colonists, it was the set of newspapers from New York City that proved to be the laggard. As was noted above, their degree of Americanism did not move from the 45 per cent level until after 1760, although in the next sixteen years the New York curve was very close to the average or composite curve. It is interesting to note, incidentally, how smoothly the pattern of Americanism in John Peter Zenger's *New-York Weekly Journal* was carried over into Hugh Gaine's *Mercury* during at least the first decade of the latter's existence.

The *Pennsylvania Gazette* started out as the journal least interested in identifying the colonies and colonists as American. Not until the 1750s did its curve rise to the level of other newspapers.[11] During the 1760s and 1770s the Pennsylvania curve differed only insignificantly from the composite curve. By itself, the *Pennsylvania Gazette's* curve is not extraordinary. But a question is raised when we consider that

---

that the former outstripped the latter in degree of Americanism in 1769. The trend line itself runs from 81.9 in 1762 (that is, the percentage of symbols of common identity in the *Boston Gazette* identifying the colonies and colonists as American was 81.9 per cent as great as the corresponding percentage for the *Massachusetts Gazette*) to 116.5 in 1775.

11. It might be well to recall that the relative paucity of such symbols of common identity rules out the possibility of establishing hard and fast principles, and that the figures used in this chapter include both explicit or direct and indirect symbols of common identity.

the period during which the *Gazette* was far below average in its Americanism comprised those years when Benjamin Franklin was its sole editor. From 1735 to 1748 only one third (34.0%) of the symbols of common identity in this journal identified the colonies and colonists as American, and it was not until Franklin retired as active editor and publisher in 1748 that this percentage rose. Was Franklin, author of the Albany Plan of Union and one of the most important creators of the American confederation and federation, uninterested in promoting an American sense of identity during these years? Such an argument is not inconsistent with what we already know about Benjamin Franklin in this period and his view of a multiple, but compatible, Anglo-American loyalty. It was not by twisting the lion's tail that Franklin was so successful as a colonial agent. Nor did his success in securing British patronage for himself and members of his family (particularly his son, William, appointed governor of New Jersey in 1762) rest on outspoken demands for American independence.

The symbol distribution of the *Virginia Gazette* is the most difficult to characterize, possibly because of the incompleteness of existing files of that journal. It would appear, however, that it was the most Americanized of the colonial prints during the years from 1735 to 1744, when seven of the twelve (58.3%) symbols in its columns identified the colonies as American. The next two decades saw a declining American identification in the *Virginia Gazette*: 57.1 per cent of the symbols of common identity labeled the colonies and colonists American in 1745–54, and 45.1 per cent did so in 1755–64. In the years after 1765, well over three fifths of all symbols of common identity in the Virginia newspapers were symbols of American identification. Thus, if the small number of extant copies of the *Virginia Gazette* permits us to generalize, it would seem that the attempt to reintegrate the colonies with the mother country through the use of symbols in the first decades of our period was most marked in the Old Dominion.

The *South-Carolina Gazette* was similar to the *Virginia Gazette* in one respect. Both were initially leaders in identifying the colonies and their population as American and, after dropping off during the middle years of the 41-year period, rose again to approximately the level of the composite trend. The major difference between the two journals was one of degree. When the Americanism of the Charleston newspaper declined, it dropped to a level below that of the others. The decade from 1745 to 1754 found the *South-Carolina Gazette* identifying the colonies and the colonists as American only six times in 20 (30.0%); during the ensuing decade it did so 66 times in 155 (42.6%). Thereafter South Carolina's curve of Americanness lagged somewhat behind the composite curve.

One final aspect of the symbols of common identity appearing in the colonial press from 1735 to 1775 remains to be discussed. As we have noted above, the Boston newspapers were the most advanced in presenting to the colonial reading public an image of Americanism, while the journals from the middle colonies lagged behind. It was not until the newspapers from New York and Pennsylvania swung into line with the Boston prints that the effective symbol revolution took place. And this growing congruence preceded such critical events as the Stamp Act crisis. In a sense this pattern parallels what William Foote Whyte observed about "street corner societies" in the modern American metropolis. Such small groups as youth gangs, Whyte noted, often contain "idea-men"—members who propose courses of action—and men who give the nod. The latter members are the true leaders: they control the commitment of the group's resources to any particular course of action.[12] We might say that Massachusetts was the "idea-man" in colonial America, proposing a greater amount of Americanism throughout the four decades that preceded the Revolution. But the Boston printers by themselves could not produce a symbol revolution. That event had to wait until the middle colonies nodded their assent, which did not come until the 1760s.

In reviewing the changeover in symbol usage in the colonial press, three general points should be reemphasized. First, the split in the territorial aspects of the Anglo-American political community of the eighteenth century was noticed and made symbolically evident before the recognition of the distinction between Englishmen and Americans. Second, in both of these processes of change, British writers and journalists (as mirrored in the colonial press) were quicker than were colonists to make the symbolic distinctions. British-datelined articles identified the colonies as American throughout the years after 1740, and by 1768 they termed the inhabitants of that continent "Americans" more often than "His Majesty's subjects" or even "colonists"; the corresponding changes in articles of American origin did not take place until, respectively, 1763 and 1773. And, third, these changing processes of symbolic identification were neither revolutionary nor evolutionary in the strictest sense of these terms. Rather, like other learning situations, they were gradual and fitful, with periods of both extremely rapid advance (or breakthrough) and more or less mild relapse.

As far as the individual newspapers are concerned, there are several differences: the New England prints led in presenting an image of Americanism; the journals of the middle colonies

12. *Street Corner Society: The Social Structure of an Italian Slum* (enlarged ed. Chicago, The University of Chicago Press, 1955), p. 262; cf. pp. 50–51, 261–62.

lagged in this respect until the 1760s; and the southern newspapers, after an initial period of rather high awareness of an
American political community, seemed to draw closer to the
British political community in the two decades between 1745
and 1764. But, even more significantly, the evidence suggests
that with the passage of time the individual newspapers not
only became more aware of the collective concept, as indicated
by the inclusion of an ever larger number of symbols of collective or common identity in their columns, but their choice
of symbols tended to become quite steady and consistent.

CHAPTER EIGHT

The Growth of American Community

In evaluating the alternative theories about the integration of the American political community, it is necessary first of all to correlate the three sets of evidence outlined in previous chapters. This is done graphically in Figures 8-1 and 8-2. At the base of the charts are listed the various formative events that were discussed in Chapter 3. The words "functional amalgamation" appear under the year 1775, the year in which the colonists formed a military alliance and in which the colonies first developed a set of unified structures performing a major portion of the functions of a national government—in short, the year in which the colonists crossed the threshold of functional amalgamation. The curved lines summarize the changing patterns of symbol usage in the colonial press, presented year by year in Figure 8-1 and as moving averages in Figure 8-2.

These three curved lines, as was suggested in Chapter 2, will be used as indicators of the growth of an American sense of community awareness in the eighteenth century. The first (a solid line), taken from Figure 5-1, represents the American share of the total number of symbols appearing in the newspapers, that is, the relative amount of attention the colonial

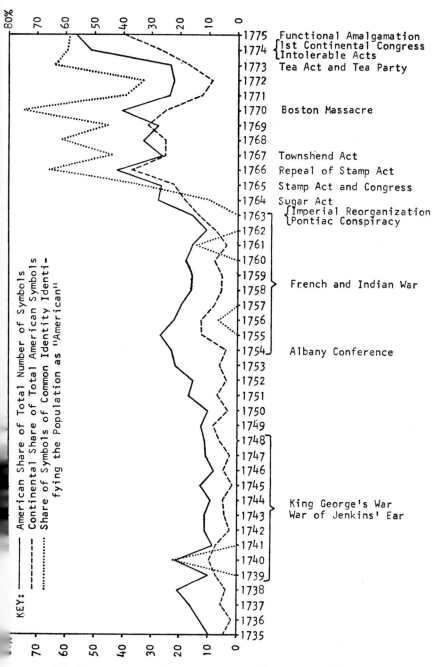

8-1. Functional Amalgamation, Formative Events,
Curves of American Community Awareness, 1735–1775
A Comparison

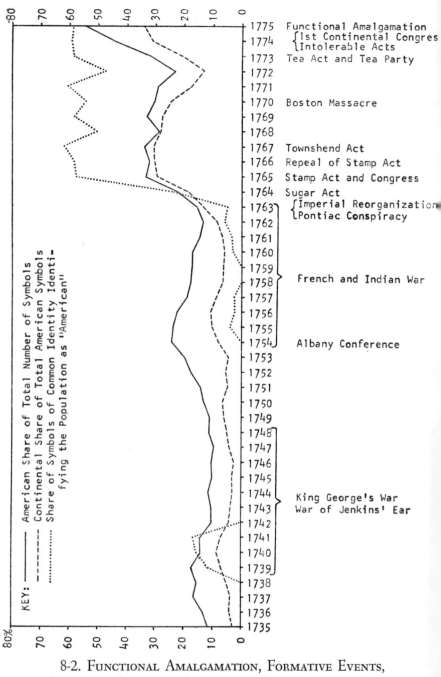

8-2. Functional Amalgamation, Formative Events,
Curves of American Community Awareness, 1735-1775
A Comparison, Using "Moving Averages"

press devoted to events taking place in the area that later became the United States of America. As is true of the others, this curve shows the composite or average distribution of symbols of all newspapers (excluding the *Boston Gazette*). The second curve (a broken line) is a partial analysis of the American symbols, showing the percentage devoted to the continent as a whole or, as we have also termed them, to symbols of common identity. Figure 6-1 compares the distribution of this latter set of symbols to other types of American symbols. Finally, the dotted line represents the share of symbols of common identity (appearing in items of both British and American as well as foreign origin[1]) identifying the population inhabiting the American colonies as members of an American political community. Examples of such symbols would be "Americans," "American colonists," "continentals," and so forth.

The curves shown in Figures 8-1 and 8-2 are strikingly similar. Instead of rising evenly and slowly, or sharply, the curves all incline somewhat fitfully, suggesting the cycles of the learning curve. There is also a certain congruence in their patterns of fluctuation: the peak and trough years are almost identical in all the curves. In fact, looked at from a statistical point of view, the degree of correlation or association among the three curves is highly significant.[2]

FUNCTIONAL AMALGAMATION AND COMMUNITY AWARENESS

The first of the theories offered by students of political communities, and which has been used to analyze the American

1. The difference between symbols of British and American origin for the years between 1764 and 1775 may be seen in Figure 7-3A.
2. The curves are far closer to one another than mere chance would lead us to suspect. In more technical terms, using the nonparametric Spearman Rank Order Correlation Coefficient, for the solid and broken lines in Figure 8-1, $r_s = .74$; for the solid and dotted lines, $r_s = .80$; and for broken and dotted lines, $r_s = .79$. These coefficients of correlation are significant for a two-tailed test at the .05 level.

example of the eighteenth century, emphasizes the importance of amalgamated political structures, arguing that a community awareness follows rather than precedes the process of amalgamation. What does the evidence of the newspapers tell us about this thesis?

During the four decades prior to the year in which the colonists crossed the threshold of functional amalgamation, the embryo American community found a constant place in the colonial press. More than one in five symbols pertained to America during these years; and in the critical decade from 1765 to 1775 the newspapers devoted one third of their symbol space to American events. In 1774 alone—the year before the colonists set up common political structures—one half of the symbols in the colonial press referred to American news.

Although the share of symbol space devoted to the mother country remained fairly constant over the 41-year period, it declined sharply relative to emphasis upon the American community. From 1735 to 1750 almost twice as many British as American symbols appeared in the colonial press; together these two categories comprised one third of the total number of symbols appearing in the newspapers. The last dozen pre-Revolutionary years saw the ratio of British to American symbols reversed. In fact, during the years from 1764 to 1775, the American community captured as great a share of symbol space as the Anglo-American community did between 1735 and 1763.

The American symbols appearing in the colonial press did not refer solely to local events but were intercolonial to a considerable degree. Well over one half of these American symbols pertained to occurrences in colonies other than the newspapers' home colonies. And during the course of the 41 years from 1735 to 1775, the home colony share of the American symbols decreased from about 40 to about 25 per cent. In the last 14 years of this period, one quarter of the total American symbol space was devoted to the colonies as a whole. Thus, by the end of the four decades, the individual colonies were not only paying more attention to other colonies than to themselves, but they were also paying substantially more attention to symbols of common identity than to home colony symbols.

The symbols of common identity appearing in the colonial press—whether of British or American origin, whether referring to the land or to the inhabitants of that land—were more likely to emphasize the American rather than the British tie long before 1775. Considered as a whole, the colonial press crossed this threshold in symbol usage a dozen or more years before the colonists successfully amalgamated some of their more important political institutions.

The evidence of the newspapers, then, renders it very difficult to maintain the belief of such writers as Merrill Jensen, Kenneth C. Wheare, John C. Ranney, Edward Frank Humphrey, and Esmond Wright, the belief that, prior to their unification, the colonies were by and large self-centered, indifferent to one another's existence and problems, and more interested in their connections to the mother country than in intercolonial affairs. Even before they crossed the threshold of extensive functional amalgamation, the colonists—at least as readers of the newspapers—had developed a fairly high degree of community awareness. However much the amalgamation of some of their political institutions may have affected the news patterns and symbol distributions in the newspapers after 1775, the assertion that no community awareness existed prior to that date is massively contradicted by the evidence surveyed in this study.

COLONIAL WARS: THE POSTPONEMENT
OF AMERICAN SEPARATISM

The curves of community awareness shown in Figures 8-1 and 8-2 do not suggest that any one of the more important events listed in Chapter 3 had a profound effect, individually, upon the development of an American sense of community awareness. This may be seen particularly clearly by examining the distribution of symbols during the last two colonial wars: the War of Jenkins' Ear and the subsequent King George's War (1739–48); and the French and Indian War (1754–63). The years encompassed by these two wars are shaded in Figures 8-1 and 8-2.

Looking first at the earlier war, there can be little doubt that the year 1740 was an early highwater mark of American community awareness. Over one fifth of the total number of symbols appearing in the colonial press in that year pertained to the colonies (although, to complete the picture, it must be added that this percentage was only one half as great in 1739 and 1741). Further, in 1740 the percentage of American symbols referring to the colonies as a whole, i.e. the continental concept, reached its highest level for the two decades from 1735 to 1754. For the first time in the period under consideration the colonial press referred to the inhabitants of the colonies as "Americans": two of the nine symbols of common identity appearing in the newspapers in 1740—to be sure, an extremely small sample—make this distinction. And, finally, looking at the symbols of common identity referring to both the land and the people, 51.5 per cent of these symbols identified the land and its population as "American" in the two years 1739 and 1740, while only 40.4 per cent did so in the four-year period from 1735 to 1738.

As the war of the 1740s progressed, however, the colonial

press became less interested in American events, less interested in the continental concept, and less interested in identifying the inhabitants of the North American continent as "Americans" rather than as "colonists" or "His Majesty's subjects." In the last three years of the war, from 1746 to 1748, the individual curves of community awareness stood at levels less than one half as high as they had in 1740. At the end of the war the curves were nonetheless beginning to rise again.

Symbol usage during the French and Indian War exhibited characteristics similar to the patterns of symbol usage during the War of Jenkins' Ear and King George's War. The years 1755 and 1756 saw peaks in community awareness, with the press devoting more than one quarter of its symbol space to American events, and one eighth of its American news space to continental symbols. In 1756, one in fifteen symbols of common identity identified the colonists as "Americans." Again, however, emphasis on American news and symbols decreased as the war went on: the curves sank in 1761 and 1762 to levels below those of the early 1750s, and to levels less than one half as high as in 1755 and 1756. After 1756, and throughout the remainder of the war, not a single symbol of common identity referred to the colonists as "Americans." As in the 1740s, the end of the French and Indian War found the curves beginning to ascend.

To get a better idea of the relationship of colonial wars to symbol usage, it would be helpful to simplify the information presented in Figure 8-1. Figure 8-3 combines the curve showing the ratio of American symbols to the total number of symbols (the solid line in Figure 8-1) with the curve indicating the share of American symbols devoted to the continent as a whole (the broken line in Figure 8-1) to produce an average curve for the period from 1735 to 1775. (Since the number of symbols of common identity referring to the population, indicated by the dotted line in Figure 8-1, was negligible in the years before 1764—the years in which the wars under discussion took place—the curve showing the distribution of these symbols will be ignored in calculating the average curve for Figure 8-3.) This average curve may then be broken into five segments—three, marked by brackets and the word "peace," encompassing the years of peace during the last four pre-Revolutionary decades; and the other two segments comprising the years of war.

Individual linear trend lines for each of the five segments (the dotted lines in Figure 8-3) bring to light an interesting fact about colonial symbol usage. During each of the three periods of peace, the trend in the levels of attention paid to American events and to the continent as a whole rose: there was an increase of eight tenths of a percentage point per year for the 1735–39 period, of nine tenths of a percentage point per year for the 1748–54 period, and of an entire percentage point for each of the thirteen years from 1763 to 1775. By way of contrast, the levels of attention dropped during each of the two colonial wars, by four tenths of a percentage point per year from 1739 to 1748, and by six tenths of a percentage point during the 1754–63 period. Thus, although the secular trend line rose throughout the four decades from 1735 to 1775, it rose more rapidly during times of peace, and fell off somewhat during war periods.

If we consider the Anglo-American wars against the French in America as single events, we can only conclude that their effect upon the growth of an American community awareness was negative. In each of the two cases encompassed by the four decades from 1735 to 1775, the outbreak of war came as the average curve of attention paid to America and continental events was ascending. (The evidence of the newspapers also indicates that the next major military conflict, the American

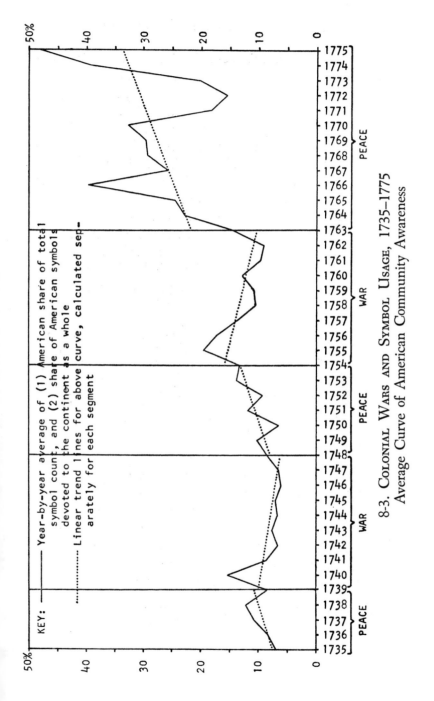

KEY: ———— Year-by-year average of (1) American share of total symbol count, and (2) share of American symbols devoted to the continent as a whole

.... Linear trend lines for above curve, calculated separately for each segment

8-3. COLONIAL WARS AND SYMBOL USAGE, 1735–1775
Average Curve of American Community Awareness

Revolution, came at a time of rising interest in the American community.) And in each case the outbreak of war arrested the trend toward greater American community awareness, and eventually resulted in lower levels of attention.

But wars, especially those enduring for as long as a decade, are social processes, not discrete events. Looking at such wars as events occurring at a given point in time is somewhat misleading in discussing the relationship between colonial wars and symbol usage. A chart placing the two wartime segments of the average curve (1739–48 and 1754–63) parallel to one another would enable us to refine our analysis of wars and levels of attention. Figure 8-4 shows the year-by-year development of the curves of awareness for both decades of war. The lower line shows symbol usage during the wars of the 1740s, while the upper curve records changes in the use of symbols during the French and Indian War.

The first point to be noticed in looking at Figure 8-4 is the striking similarity of the two wartime curves. The levels of attention during the War of Jenkins' Ear and King George's War were, to be sure, lower than those of the French and Indian War. Otherwise, except most notably for the fifth year of the two wars (1743 and 1758 respectively), their cyclical patterns moved together in a parallel manner.[3]

Second, the curves in Figure 8-4 point to a definite pattern of symbol usage during the colonial wars. It has already been noted that the curves of American community awareness were rising before the wars erupted. The first period of each war, approximately two years in each case, saw the curves continue to rise, achieving new heights. This was a period of increased interest both in American symbols and in events affecting the colonies as a whole—a period of increased American commu-

3. In fact, using the nonparametric Spearman Rank Order Correlation Coefficient, $r_s = .76$ (significant at the .05 level for a two-tailed test).

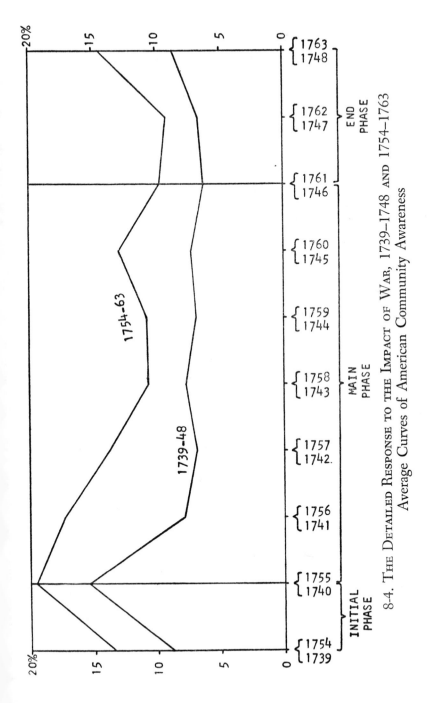

8-4. THE DETAILED RESPONSE TO THE IMPACT OF WAR, 1739–1748 AND 1754–1763
Average Curves of American Community Awareness

nity awareness. The decline of the curves during the ensuing six years constitutes the second period. Toward the end of these years the cycles of American community awareness were at an ebb, in spite of slight reversals of the dominant trend in the seventh year of the wars. Finally, during the last two years of each war there was an upsurge of interest in the American community. In the last year of each war, by the way, the curves were at almost the same levels as in the first year of the wars: the lower curve on Figure 8-4 dropped from 8.7 per cent in 1739 to 8.6 per cent in 1748; while the upper curve climbed from 13.4 per cent in 1754 to 14.5 per cent in 1763.

If we consider wars as social processes rather than as single events, then, what do the patterns summarized in Figures 8-3 and 8-4 tell us about symbol usage during the different phases of the processes? First, as was already noted, the wars took place in contexts of rising levels of attention paid to American events and symbols. Throughout the four decades from 1735 to 1775 there was a secular trend toward increased interest in the American community—a trend most dominant during the years of peace and receding somewhat during the war years. And, second, symbol usage during the war years indicates that the colonists' mood and foci of attention passed through three separate and distinct phases.

(1) The initial phase was a period of drag as far as symbol usage was concerned: the press continued the patterns and trends already in existence at the beginning of the war, that is, the newspapers maintained the rising pattern of the secular curve. It was in the early years of the War of Jenkins' Ear that Albert Harkness, Jr. found evidence of a rising sense of American separateness.[4] And symbol usage emphasizing the sep-

4. Harkness, "Americanism and Jenkins' Ear," *Mississippi Valley Historical Review,* 37 (1950), 88–90.

arateness of the American community during the first two years of the French and Indian War was in accord with Benjamin Franklin's appraisal of the colonists' mood during those years. If the colonies had accepted the Albany Plan of union in 1754, Franklin wrote thirty-five years later, they "would have really been, as they then thought themselves, sufficient to their own Defence." [5] These were also the years of which Carl Lotus Becker wrote when he argued that the French and Indian War "generated a sense of spiritual separation from England" among the colonists:

> Who shall estimate the effect upon the proud and self-contained Washington of intercourse with supercilious British officers during the Braddock expedition? . . . Who were these men from oversea to instruct natives in the art of frontier warfare?—men who proclaimed their ignorance of the woods by standing grouped and red-coated in the open to be shot down by Indians whom they could not see! [6]

(2) As the war progressed, however, and as the adverse turn of events seemed to cast doubt upon the ability of the colonists to fight their own battles and even upon the strength of the Anglo-American alliance in the New World, sentiments of separateness subsided. By the end of this phase of the French and Indian War, Franklin found himself rejoicing at the reduction of Canada, not merely because he was a colonist, but because he was a Briton. [7] If we may judge from symbol usage in the colonial press, Franklin's view of his Anglo-American multiple loyalties as compatible and complementary

5. Cited in George Louis Beer, *British Colonial Policy, 1754–1765* (reprinted from 1907 ed. New York, Peter Smith, 1933), p. 314.
6. Becker, *Beginnings of the American People*, p. 192.
7. Cited in Greene, *The Revolutionary Generation*, p. 181.

in 1760 reflected the mood of the politically relevant strata of the population as a whole.

(3) Not until victory was in sight, but well before the formal conclusion of the war, did the colonists begin to reassert their interest in a purely American community. But even this increased interest only brought the levels of attention to American events up to the height existing at the outbreak of the war.

At best, the colonial wars postponed the emergence of sentiments of national separateness in America. In looking at the testimonials of the colonists themselves (or at the judgments of more recent students of the American political community) about the effect of these wars upon the moods and perceptions of the colonists, it is necessary to place such remarks and opinions in sequence. During the initial phase of the French and Indian War, for example, when the image of an American separateness was rising, a haughty attitude toward British methods of warfare may have been in keeping with the prevailing mood. We would not expect to find a similar attitude among the colonists toward General James Wolfe's victory on the Heights of Abraham in 1759, when the mood of Anglo-American solidarity was predominant in the colonies. But regardless of shifts in prevailing moods, the ultimate effect of the cycles left the colonists, at the end of the wars, using essentially the same symbol patterns in existence at the outset of the wars.

Before leaving the French and Indian War years, we might briefly consider the Albany Congress of 1754 as a formative event. The Albany Congress did not seem to have much effect upon the distribution of symbols in the early American newspapers. On the curve representing the American share of the total number of symbols (in Figure 8-1), the year 1754 is merely another point in an ascending slope. At the same time, that year was a low point in the curve showing the continental share of the total number of American symbols. It is, perhaps, ironic that the year in which Benjamin Franklin was encouraging his fellow colonists to form a union was a year in which the emphasis of the colonial press (including Franklin's own newspaper) was on almost anything but the collective concept. And neither in 1754 nor in the following year did a single reference to the colonists as a whole identify them as Americans.

THE STAMP ACT CRISIS: THE JUNCTURE OF EVENTS AND INTEGRATIVE PROCESSES

The formative event most often singled out by historians and political scientists in accounting for the growth of an American sense of community is the Stamp Act crisis. And, as may be seen in Figures 8-1 and 8-2, it is indeed undeniable that the sharpest upward swings of the curves of American community awareness, as well as their highest points in the 1760s, seem to coincide with the development of the Stamp Act crisis.

Two sets of facts, however, one to be found in the quantitative data analyzed in this study and the other implicit in the standard, nonquantitative interpretations of American history, argue against a causal relationship between the crisis and the growth of community awareness in the colonies.

The first set of evidence has been discussed: the Stamp Act crisis took place after the curves of community awareness had already begun to ascend, and the curves turned downward immediately after the repeal of the measure. If the crisis had in fact set the symbol revolution of the early 1760s in motion, we would expect that the force of inertia alone in the colonists' patterns of self-imagery and attention would have carried this revolution forward at least to some extent in the months after March 1766.[8] Instead, there was a sharp drop in all of the curves that continued until 1768.

The second fact is that the parliamentary measures of 1764 and 1765, the Sugar Act and the Stamp Act, were not unique events in colonial history. Nor were they the first such measures to arouse the ire of the colonists. Of the Molasses Act, for example, Oliver M. Dickerson has written:

> The act of 1733 sought to eliminate outside competition in the American colonial market and confine this trade to the products of the British sugar plantations by an import duty of six pence a gallon on the foreign product. This act was opposed by the New Englanders before its passage, but does not seem to have received especial attention when it was re-enacted at successive intervals down to 1764.[9]

Historians seem to agree that the colonists generally ignored this measure: indeed, the cost of collecting the import duties

8. From current analyses of public opinion, we know that changes of image in response to a dramatic event are likely to be quite durable, unless they are counteracted by equally dramatic events or by governmental or mass media pressures in the contrary direction. Favorable opinion among Western Europeans about the Soviet Union, for instance, dropped 20 percentage points after the Soviet suppression of the Hungarian Uprising in 1956; it took two years (and, possibly, the impact of Soviet space accomplishments) before attitudes toward the USSR regained the level of early 1956. See Karl W. Deutsch and Richard L. Merritt, "Effects of Events on National and International Images," in Herbert C. Kelman, ed., *International Behavior: A Social-Psychological Analysis* (New York, Holt, Rinehart, Winston, 1965). It seems reasonable to assume that a similar lag in image or attitude change would have followed the Stamp Act crisis if its salience among the colonists had been as high as some writers suggest.

9. Oliver M. Dickerson, *The Navigation Acts and the American Revolution* (Philadelphia, University of Pennsylvania Press, 1951), p. 83.

on foreign molasses outweighed fourfold the amount of the duties collected.[10]

Of more importance in assessing the role of the Molasses Act, however, are three other considerations. First of all, the argument, so significant during the last pre-Revolutionary decade, that the Stamp Act and similar parliamentary measures violated the colonists' "constitutional right" of "no taxation without representation," had a prominent forerunner in the reasoning of those opposing the passage of the Molasses Act. The latter, as a colonial agent in England wrote to the Duke of Newcastle in March 1733, "is divesting them of their Rights & prividges as ye Kings Natural born Subjects and Englishmen in levying Subsidies upon them against their Consent when they are annexed to no County in Great Britain, have no Representatives in parliam^t nor are any part of ye Legislature of this Kingdom." [11]

Second, the ample opportunities open to the colonists to evade the duties imposed by the Molasses Act of 1733 doubtless contributed to a breakdown of one of the most important attributes of a political community: the feature of voluntary compliance complemented by an adequate system of enforcement. And, third, the Molasses Act was, at least potentially, as important a measure of taxation as the Stamp Act of 1765 promised to be. In 1763 British treasury officials estimated that the revenue from the original, or a modified, Molasses Act, if strictly enforced, would range between £60,000 and £100,000 per year.[12] By way of contrast, according to Chester

10. Beer, *British Colonial Policy,* p. 230.
11. Ibid., p. 41.
12. According to Dora Mae Clark, *The Rise of the British Treasury: Colonial Administration in the Eighteenth Century* (New Haven, Yale University Press, 1960), p. 116 n.: "Nathaniel Ware estimated that foreign imports might amount to 23,625 hogsheads a year, and thought the

W. Wright, British officials expected that the Stamp Act of 1765 "would yield between £60,000 and £100,000 of revenue, possibly half coming from the West Indies." [13] Though unenforced, the Molasses Act proved costly to the colonists because of the generally increased price of sugar and sugar products resulting from a growing demand in England and the colonies and the inability of the British sugar islands to keep pace.[14]

Similarly, if less directly, the Iron Bill of 1750 could have had a tremendous influence upon colonial society—if the Crown had enforced it rigidly. It prohibited the establishment of new steel mills, slitting mills, and tilt hammers in the colonies. Wright has termed this measure the most important of the parliamentary restrictions upon economic development in the New World,[15] although some historians view it "chiefly as a measure to encourage an infant steel industry in England rather than an attempt to destroy a colonial enterprise." [16]

What was it about the Sugar and Stamp Acts of 1764 and 1765 that was not present in the '30s and '50s and that now led the colonists to meet in joint congress in New York City and protest loudly? Why was the conflict over these measures of a magnitude never attained during previous periods of stress in the relations between the colonies and the mother country?

6*d*. might be collected if local duties were eliminated. According to another calculation a tax of 3*d*. a gallon from an estimated 80,000 hogsheads might produce £100,000 or somewhat less." Professor Dickerson reported that the colonial imports of foreign molasses in 1768 amounted to 2,824,060 gallons, and in 1772 to 4,878,794 gallons. *The Navigation Acts*, p. 86. A tax of 6*d*. would have produced £70,601 in revenues in 1768, and £121,969 in 1772; a tax of 3*d*. per gallon would have produced £35,301 in 1768 and £60,985 in 1772.

13. Chester W. Wright, *Economic History of the United States* (New York, McGraw-Hill, 1941), p. 192.

14. Ibid., p. 145.

15. Ibid., p. 103.

16. Dickerson, *The Navigation Acts*, p. 20.

The Growth of Community

The Events of 1763 One possible explanation of the increased degree of colonial sensitivity to parliamentary interference in what the colonists felt were their rights in 1764 and 1765 pertains to the discrete and yet not unrelated events preceding the enactment of the Sugar and Stamp Acts. The fact that major shifts in symbol usage took place during the latter half of 1763 lends considerable plausibility to this explanation.

THE TREATY OF PARIS of 1763, which concluded a successful war against the French, is one of these events. It must be noted at the outset that the actual peace treaty negotiated by the King's ministers did not differ significantly from the colonists' expectations. The warmth with which the Americans received news of its terms leads us to discount the treaty itself as a basis of conflict between them and their English brethren.[17]

Some have argued, however, that the elimination of French influence from the North American continent reduced the colonists' reliance upon the mother country.[18] This sounds reasonable. But it raises the question of the extent to which the French threat was uppermost in the colonial minds of, let us say, 1733 and 1750. After all, two decades had intervened between the most recent clash of English and French arms in

17. At a reception for New Jersey's newly appointed governor, William Franklin, on 10 June 1763, a member of the welcoming committee stated: "The Commencement of your Excellency's Administration, will ever stand distinguished by the most Brilliant Aera, in the Pages of British Story: a War, terminated after a serious [sic] of Conquests, unequalled in the Revolution of past Ages; and Peace, with an immense acquisition of Territory, established on the Basis of the firmest Security to his Majesty's Empire in America." *New-York Mercury,* no. 608 (20 June 1763), p. 1.

18. A Swedish traveler in America, Peter de Kalm, wrote in 1750 that the presence of the French in America gave the best assurance to Great Britain that the colonies would remain in due subjection; cited in Francis Parkman, *Montcalm and Wolfe* (3 vols. Boston, Little, Brown, 1898) (Part Seventh of his multivolume work, *France and England in North America*), 3, 250. Cf. also Esmond Wright, *Fabric of Freedom,* p. 2.

North America and the passage of the Molasses Act; and the Iron Bill followed the Peace of Aix-la-Chapelle by two years. These two acts, then, came at a time when the colonists were not directly dependent upon the presence of Redcoats to preserve peace. If the sole factor keeping the Americans from protesting to the Crown against unwanted trade restrictions had actually been their reliance upon the force of British arms, we might wonder at their acquiescent serenity in the 1730s and the early 1750s.

As a formative event capturing the imagination of the colonists, the effect of the Treaty of Paris seems to have been short-lived indeed. At best, its influence upon the distribution of symbols in the colonial press produced only a brief flurry of interest in American and continental symbols. The intensive analysis of the *Boston Gazette* and the *New-York Mercury* for the years from 1762 to 1766 demonstrated that, although the curves of American community awareness rose sharply in the two months after the conclusion of the peace treaty, they fell off just as sharply before the summer of 1763 (Figures 5-4 and 6-3).

PONTIAC'S CONSPIRACY was one of the most important colonial foci of attention during the latter half of 1763. Not only did this event find a prominent place in the newspapers from all of the colonies, but the different journals shared a common perception of the uprising.[19] There seems to have been little doubt in the mind of the colonial printer that the Indians themselves had begun the rebellion (probably with the aid or at least the encouragement of the remaining French

19. Because of the apparent importance of the months from June to December 1763 in the changing symbol usage of the colonists, I read every issue of each of the newspapers included in our sample for these months. The above remark is my impression, based on this reading; it is not based on an actual counting of items. I feel sure, however, that any sort of quantitative analysis of all newspapers during these months would verify my impression.

in the western lands), and that the colonists were justly defending their homes and farms against the marauding savages. Individual news reports and atrocity stories, many of them quite possibly true, about the inhumanity of the Indians often found a place in several different newspapers.

The role played by Pontiac's Conspiracy in the growth of an American political community is not at all clear. On the one hand, the colonists never developed a sense of involvement matching the amount of attention that they paid to the uprising; the colonial governments, while most assuredly deploring the butcheries on the western frontier, were for the most part unwilling to allocate men or other resources to quell the rebellion.[20] This inability to act or cooperate in the face of a common threat dealt a severe blow to the cause of intercolonial integration.

On the other hand, however, Pontiac's Conspiracy made crystal clear certain aspects of divergent colonial and British

20. This was particularly true with respect to the colonial government of Pennsylvania. That the attitude of the colonial governments as a whole irritated the Ministry in London is clear from Lord Halifax's letter of 19 October 1763 to General Jeffery Amherst, commander of the British troops in North America: "It is Matter of Concern to His Majesty to find that the Measures You had taken for putting an End to the Indian War, have not yet produced the desired Effects, but that, on the contrary, the Insurrections of the Indians are considerably increased, and almost become general. Upon this Extension of the War, & Increase of Danger, His Majesty judges it proper to enable You, (in Case You should find it absolutely necessary) in the most efficacious Manner to call upon the Colonies, (the want of whose Assistance is regretted in several of the Papers You inclose) to contribute to the general Defence of the Country, & Annoyance of the Indians, by raising & employing such Numbers of Provincial Troops, or Militia, as You shall find requisite. I, therefore, inclose to You Letters for that purpose, not only to the Governor of Pennsylvania, signifying His Majesty's Displeasure at that supine and neglectfull Conduct, which You so justly blame in the Legislature of that Colony, but also to the Governors of New Hampshire, Massachusetts, Connecticut, Rhode Island, New York, New-Jersey, and North & South Carolina." Clarence Edwin Carter, compiler and ed., *The Correspondence of General Thomas Gage, 1763–1775* (2 vols. New Haven, Yale University Press, 1931), 2, 3–4.

perceptions and interests. Newspaper articles reprinted from British journals seemed unanimous in blaming the uprising upon the colonists' abuse of the Indians, and condemned the colonists for encroaching upon the Indian territories. As a letter from London, dated 5 August 1763, noted, "If we search into the Beginning of some of the late Indian Wars, we shall find they have taken Rise from some of our Colonists over-reaching them in their Treaties, and getting Possession of their hunting and fishing grounds, without which they cannot possibly subsist." [21] That at least some of the colonists had different ideas about the origin of the conspiracy is clear from the correspondence of such men as His Majesty's Superintendent of the Northern Indians, Sir William Johnson, and his fellow New Yorker, William Livingston. In March 1764, Livingston wrote that it was the British commander in North America, General Jeffery Amherst, whose "blundering and disdainful Conduct towards the distant Tribes" lay at the bottom of the uprising.[22]

More significantly, the measures proposed by articles of British origin appearing in the colonial press found the key to peace in curbs upon the colonists' activities: a delineation of the colonists' territorial limits coupled with measures to prevent their encroachment upon the Indian lands; regulation of trade with the Indians and punishment for those colonists who would take advantage of the Redskins; and so forth.[23] It

21. This letter appeared in the *Massachusetts Gazette*, no. 1314 (27 Oct. 1763). Cf. also the proposals submitted to the *Gentlemen's Magazine* for September 1763 by Peter Collinson, Esq., F.R.S., reprinted in the *New-York Mercury*, no. 634 (19 Dec. 1763).

22. Cited in Knollenberg, *Origin of the American Revolution*, pp. 110–11, 245. Knollenberg also cites the similar opinions of several Englishmen; but their opinions did not reach the newspapers included in the present study.

23. *Massachusetts Gazette*, no. 1314 (27 Oct. 1763). *New-York Mercury*, no. 634 (19 Dec. 1763).

must have been with dismay that the Americans learned from the Royal Proclamation of October 1763 that such sentiments had become official doctrine. What amounted to giving a great part of the American continent over to the Indians was certainly a severe blow to the colonists' expectations.

Like the Sugar and Stamp Acts, the Indian uprising of 1763 was not without precedent in colonial history. Nor was it the most devastating series of engagements that the colonists had fought. George Croghan, an Irish trader and Deputy Superintendent of Indian Affairs under Sir William Johnson, estimated that the Indians "killed or captivated not less than two thousand of His Majesty's subjects and drove some thousands to beggary and the greatest distress." [24] Modern writers, however, have discounted Croghan's figure; and one historian has placed the loss of life in the period of Pontiac's Conspiracy as low as two hundred.[25] Nor did the Indians penetrate far enough eastward to pose a real danger to the urban areas huddled along the Atlantic seaboard.

Earlier battles and wars had threatened the colonists more seriously, but the response, in terms of symbol usage in the colonial press, to those conflicts did not begin to equal the newspapers' coverage of the uprising led by the Ottawa chief. Disease, Spanish bullets, and British bungling, for example, were responsible for the death of 90 per cent of the 3600 American volunteers serving in the Caribbean phase of the War of Jenkins' Ear.[26] The siege of Louisburg in 1745, and the tragic winter that followed it, cost more than one thousand

24. Cited in Howard H. Peckham, *Pontiac and the Indian Uprising* (Princeton, Princeton University Press, 1947), p. 214.
25. The low estimate comes from Esmond Wright, *Fabric of Freedom*, p. 44. Cf. also Knollenberg, *Origin of the American Revolution*, pp. 112, 245.
26. Harkness, "Americanism and Jenkins' Ear," *Mississippi Valley Historical Review*, 37 (1950), 87 n.

colonial lives.[27] In part as a response to the loss of Louisburg, the French undertook two sea attacks on Boston in the last years of King George's War (the first thwarted by gales and the second by the British navy) in addition to raiding and burning towns and farms all the way from Maine to Saratoga. Pierre François de Rigaud, Marquis de Vaudreuil, in his account of his attack upon northwestern Massachusetts, wrote:

> I divided my army between the two sides of the Kaskékouké [Hoosac], and ordered them to do what I had not permitted to be done before we reached Fort Massachusetts. Every house was set on fire, and numbers of domestic animals of all sorts were killed. French and Indians vied with each other in pillage, and I made them enter the [valleys of all the] little streams that flow into the Kaskékouké and lay waste everything there. . . . Wherever we went we made the same havoc, laid waste both sides of the river, through twelve leagues of fertile country, burned houses, barns, stables, and even a meeting-house,— in all, above two hundred establishments,—killed all the cattle, and ruined all the crops. Such, Monseigneur, was the damage I did our enemies during the eight or nine days I was in their country.[28]

While Rigaud was incinerating Fort Massachusetts, however, colonial printers were all but ignoring American symbols and the collective concept.

Nor did the curves of American community awareness sky-

27. Parkman, *A Half-Century of Conflict* (Part Sixth of *France and England in North America*), 2, 133, 150. Deaths during the siege itself amounted to 130, of which about 30 were from disease; pestilence and exposure carried away 890 men during the ensuing winter.
28. Ibid., 2, 253.

rocket when the French and their Indian allies attacked and captured the trading post of Pickawillany, located in a part of the wilderness that later became Pennsylvania, in a year of peace, 1752. The colonial printers may have shuddered upon learning how the victorious Ottawa and Ojibwa warriors boiled and ate La Demoiselle, Great Chief of the Miami Confederacy and friend to the colonial traders at Pickawillany, but in terms of the symbols they used in their journals these printers did little else.

Although the loss of life and the devastation of settled areas in the French and Indian War were more extensive, and the threat to the colonies greater, than in the Indian uprising of 1763, the war of the late 1750s did not occasion the dramatic shifts in attention and American community awareness that accompanied the latter event. Thousands of colonists died from French shot and shell, from Indian scalping knives and hatchets, from scurvy, dysentery, and a host of other diseases.[29] And, with French support, the Indian menace was without doubt greater during this war than during the period of Pontiac's Conspiracy. The French navigator, Louis Antoine de Bougainville, wrote of his Indian allies: "The very recital of the cruelties they committed on the battlefield is horrible. The ferocity and insolence of these black-souled barbarians makes one shudder. It is an abominable kind of war. The air one breathes is contagious of insensibility and hardness." [30]

29. To my knowledge there is no compilation of battle casualties in the French and Indian War. The meager information on this topic in Parkman, *Montcalm and Wolfe*, 1, 2, 3; J. W. Fortescue, *A History of the British Army* (13 vols. London, Macmillan, 1910–30), 2; and Matthew Forney Steele, *American Campaigns* (2 vols. Washington, Byron S. Adams, 1909), 1, suggests that a figure between 5,000 and 10,000 colonial deaths attributable to the war or war service would not be excessive. This figure omits British casualties.

30. Cited in Parkman, *Montcalm and Wolfe*, 2, 118. Of the attitude of Rigaud, Marquis of Vaudreuil, toward the Indians, Parkman wrote: "He owns that they committed frightful cruelties, mutilating and some-

The French themselves, if possibly more humane, nonetheless wreaked havoc along the western frontiers. Captain Dumas, for example, swept across the frontier after defeating General Braddock in the Battle of the Wilderness. Varying his means "in every form to suit the occasion," Dumas claimed success "in ruining the three adjacent provinces, Pennsylvania, Maryland, and Virginia, driving off the inhabitants, and totally destroying the settlements over a tract of country thirty leagues wide, reckoning from the line of Fort Cumberland." [31]

THE ROYAL PROCLAMATION OF OCTOBER 1763 has also been cited by some scholars as an important source of irritation between the colonists and the mother country—an irritation that, they believe, developed into the Revolutionary War.[32] Ostensibly to provide for the administration of the newly conquered territories in America, the Proclamation erased the colonists' territorial claims in the western lands, restricted their trade with the Indians, and prohibited them from buying land or settling west of the Alleghenies. The costs of maintaining some 10,000 British soldiers (General Amherst was reported to have desired 16,000 troops "to maintain his footing" in North America[33]) that would be used to enforce the Proclamation's provisions were to be borne by the colonists.

In looking at the later colonial years as a whole, it seems somewhat difficult to justify the importance that has been

times burning their prisoners; but he expresses no regret, and probably felt none, since he declares that the object of this murderous warfare was to punish the English till they longed for peace." Ibid., pp. 114–15.

31. Dumas, quoted in ibid., p. 15.

32. Esmond Wright and others, however, have seen the Proclamation as an indirect result of the Treaty of Paris. *Fabric of Freedom*, p. 2.

33. Reported, inter alia, in the *New-York Mercury*, no. 626 (24 Oct. 1763); and the *Massachusetts Gazette*, no. 3122 (20 Oct. 1763). The decision to station troops in America came quite some time before news of Pontiac's Conspiracy reached British ears. Cf. Charles S. Grant, "Pontiac's Rebellion and the British Troop Moves of 1763," *Mississippi Valley Historical Review*, 40 (June 1953), 75–88.

assigned to the Royal Proclamation as a formative event in the embryo American political community. The months prior to its enunciation found rumors circulating throughout the colonies about its content—the press took notice of reports that 10,000 men were to be stationed in America at the colonists' expense—but, after its appearance, discussion of the measure in the colonial press quietly disappeared. The consensus among modern historians of colonial America seems to be that its provisions were generally unenforceable and for the most part left unenforced. It is probably also true, however, that the Proclamation caused some inconvenience to some colonists, who had to find ways of evading its provisions. Whatever the inconveniences, though, the westward advance of the colonists across the Proclamation Line continued, and the colonists continued to trade with the Indians, probably cheating and otherwise taking advantage of them to no lesser degree than before October 1763.

THE EVENTS OF 1763, then, do not explain the critical nature of the Stamp Act crisis. Clearly these events "caused" neither the Stamp Act crisis nor the symbol revolution that took place in the colonial press in the early 1760s. We must look elsewhere for clues about the timing of changes in symbol usage. And we must look elsewhere for answers to certain types of questions about these events. If, for example, a newly found sense of security emboldened the colonists to make demands of the mother country after the Paris Treaty of 1763, why did not a similar sense of security lead them to make similar demands after the Peace of Aix-la-Chapelle in 1748? What had intervened in the sixteen years from 1747 to 1763 that made news of Pontiac's Conspiracy in the northwest so important in the colonial press, while earlier French depredations in the northeast had failed to secure widespread newspaper coverage? Notice was scarcely taken of the Iron Bill of

1750 during the year of its passage. "Iffing" is always danger-ous in analyzing historical events and processes, but I would suggest that, if the Iron Bill had been enacted in 1767 or even 1764, it would have met with vociferous colonial opposition. Instead of a "Stamp Act crisis," the colonists would have rallied to the clarion call for intercolonial cooperation in the midst of an "Iron Bill crisis." A spark that would have gone un-noticed in the previous decade could have kindled the flames of patriotism in the 1760s.

Changing Levels of American Community Awareness A second approach to the question of increased colonial sensi-tivity to parliamentary measures of control in the 1760s centers on the growth of habits and facilities of intercolonial com-munication. Attention to American events and problems is an important aspect of this approach, as is the emergence of trading patterns, communication systems, and intercolonial contacts.

THE LEVELS OF ATTENTION paid to American symbols and the collective concept (the solid and broken lines, respectively, in Figures 8-1 and 8-2) increased steadily if somewhat fitfully throughout the twenty-eight years preceding the Treaty of Paris and Pontiac's Conspiracy. The level of attention paid to American symbols increased by 49 per cent from 1735 to 1762 (based on a linear trend line), while the level of attention paid to continental symbols increased by 77 per cent.

Taking the fluctuations in the curves of American commu-nity awareness into account does not alter our conclusion about the increased levels of attention to American symbols. In fact, the cycles of the curves shown in Figures 8-1 and 8-2 took place on progressively higher planes. And even the low points in 1761 and 1762 were at higher levels than the lowest points of previous cycles.

Two other facts about the level of attention will also be recalled from earlier sections of this study. First, the symbol distributions of the newspapers from different colonies became increasingly congruent as the colonial years passed. And, second, by 1763, references to the colonies as a whole were more likely than not to identify them as an area separate from the British political community.

EXPANDING FACILITIES OF INTERCOLONIAL COMMUNICATION characterized the context in which changes in the levels of attention took place. Illustrative of this expansion is the colonial press itself. The number of newspapers, for example, mushroomed in the decades between 1735 and 1775. At the time of John Peter Zenger's trial for seditious libel there were only nine newspapers in all America; by the end of the French and Indian War their number had more than doubled, and 38 were in existence on the eve of the Revolution.[34] Furthermore, the size and news coverage of the journals kept pace with their numbers: the linage in the average newspaper doubled, and the number of symbols increased almost three-fold, from the 1730s to the 1760s.[35]

Another indication of the colonists' changing patterns of communication lies in their choice of trading partners. The number of ships plying between the major American ports of New York, Philadelphia, Hampton, and Charleston, on the one hand, and harbors in Great Britain or Ireland, on the other hand, doubled from 1734 to 1772 (increasing from 264 to 556), but the number of ships engaged in the coasting trade

34. According to Clarence S. Brigham, *History and Bibliography of American Newspapers, 1690–1820* (2 vols. Worcester, Massachusetts, American Antiquarian Society, 1947), nine newspapers existed in January of 1735, twenty in January of 1763, and 38 in April of 1775.

35. In the five years from 1735 to 1739, the average newspaper contained 79 symbols; in the 1762–66 period, it contained 206 symbols. The average newspaper included in the sample for 1738 had 349 lines of news; the average journal of 1768 had 650 lines.

quadrupled (from 402 to 1,750) during the same period. Comparable figures for the port of Boston are even more dramatic: the number of ships sailing from Boston to the mother country rose from an average of 48 a year in the period between 1714 and 1717 to 59 a year in the four years from 1769 to 1772 (an increase of 23%); the number of coastal vessels jumped from 117 to 451 (an increase of 286%). Of the total annual tonnage shipped from Boston, 19 per cent (3,985 tons) went to Great Britain or Ireland from 1714 to 1717, whereas 16 per cent (6,171 tons) of the yearly tonnage did so from 1769 to 1772. The share of the total tonnage shipped each year from Boston to other colonial ports rose from 17 per cent (3,583 tons) in the four-year period from 1714 to 1717 to 43 per cent (16,766 tons) from 1769 to 1772.[36] In short, although the shipping facilities of the colonies expanded generally during the course of the eighteenth century, coastal shipping grew at a much more rapid rate than did trade with the mother country.

Population expansion accompanied the growing intercolonial commercial ties. From 1700 to 1775, the American population multiplied tenfold. Along with a general movement west, people began to fill in the gaps separating the urban clusters scattered along the Atlantic seaboard. By the middle of the 1770s, according to census data currently available, a fairly continuous line of settlement ran from Penobscot Bay to Savannah.[37]

36. The remainder went to the Caribbean and other colonies in the New World (58% in 1714–17, 38% in 1769–72) and to Europe and Africa (6% in 1714–17, 3% in 1769–72). Computed from data given in U. S. Bureau of the Census, *Historical Statistics of the United States, Colonial Times to 1957* (Washington, D. C., U. S. Government Printing Office, 1960), Series Z 56–75, pp. 759–60. The earlier figure for the port of Hampton is 1733 rather than 1734.

37. Cf. Stella H. Sutherland, *Population Distribution in Colonial America* (New York, Columbia University Press, 1936).

The Growth of Community

With the expansion of the population came the construction of post roads, ferries, and other means to facilitate intercolonial travel and communication. This is not to say that the transportation system was complete or ideal; some of the roads were almost impassable in bad weather. But two facts stand out: the roads multiplied and were considerably improved during the eighteenth century (a good indication of this fact is the amount of time it took to travel between two cities: post office records report that a letter required three days to go from Philadelphia to New York in 1720, but only one day in 1764[38]); travel between colonies was often faster and cheaper than that between coastal and inland population clusters within the same colony.

Intercolonial mobility made increasingly possible the exchange of ideas among the colonists. Among the many colonial travelers, one of the more notable was the evangelist George Whitefield. From 1738 until his death in 1770, he made seven journeys throughout the colonies, five of them extending from Georgia to New England. The religious revival that he occasioned, termed the "Great Awakening," was perhaps the first mass movement to sweep America. It was the spirit engendered in this movement that helped Whitefield to collect money throughout the colonies (and even in England) for such worthy causes as an orphanage in Georgia, the construction of Dartmouth and Princeton colleges, and the reconstruction of the Harvard College library after a fire in 1764.

The end of the French and Indian War found the colonists with communication habits and facilities considerably better than those of the 1730s or even the early 1750s. The politically relevant strata of colonial society had a wider range of opportunities to learn about events and attitudes affecting and in-

38. Seymour Dunbar, *A History of Travel in America* (4 vols. Indianapolis, Bobbs-Merrill, 1915), *1*, 177 n.

fluencing their fellow colonists than had been possible prior to that time.

And, if we are to judge from symbol usage in the colonial press, a new set of perceptions and foci of attention accompanied these changed habits and facilities of communication. American events were becoming increasingly more important in the attention patterns. The idea of referring to the colonies as a single unit was gaining favor. The newspapers began separating the colonies from the mother country through their symbol usage more often than identifying the colonies as a part of a British political community. Slow to develop, the trends toward increased American community awareness and an enhanced sense of American community were well under way.

With their changing self-images and attention patterns, the colonists began to perceive new common interests. Events that in earlier years might have seemed unimportant took on a new aura of significance in the context of changing perceptions and new trends toward intercolonial habits and facilities of communication. The grumbling responses in the 1730s and 1750s that the Molasses Act and the Iron Bill may have elicited from the colonists were isolated, and hence to a large measure ineffective. As the facilities for intercolonial communication improved, however, and as the colonists began to focus more and more of their attention upon the American community, such tones of dissatisfaction could find echoes throughout the continent. An Indian uprising in 1763, much less threatening than other attacks upon the colonists during the course of the previous two decades, could become a major topic of discussion in the press. The rapidly expanding newspapers could spend a larger amount of space on differences between the perspectives and interests of the colonists and those of the mother country. Given these circumstances, then, it seems less likely that the Stamp Act crisis itself generated bonds of community awareness among the colonists than that the rapidly growing ties of communication and community enabled the colonists to voice the effective opposition to parliament that has come to be called the "Stamp Act crisis"—which, in its turn, made a further contribution to the developing sense of American community.[39]

The Interaction of Formative Events and Levels of Community Awareness The evidence does not bear out a direct causal relationship between any *single* event and trends in American community awareness. Could it be, however, that it was the *cumulative impact* of the colonial wars or of the events in the years from 1763 to 1765 that created ties of community among the colonists?[40] To what degree did the "formative events" of the pre-Revolutionary era interact with levels of American community awareness?

By the summer of 1763, judging from their symbol usage, the colonists had reached what might be described as the "takeoff" stage of political integration—"a period in which small, scattered, and powerless movements" directed toward integration "change into larger and more coordinated ones with some significant power behind them." [41] Before those crucial months, the colonial press revealed a slow and often unsteady—but nonetheless increasing—interest in American

39. For the contribution of the Stamp Act crisis to a growing sense of Americanism, the best summary is Morgan and Morgan, *The Stamp Act Crisis.*

40. In shifting our focus from uni- to multicausality, it is worth stressing explicitly that we are abandoning the search for single causes—events, such as the War of Jenkins' Ear or the Stamp Act crisis itself, that stand out sharply and distinctly from the background, hence producing special effects —and turning to the scientist's analysis of systems.

41. "Before take-off, the proposal for integration is a matter of theory; after take-off, it is a political force." Deutsch et al., *Political Community and the North Atlantic Area,* pp. 83–84.

events, a growing interest in events affecting the colonies as a whole, and an ever greater tendency to identify the colonies as American rather than as British.[42]

The significance of these trends lies in the realm of inference and judgment. It is by no means clear, for example, that the colonists' moods and perceptions in the spring of 1763, although considerably different from previous decades, committed them irrevocably to a course ultimately leading to rebellion and independence. A more accurate appraisal of the Americans' mood might have led parliament to alter its own attitude and policy. But the order of magnitude of any parliamentary shifts would have to have been commensurate with the order of magnitude of the cumulative changes in the colonial mood and perceptions that had already occurred. It would have required major concessions to reverse the trend of a growing American sense of community. It would have required, for instance, substantial concessions in terms of the arguments then current in the colonies: freer trade, defense against the Indians, "no taxation without representation," and so forth. And it would have required substantial changes in the imperial policy-making mechanism to accommodate greater colonial participation.

However justified its reasons may have been, Great Britain rejected the path of conciliation.[43] At a time of changing moods and perceptions in the colonies, the mother country in-

42. In one sense these findings can be interpreted as matching the image of political integration and of takeoff discussed in the Princeton study (Deutsch et al., *Political Community and the North Atlantic Area*). In pointing to the rough and cyclical nature of the curve of community integration, however, the present study refines the concept developed in the Princeton study.

43. It is interesting to note that Great Britain did not follow its eighteenth-century pattern in dealing with Canada in the nineteenth century or with other Commonwealth members in the twentieth century.

stituted measures that underscored the cross-pressures already existent in the imperial system. By April 1763 the colonists had read rumors that 10,000 British regulars were to be posted in America, with "every Article of Expence" after the first year "to be defrayed by the Colonies." [44] Three months later followed the publication of "An Act for the further Improvement of His Majesty's Revenue of Customs; for the Encouragement of Officers making Seizures; and for the Prevention of the clandestine Running of Goods into any Part of His Majesty's Dominions." [45] There could have been little doubt that the act was aimed in large part at the rum, molasses, and sugar trade carried on between the colonies and the French Caribbean islands. Lest there be any doubt, however, many newspapers also published lists of British naval vessels ordered to the American station—45 newcomers in all, of which 17 were to range off the coast between Canso and Cape Florida.[46] Nor could British accounts of Pontiac's Conspiracy have provided pleasant reading for the colonists. The solution to the Indian problem? Articles of British origin appearing in the colonial press generally envisioned curbs to be imposed upon the colonists, not the Indians! The Royal Proclamation of

44. *New-York Mercury*, no. 600 (25 April 1763), no. 602 (9 May 1763), no. 605 (30 May 1763); *Pennsylvania Gazette*, no. 1792 (28 April 1763), no. 1794 (12 May 1763), no. 1795 (19 May 1763), no. 1797 (2 June 1763). An article in the *New-York Mercury*, no. 611 (11 July 1763), citing a report datelined Charles-Town, South-Carolina, on 14 June, reported that such a British move was "pretty certain." The timing of the rumors, no less than their persistence, suggests the possibility that they prompted the rise in symbol consciousness charted above. This possibility deserves to be pursued farther in other quantitative and qualitative analyses for, if it is true, it would lead to some shifts in our thinking about the importance of events leading up to the Stamp Act crisis.

45. Printed in full in the *Massachusetts Gazette*, no. 3118 (22 Sept. 1763), in what appears to be a special supplement.

46. *Massachusetts Gazette*, no. 3118 (22 Sept. 1763); *New-York Mercury*, no. 623 (3 Oct. 1763).

October 1763, which reached colonial ears some two months later,[47] incorporated these ideas and went one step further: it verified the rumors, circulating since the spring of 1763, and provided for the stationing of 10,000 Redcoats in America at the colonists' expense. These British measures and sentiments, coming at a time of accelerating trends toward higher levels of community awareness among the colonists, gave impetus to a moving political force already under way.

In analyzing the psychological basis of opinion change, Carl I. Hovland, Irving L. Janis, and Harold H. Kelley write that "heightened conflict" at the time of a communication designed to change a person's mind "can lead to certain types of resolution which increase long-term effectiveness." [48] This relationship of communication, persuasion, and counterpressures in personal behavior is extremely pertinent to the situation of the American colonies in 1763. Each new measure instituted by the British government in the latter half of that year (and in the subsequent years) constituted a challenge to the colonists' changing set of moods, images, habits, and attitudes. Each new measure, in effect, was a counterpressure that in the long run only served to increase the persistence with which the colonists clung to their new perceptions and patterns of behavior. And, as Merle Curti has written, "when the shoe began to pinch, the conviction that British and American interests differed became an important factor in the growth of American self-consciousness." [49]

47. *Massachusetts Gazette*, no. 3120 (9 Dec. 1763); *New-York Mercury*, no. 633 (12 Dec. 1763).

48. Carl I. Hovland, Irving L. Janis, and Harold H. Kelley, *Communication and Persuasion: Psychological Studies of Opinion Change* (New Haven, Yale University Press, 1953), p. 284.

49. Merle Curti, *The Roots of American Loyalty* (New York, Columbia University Press, 1946), p. 10. Cf. Harold D. Lasswell's remark, "the intensity of collective emotions and the broad direction and distribution of collective acts are matters of the changing total context." *Politics: Who Gets What, When, How* (New York, McGraw-Hill, 1936), p. 51.

The Growth of Community

By the end of 1763 the colonists' takeoff toward political integration was well under way. The movement toward an American political community waxed strong during the years of the Stamp Act crisis. The repeal of that act, while removing the most immediate cause of colonial grievance, did little to alter the basic moods and perceptions that in large part had been responsible for the crisis, and which had conditioned the colonists' responses during the struggle itself. That the levels of American community awareness dropped off after the repeal of the Stamp Act does not mean that American community awareness sank to the level prevalent during the 1740s: in most cases, the curves after 1766 were higher than in any year prior to the Stamp Act crisis.[50]

Judging from symbol usage in the newspapers, the remaining decade of the colonial era witnessed an intense interaction of increasing American community sentiments and events. On the one hand, the colonists' mood became increasingly more sensitive to actual or perceived abridgments of their rights, or what they perceived their rights to be. Milder provocations began to arouse stronger responses. And, on the other hand, each new event—the Townshend Act, the Boston Massacre, the Tea Act, the Intolerable Acts—only served to bring the complex of images and attitudes into sharper focus.

THE GROWTH OF AMERICAN COMMUNITY

The data surveyed in this study tell us much about the timing and patterns of growing national consciousness in the eight-

50. Linear trend lines for the three curves from 1763 to 1775 only, all start out at about the 22 per cent level in 1763. The linear trend line for the curve depicted in Figure 8-1 as a solid line rose to the 42 per cent level in 1775 (or 1.6 percentage points per year); that for the broken line in Figure 8-1 rose to the 26 per cent level in 1775 (or .4 percentage points per year); and that for the dotted line in Figure 8-1 rose from the 25 per cent to the 66 per cent level in 1775 (or 3.4 percentage points per year).

eenth-century American colonies. They indicate, for instance, the more significant changes in the colonists' perceptions of and attitudes toward their community. Some were essentially quantitative: the amount of intercolonial news carried by the newspapers increased sixfold and more from the late 1730s to the early 1770s; the distributions of symbols in the newspapers of different colonies were increasingly parallel (even if not always symmetrical); the major shifts in symbol usage occurred during the latter half of 1763. A change in quality attended these changes in quantity: a growing propensity to pay attention to American events, an ever greater willingness to refer to Americans as a single group, the increasing use of terms identifying the colonists as Americans rather than as members of a British political community—all these suggest aroused expectations about group membership in a distinctly American political community.

Second, concomitant changes in the structure of intercolonial communication, such as the expansion of trade among the colonies, the emergence of interlocking elites, and the construction of post roads and other means to facilitate communication and transportation, reinforced the developing image of an American community. Which came first—the ties of social communication and identity, or improved facilities—is a chicken-and-egg question that must remain unanswered for now.

Third, the growth of far-reaching habits of and facilities for intercolonial communication preceded the creation of unified political institutions among the colonists. However much the structures created in 1775 and later may have furthered a sense of Americanism and given the colonists a concrete as well as symbolic focus around which to rally, the structures themselves did not generate this Americanism; more probably, it was the changed climate of opinion that permitted the institutions to be created in the first place.

Fourth, the emergence of American community consciousness seems to explain, rather than to be explained by, the occurrence of single, dramatic events in the later colonial years. Wars against the French and their Indian allies merely postponed the emergence of sentiments of Americanism. Other "formative" events, such as the Stamp Act crisis, came well after American community awareness had begun to increase. Such events as these, however, even if they did not furnish the original impetus, most assuredly reinforced the colonists' growing sense of American separatism. It was this interplay that, more than anything else, led to the Revolution and the formation of the American Union.

What the data surveyed in the study cannot do is to account for such changes in the colonists' communication patterns. They cannot answer the question: What impulses led the eighteenth-century Americans to pay more rather than less attention to one another as time passed, to trade, correspond, and visit more with one another, to view themselves as a community apart from the British or even the Anglo-American political community? Neither can they give us clues about the motivations of His Majesty's Government in London. What was it, for instance, that prompted the Royal ministers to institute such measures as the Stamp Act and the Boston Port Bill which, in retrospect at least, seem to have been calculated to stir up colonial hostility and resistance? The answers to such questions do not lie in the raw data but in inference and interpretation based upon the information they supply, as well as in the confrontation of these data with other types of information about community sentiments in colonial America. Some of these interpretations and analyses lie outside the scope of this study;[51] others have been discussed briefly in the preceding pages.

The increasing intercolonial communication load accompanied extensive changes in the colonists' habits of and facilities for intercolonial communication and decision-making. The data surveyed above indicate growing colonial interaction from 1735 to 1775, together with a high rate of mutually beneficial transactions, compared to the total number of intercolonial transactions of all sorts. To be sure, they indicate that the emergence of an American community consciousness was a slow process, retarded at times by developments that emphasized the colonists' psychic distance from one another and their reliance upon the mother country, and occasionally hastened by developments highlighting conflicts within the imperial relationship. But, what is more important, these data indicate that, by the early 1770s, the colonists were sufficiently different from their English contemporaries that they comprised a political community—embryonic in some respects, perhaps, but nonetheless a distinct American political community.

51. For some interpretations, see my "Systems and the Disintegration of Empires," *General Systems: Yearbook of the Society for General Systems Research,* 8 (1963), 91-103, and my "Distance and Interaction among Political Communities," in *General Systems: Yearbook of the Society for General Systems Research,* 9 (1964), 255–63.

CHAPTER NINE

Toward a Theory of Political Integration

A main purpose of this study was to develop a systematic, analytical framework useful not only for examining the American case study, but also in considering the development of other political communities in the international arena. This imposes two tasks. First, it is necessary to narrow the set of relevant problems. From a wealth of historical data, the student of political communities must extract the processes and interacting changes that are at once significant for the particular case study and capable of a more universal application. Second, it is necessary to describe as accurately as possible the timing of significant, interacting changes.

This book concentrated upon shifting political demands in colonial America—demands, whether explicitly stated or dimly felt, that resulted in the disintegration of community ties between the colonies and the mother country, and in the integration and eventual political amalgamation of the colonies themselves. After selecting two variables basic to the changing patterns of demands, I sought to pose a series of sharply defined questions, to use empirical, quantitative data in answering these questions, and to point to a need for the reinforcement or contradiction of these findings through similar analyses of other sources and communication media in eighteenth-century America.

The symbol analysis of the colonial press produced a number of hypotheses about the interaction of patterns of attention and self-perceptions with the more important events of the pre-Revolutionary decade. (1) The growth of a rich community life in colonial America was a slow process, resting to a large measure upon the development of common perceptions and experiences. (2) With the passage of time, the colonies and the mother country tended to develop distinctive ways of looking at themselves and to find distinctive foci of attention. (3) A curve representing the growth of an American community awareness was not strictly linear, rising steadily if slowly throughout the colonial years. Rather, it was cyclical, resembling a typical learning curve, with periods of decline interspersed with periods of incline and rapid breakthroughs. (4) English newspapers symbolically differentiated the colonies from the mother country before colonial newspapers made this distinction. (5) The development of a sense of community among the colonists preceded a demand for the functional amalgamation of their political institutions. (6) As more attention was devoted to American events, attention to British symbols did not falter, while the amount of space devoted to European symbols dropped sharply. (7) As the colonial press paid more attention to intercolonial (that is, continental) symbols, attention to home colony symbols declined. (8) With the passage of time the attention patterns of the individual colonies grew more congruent. (9) In their perceptions of American news and each other, the southern colonies seemed to stress the collective character of colonial society, the middle colonies emphasized the other colonies as individuals, and Massachusetts was comparatively self-centered. (10) In the later colonial years Massachusetts was a primary source of news for other colonies. (11) Colonial wars, with the British and the Americans allied militarily against a common enemy, slowed the development of sentiments of American unity in the colonies. (12) Symbol usage in the colonial press during periods of colonial wars went through three distinct phases: an initial period of drag, in which the symbol usage of the prewar period was continued; an intermediate phase in which sentiments of American unity played a role of decreasing importance in the colonial press; and a final phase, simultaneous with or shortly after the decisive stages in the wars, in which symbols of American community awareness began to capture larger shares of newspaper space. (13) As the level of attention to the American community rose, the colonists became increasingly more sensitive to what they perceived to be either interference from the mother country or abrogations of colonial rights and privileges. (14) The mother country followed policies that emphasized divergent British and American perceptions, interests, and moods. (We might speculate that, if the Crown had made substantial efforts to reintegrate the colonists into the British political community in the early 1760s, it might have prevented or at least postponed the disintegration of the eighteenth-century Anglo-American political community.)

These hypotheses, which the data gathered for this study affirm, are nonetheless tentative. They stand in need of further verification (or even contradiction) through empirical analyses of other media of communication in colonial America or through empirical studies, for instance, of other variables in the integrative processes. Patterns of mutual attention and self-perceptions are only two of the many important variables in the ecology of demands for change in colonial America. In effect, by sharpening the data relevant to these two patterns, I am suggesting that other historians and political scientists might wish to be equally sharp in their discussions of the timing of other changes and processes that culminated in the integration of the American political community.

What are these other variables? What would a systematic analysis of the ecology of political demands for the disintegration of the Anglo-American community and the integration of a purely American political community have to take into consideration? The most complete list of such variables was given by Karl W. Deutsch and his associates:

> Altogether we have found nine essential conditions for an amalgamated security-community: (1) mutual compatibility of main values; (2) a distinctive way of life; (3) expectations of stronger economic ties or gains; (4) a marked increase in political and administrative capabilities of at least some participating units; (5) superior economic growth on the part of at least some participating units; (6) unbroken links of social communication, both geographically between territories and sociologically between different social strata; (7) a broadening of the political elite; (8) mobility of persons, at least among the politically relevant strata; and (9) a multiplicity of ranges of communication and transaction. And we have found indications that three other conditions may be essential: (10) a compensation of flows of communications and transactions; (11) a not too infrequent interchange of group roles; and, (12) considerable mutual predictability of behavior.[1]

1. Deutsch et al., *Political Community and the North Atlantic Area,* p. 58. Some scholars have analyzed these variables in the light of current attempts at political integration on the international level. Cf. Ernst B. Haas, "The Challenge of Regionalism," *International Organization,* 12 (Autumn 1958), 440–58, reprinted in part in Stanley H. Hoffmann, ed., *Contempo-*

Political Integration

One of the tasks of interdisciplinary research in history and political science would be to find ways to measure trends in such variables, and the way in which they interacted during the later colonial years. The data gathered for the present study indicate trends in certain aspects of these variables. It is necessary, however, to investigate how changes in perceptions and symbol usage were related to the other variables in the inchoate American community. And, to find this out, we need more precise descriptions of the other variables.

The ecology of the demands, of course, is not the sole problem in considering the rise of an American political community. We must also examine the conscious elements in the formation of demands for political change. What in fact were the demands for change in the colonies? What persons or groups were demanding changes? What rewards did they expect if they were effective? What was the relative strength of competing demands, such as that for continued unity with the British political community, or the demand for a greater measure of autonomy within the British imperial system? With what amount of intensity were the demands for unity or reorganization made? What role did such factors as price and market changes play in the formulation of the demands? What resources—physical, intellectual, or even spiritual—were at the command of the persons or groups demanding changes? What strategies were available to them? Under what conditions might we expect such strategies to have been successful? What conditions would have been necessary for the maintenance of multiple, Anglo-American, loyalty in the colonies? What factors worked toward the disintegration or increased

rary *Theory in International Relations* (Englewood Cliffs, Prentice-Hall, 1960), pp. 223–40. Cf. also John G. Stoessinger, *The Might of Nations: World Politics in Our Time* (New York, Random House, 1961), pp. 307–42.

integration of the colonies as a group after their secession from the British political community?

A systematic analysis of the conscious elements of demands for change in the American colonies, and of the ecology of those demands, would also be helpful in developing a more general theory of political integration. The questions and hypotheses presented in the previous paragraphs comprise an effort to extract from the vast stream of American history the concepts that can be used in analyzing large-scale political integration on the international level. They represent an effort to get the type of information that we would need to perform a systematic comparison of emerging political communities, such as Germany or Italy of the nineteenth century or the North Atlantic community of our own generation. Such a comparison would be useful not only intrinsically, that is, in the analysis of each community by itself, but also as a basis for policies aimed at reducing tensions in specific regions (such as Western Europe).

In short, we need to begin discussing past examples of political communities in terms that will enable a better understanding of current trends toward political integration or disintegration. We want to make the American case study more meaningful and fruitful through reinterpreting it in terms of a general theory of political integration. We want to know how political communities, such as the Anglo-American community of the early eighteenth century, break up, and how communities are formed or re-formed.

Some of the hypotheses suggested above could serve as a useful starting point for cross-national studies of political integration. Their verification, rejection, or improvement through studies of other political communities would enrich the hypotheses, making them more suitable as bases of an empirical theory of political integration.

Political Integration

How could we generalize the hypotheses about community awareness in colonial America? In a sense, the Anglo-American political community of the early eighteenth century is a paradigm of noncontiguous political communities; and the subsequent integration of the thirteen colonies is a model of integrative processes uniting separate groups or communities. Thus, for example, we might hypothesize: noncontiguous members of a political community tend to develop distinctive ways of looking at themselves and to find distinctive foci of attention. Clearly such a proposition has serious implications for policy-makers in modern Pakistan, Malaysia, and the North Atlantic Treaty Organization. If this proposition is true, and if these policy-makers would seek to maintain or to increase existing levels of integration in their respective communities, some means to combat the tendency toward separate identification and attention patterns must be found.

Similarly, as the level of separatist sentiment in an outlying member of a noncontiguous political community rises, there is increasing sensitivity to actions by the old core area that are perceived as interference. Such a proposition is not dissimilar from Alexis de Tocqueville's observation about the origins of the French Revolution: "Evils which are patiently endured when they seem inevitable become intolerable when once the idea of escape from them is suggested." [2] If this is true, policy-makers in the community's core area must be alert to shifts in the perceptions and moods of the outlying members, either making allowance for the shifts or finding some means to accommodate them.

Consider one more hypothesis: the development of a sense of community among different groups or countries precedes a popular demand for the functional or complete amalgamation

2. Cited in Davies, "Toward a Theory of Revolution," *American Sociological Review*, 27 (1962), 6.

of their political institutions. If this is true, those who would unite the entire world (or even Europe) into a single, amalgamated political community should direct their attention most immediately to improving the climate of community awareness or a sense of community in the world (or in Europe).

Such hypotheses as these are basic to the development of an empirical theory of political integration. Subjecting these hypotheses to the test of quantitative evidence and rigorous qualitative analysis is one of the most important tasks facing modern students of political communities.

A Design for Symbol Analysis Research

In designing a symbol analysis of colonial newspapers there are certain basic decisions to be made at the outset: What time period would give the optimum amount of information? From what towns in British North America should newspapers be selected? Which newspapers from these towns would be best suited for a symbol analysis? How many issues of each newspaper should be included in the analysis? What should be the method of sampling? What symbol list should be used, that is, what should be counted?

ORGANIZING THE PROJECT

The Time-Span   The decision to limit the scope of the analysis to the years from 1735 to 1775 inclusively stems from a number of considerations. Before the 1730s, first of all, there were very few newspapers in the colonies. The introduction of newspaper printing in colonial America came as late as 1704 when, on 24 April of that year, John Campbell of Boston, because of widespread popular demand for his handwritten newsletters, first printed the *Boston News-Letter*.[1]

1. We may ignore Benjamin Harris' *Publick Occurrences Both Forreign and Domestick,* only one issue of which (25 Sept. 1690) appeared before the government of Massachusetts Bay ordered its cessation.

Boston's and America's second newspaper, the *Boston Gazette*, printed originally by James Franklin for William Brooker, did not appear for another 15 years;[2] 1719 also saw the initiation of a newspaper in Philadelphia, the *American Weekly Mercury*, published somewhat sporadically by Andrew Bradford from 1719 to 1747. The first enduring newspaper did not appear in that city for another decade, however, when Benjamin Franklin and Hugh Meredith bought out Samuel Keimer's rapidly failing *Universal Instructor in all Arts and Sciences: and Pennsylvania Gazette,* and changed its title by omitting the rather pretentious first eight words. New York had no newspaper until 1725, Virginia until 1736, and Connecticut until 1755.

That the earliest files of many newspapers—and this is particularly true of numerous short-lived ventures—are often incomplete in today's libraries is a second reason for limiting the analysis to the years after 1735. Beginning with the late 1730s, the percentage of issues that have survived rises considerably. In one case, the incompleteness of the files was great enough to reduce the relevance of the newspaper for this inquiry, in spite of its importance in colonial history. This indicates that the reduced sample size of this particular newspaper must be considered when looking at the results of the analysis.

The period from 1735 to 1775 includes what I would term the most important formative events of the pre-Revolutionary years. With the possible exception of the Molasses Act of

2. James Franklin is chiefly remembered as the older brother of another future newspaper publisher, Benjamin Franklin; in his *Autobiography,* the latter recalled his brother's newspaper venture, commenting, "I remember his being dissuaded by some of his friends from the undertaking, as not likely to succeed, one newspaper being, in their judgment, enough for America." *Autobiography,* ed. Dixon Wecter (New York, Rinehart, 1948), p. 17.

Appendices

1733, which the colonists generally ignored and the Crown did not enforce, there were few events that could be termed "formative" in the period prior to 1735; to reach back further into American history would be to multiply the amount of work with little hope of receiving much more useful information for the analysis of integrative processes and political communities.

The terminating date of 1775 for the study is arbitrary; the present study could be extended into a larger inquiry analyzing the effect of the Revolution itself upon the news distribution and identity patterns of the American newspapers. The year 1775 is nonetheless important in the analysis of integrative processes: it was in that year that the colonists crossed what I have termed the threshold of functional amalgamation. It would be the rare newspaper, we might anticipate, that would refer to the inhabitants of America as "British subjects" after the Declaration of Independence. The extent to which that did occur is a matter for further testing.

The Areas The centers of the five largest population clusters in the colonies—Boston, New York City, Philadelphia, Williamsburg in Virginia, and Charleston in South Carolina—were chosen as the areas of concentration. These cities are representative of their respective regions and, considered together, of the thirteen colonies as a whole. Consideration of these areas alone builds an unavoidable bias into the research project, however; each of the cities was large, and each contained important Patriot or antigovernment groups in the later colonial years.[3] Counterbalancing this bias to some extent is

3. In fact, according to estimates made by the U. S. Bureau of the Census, only 5.1 per cent of America's population lived in urban areas in 1790, the remainder residing in rural farming and nonfarming areas. U. S. Bureau of the Census, *Historical Statistics of the United States, Colonial Times to 1957*, Series A 34–50, p. 9.

the fact that nonurban areas generally did not have their own newspapers; they relied upon the metropolitan centers for their news and advertising. It would, of course, be impossible to include all of the towns and cities that were important in colonial America and which published newspapers:[4] Hartford and New Haven in Connecticut, Providence and Newport in Rhode Island, Baltimore and Annapolis in Maryland, New-Bern and Wilmington in North Carolina, and Savannah in Georgia. Many of these towns began their newspapers only in the later colonial years; most of them were also reasonably close to the large population centers that are included in the study.

The Newspapers The selection of newspapers to be analyzed proved to be one of the thorniest problems. Some newspapers important in colonial history, such as John Peter Zenger's *New-York Weekly Journal,* were relatively short-lived. Incomplete files in the libraries of today destroyed the usefulness of other journals for this project. Still others were official organs, neither widely read nor accepted by the populace. Such was the case with John Campbell's *Boston News-Letter* and its successors, which propagated strong pro-governmental views for the better part of 72 years. Dubbed "the Court Gazette" by the citizens of Boston, it fell into severe disrepute before ceasing publication early in 1776.

The criteria for selecting one newspaper from each of the four cities were: (a) continuity of the newspaper during the entire period, 1735–75; (b) availability and completeness at the present time; and (c) the prestige of the newspaper, insofar as it can be determined. In considering the various alternatives, I relied upon the standard works on early American

4. In April 1775, twenty different towns in colonial America published newspapers. Brigham, *History and Bibliography of American Newspapers,* passim.

journalism by Isaiah Thomas, James Melvin Lee, Frank Luther Mott, and Clarence S. Brigham.[5]

The *Virginia Gazette* fulfilled the requirements of the first criterion. William Parks began the publication of the first *Gazette* on 6 August 1736, and it continued until some months after his death in 1750. William Hunter, later to become Joint Deputy Postmaster General for North America along with Benjamin Franklin, reestablished the *Gazette* in January of the following year and, after his death in 1761, his step-son, Joseph Royle, continued its publication until his own death in 1766. Alexander Purdie and John Dixon then took over the *Gazette,* continuing the same numbering that Hunter and Royle had followed. When Purdie went out on his own to found a rival *Virginia Gazette* in 1775, Dixon formed a new partnership with William Hunter, the son of the former publisher, and continued the *Gazette* in the same form until 1778. Thus the continuity of the *Virginia Gazette* was maintained under five editorships—Parks, Hunter, Royle, Purdie and Dixon, and Dixon and Hunter—for some forty-two years. However, the present-day files of this newspaper are rather incomplete in the middle years of our period.

The selection of a newspaper from Philadelphia proved an easy matter. Although not the first published in the city, the *Pennsylvania Gazette* fulfills all three criteria. The files are complete from 1729, when Franklin and Meredith purchased it from Samuel Keimer, until its transformation, long after

5. Isaiah Thomas, *The History of Printing in America* (1st ed. Worcester, Massachusetts, From the press of Isaiah Thomas, Jun., 1810; 2d ed. Albany N. Y., Joel Munsell, Printer, 1874). James Melvin Lee, *History of American Journalism* (Boston and New York, Houghton Mifflin, 1923). Frank Luther Mott, *American Journalism, A History: 1690–1960* (3d ed. New York, Macmillan, 1962). Brigham, *History and Bibliography of American Newspapers.* Cf. my "Public Opinion in Colonial America: Content-Analyzing the Colonial Press," *Public Opinion Quarterly,* 27 (1963), 356–71.

the turn of the century, into the *Saturday Evening Post.* Perhaps no colonial newspaper enjoyed as much prestige as did the *Pennsylvania Gazette* under the editorship of Benjamin Franklin, nor was any more active in the promotion of public welfare projects. The editorship of this newspaper changed hands several times during the pre-Revolutionary period: Franklin eased Hugh Meredith out of the partnership in 1732; sixteen years later, in 1748, he formed a partnership with David Hall and, although he continued to write for it and to direct its activities from afar, Franklin moved into semi-retirement from the newspaper world; after Franklin sold out his interest completely in 1766, Hall continued its publication in partnership with William Sellers; and when Hall died in 1772, his sons, William and David, took over his share of the partnership.

Similarly, the *South-Carolina Gazette* was the obvious choice for a newspaper from that colony. In spite of some publishing lapses in the middle 1760s, it satisfied all three criteria used for selecting newspapers. Although not the first newspaper printed in Charleston, the *Gazette* was the only one to cover a substantial portion of the colonial era. Moreover, by encouraging original contributions from its subscribers and by reprinting extensively from such English papers as the *Spectator,* it gained a reputation as a leading colonial literary journal. Thomas Whitmarsh established the original *South-Carolina Gazette* in January 1732, but it died twenty months later when Whitmarsh fell victim to yellow fever. Lewis Timothy, Franklin's protégé and former associate, reinstituted the journal (with new numbering) in April 1734. His death in 1738 left it in the hands of his widow, who eventually sold it to their son Peter. Under Peter Timothy's editorial supervision, which lasted from 1739 to 1775 (except for a few months in 1772–73, after Timothy had been appointed Deputy Postmaster General for the Southern Provinces), the *South-Carolina Gazette* became a leading voice of the southern colonies. Timothy revived the journal under a new title early in 1777, but he was soon arrested for his Patriotic sentiments.

The availability and prestige criteria suggested the selection of Zenger's *New-York Weekly Journal* despite its short 18-year duration (1733–51). A strong pro-government bias marked Zenger's chief rival, the *New-York Gazette*, published from 1725 to 1744. Zenger's columns, by way of contrast, had an independent and even saucy approach—one so offensive to New York's aristocratic government that he was arrested in the fall of 1734, held in jail for 35 weeks, and tried for seditious libel. His acquittal was a turning point in American journalism and the freedom of the press. After Zenger's death in 1746 his widow, Catherine, and later her stepson, John Zenger, published the newspaper; but with the latter's death in 1751, the publication of the *New-York Weekly Journal* ceased. For the sake of continuity, it was necessary to select another newspaper, the *New-York Mercury* (later the *New-York Gazette, and Weekly Mercury*), published by Hugh Gaine from August 1752 until 1783. For convenience, Gaine's newspaper is referred to solely as the *New-York Mercury* throughout this inquiry.

Finding a Boston newspaper was not such a simple matter. In terms of continuity and availability there was an obvious choice: the *Boston News-Letter*, later published under other names (including the *Massachusetts Gazette; and Boston News-Letter*), which appeared from 1704 to 1776. As noted above, this journal generally expressed the point of view of the royally appointed governor of the Bay Colony; in fact, for some years it bore the inscription "Published by Authority" on its masthead. Other Boston newspapers are currently unavailable, and many of them were too short-lived to be useful for this study. An exception is the *Boston Gazette and Country Journal,* published regularly during the four decades prior to the outbreak of revolution, and generally oriented toward the Whig or Patriot party. It was this journal about which Governor Hutchinson lamented, "seven eighths of the people read none but this infamous paper, and so are never undeceived." [6] A modern authority on colonial journalism has written that the *Boston Gazette* was "the best Whig paper in the country." [7] An analysis of the *Boston Gazette* for the last third of our period, I felt, would not only balance the analysis of the *Massachusetts Gazette* (as the *Boston News-Letter* or the *Massachusetts Gazette; and Boston News-Letter* will be termed in this inquiry), but could also serve to test the differences in attention and identity patterns between Tory- and Whig-oriented newspapers in the American colonies.

It might be worth noting at this point that, of the seven newspapers included in the survey, four (the *Virginia Gazette,* the *Pennsylvania Gazette,* the *New-York Mercury,* and the *Massachusetts Gazette*) tended to be conservative and pro-British in their editorial policy. Only three (Zenger's *New-York Weekly Journal,* Timothy's *South-Carolina Gazette,* and the *Boston Gazette,* published by Benjamin Edes and John Gill) were critical of the colonial government and its policies. Thus, if anything, a slight pro-Tory and anti-Patriot bias was built into the study. If a difference in the attention and identity patterns between Tory- and Whig-oriented newspapers actually existed, and if, as we might suspect, the Whiggish journals were indeed more inclined than the Tory prints to recognize and to encourage the existence of

6. William V. Wells, *The Life and Public Services of Samuel Adams* (3 vols. Boston, Little, Brown, 1865), *1,* 244.

7. Philip Davidson, *Propaganda and the American Revolution, 1763–1783* (Chapel Hill, University of North Carolina Press, 1941), p. 227.

a distinct American political community, then the present study underestimates the drive toward independence in symbol usage to a slight degree. In viewing the results of the survey, this fact must be kept in mind.

The Sample   Symbol analysis research bases the size of samples upon the degree of sensitivity to trends needed for testing a set of hypotheses. If it is necessary to measure week-by-week shifts in symbol usage precisely, the research design must include each weekly issue of a selected number of colonial newspapers. The present project, however, does not require such a precise analysis of weekly trends in symbol usage. First of all, subjecting every single issue of the selected newspapers to a complete symbol analysis would be too time-consuming for our present purposes. Second, and more important, such a large sample would bury the long-range trends in a mass of weekly fluctuations. A smaller sample—sufficient to give us a picture of year-by-year changes in the use of symbols—would serve in evaluating the alternative theories of political integration discussed in previous chapters.

This study uses a random sample of one issue per quarter-year (or four per year) from each of the selected sets of newspapers. Clearly a sample of this size, however representative, would not tell us as much as a sample of twelve issues per year about fluctuations in symbol usage during the course of a single year. For measuring the overall trend for an entire year, however, a random sample of four issues per year is almost as adequate as an independent random sample of twelve issues per year.[8]

8. Independent samples of four and twelve issues per year for ten different years were compared, using the nonparametric "Mann-Whitney *U* Test." In nine of the ten cases, the tests indicated that no significant difference between the two samples existed. More properly speaking, in nine of ten cases (significant at the .05 level for a two-tailed test) the tests did not

If all of the issues of a particular newspaper for the years from 1735 to 1775 were available, as was the case with the *Pennsylvania Gazette*, the sample size would have constituted 164 issues, or 7.7 per cent of the total number of issues printed over the 41-year period. Where the files were incomplete, however, the percentage size of the sample increased: thus 10.3 per cent of the available issues of the *Virginia Gazette* and 10.9 per cent of the available issues of the *New-York Weekly Journal* were included in the analysis.

In terms of procedure, the number of newspapers extant for each quarter was tabulated, and one of these was selected at random according to a standard procedure.[9] Where there were no extant issues for a given quarter, it was necessary to select at random another issue from the same year.

In the pretest it was found that the crucial years for the study were those from 1762 to 1766. To get a closer look at newspaper content for those five years, it seemed necessary to take an independent random sample of two sets of news-papers—the *New-York Mercury* and the *Boston Gazette*—on a monthly, rather than a quarterly, basis. The New York and Boston journals were selected as representative of news-papers paying, respectively, less and more than average attention to American events relative to news of British or foreign occurrences. Using the procedure described above, one issue per month was selected for each of these publications.

Coding Reliability To check on the reliability of coding, I used a simple percentage agreement index: $r = \dfrac{2p_{ab}}{p_a + p_b}$, where r is the observed percentage agreement between two

---

reject a null hypothesis asserting that there was no significant difference between the sample of four and the independent sample of twelve issues. Cf. Siegel, *Nonparametric Statistics for the Behavioral Sciences*, pp. 116–27.

9. The RAND Corporation, *A Million Random Digits* (Glencoe, Illinois, The Free Press, 1955), p. xxiv.

coders coding the same material, p_a is the number of observations recorded by coder A, p_b the number of observations recorded by coder B, and p_{ab} the number of observations recorded jointly by coders A and B. The percentage agreement between the two coders coding the Massachusetts newspapers was $r = .92$. The percentage agreement between my coding at the outset of the project and a recoding of the same material after the project was completed is $r = .96$.

SYMBOLS OF COMMUNITY

The analysis included all of the news items in each selected newspaper issue, omitting only advertisements and notices of ship movements (that is, official port entries stating which ships had arrived and which had been cleared by port officials for departure). I had originally intended to perform a complete symbol analysis for each of these classifications, but the pretest revealed that the information derived from the latter two categories—which in later years comprised between fifty and seventy-five per cent of the total column space in each issue—was not a large enough increment to the total amount of useful information to warrant spending the time and labor that such a task would require.

Symbols of the Focus of Attention   A symbol list of place-names seemed to be most suited for an analysis of attention patterns in the colonial newspapers. Each observation of such a symbol—specific place-names throughout the world, such as "Boston" or "Africa"—was recorded.

Geographic references per se seemed too remote from the main purpose of this study, which is limited to specific political units and the symbols for those units. Thus the names of rivers, mountains, lakes, and bays were not included in the symbol list unless those place-names were also the names of political units (e.g. "Massachusetts Bay"). Neither the names of ships (such as "the Sloop *Virginia*") nor the names of persons ("William Paris," for example) were counted, even though those names corresponded to the symbol categories. An exception to this rule was the inclusion of names which were in actuality titles, such as "the Duke of Tuscany" or "the Prince of Wales," provided that the place-name symbol was included in the title. Finally, it did not seem necessary to tabulate place-names in the following instances: (a) when they appeared as the city of publication of a newspaper (e.g. "Printed in New-York City by John Peter Zenger"); or (b) when they appeared in the title of the newspaper at the masthead.

To secure a more complete picture of the focus of attention within America, it seemed necessary to include indirect references to place-names in the American colonies as well as direct references. Thus a news item may have referred to "Williamsburg" (direct reference) or to "this colony" or "here" (indirect references). By keeping separate tabulations of direct and indirect symbols it was possible, in the analysis stage of the project, to include the indirect symbols in the consideration of the newspapers' focus of attention on American events only, and to exclude them when the focus of attention on American events was to be contrasted to the amount of symbol space given to, for example, England or Europe.[10]

10. The use of place-name symbols underestimates the total amount of linage devoted to American events in the colonial press. In 1738 the average line of news about events taking place in or primarily affecting the colonies contained .13 symbols (or roughly one symbol for every eight lines of print); while the average line of news about European events contained .34 symbols (or about one symbol for every three lines). In 1768 these figures were, respectively, .19 symbols for each line of print about American events (one symbol in five lines) and .40 symbols for each line of print about European events (two symbols in five lines). Thus the distribution of place-name symbols in the colonial press cannot be taken as an exact measure of those newspapers' distribution of linage. This fact, however, does not

Appendices

The symbol list used in analyzing the news and editorial content of the colonial newspapers was divided into seven categories:

1. *Symbols of Common Identity (Continental Symbols)* These are generic terms applied to the entire area later comprising the United States of America, and to the inhabitants of that geographic entity: "His Majesty's Colonies," "the colonies," "America," "British Americans," "colonists," "Americans," and so forth. Indirect references to such symbols were tabulated separately. This category does not include references to "America" that clearly pertained to Spanish America or to the French colonies in North America.

2. *Home Colony Symbols* This category contains references in a newspaper pertaining to the newspaper's own colony or to places within that colony. In the analysis of the *Virginia Gazette,* for example, references to both Virginia and to Charlottesville would appear in this category. Here, too, a separate tabulation was kept of such indirect references ("this colony," "this city," "here") that pertain to place-names in the newspaper's own colony.

3. *Other Colony Symbols* All of the colonies that joined the American union by 1791, that is, the original thirteen colonies and Vermont, are included in this category. Again, subcategories include references to "this colony" and "here" when they apply specifically to some place within these colonies or to one of the colonies by itself. For convenience this category is divided into four main groups: the northern colonies (New Hampshire, Vermont, Massachusetts Bay, Rhode Island, and Connecticut); the middle Atlantic colonies (New York, New Jersey, Pennsylvania, Maryland, and Delaware); the southern colonies (Virginia, North Carolina, South Caro-

---

affect the value of using place-name symbols as an indication of the journals' focus of attention.

lina, and Georgia); and other (including such places in the western country as "Ohio" and "Detroit" as well as unidentifiable place-names definitely somewhere in the colonies).

4. *British Symbols* Great Britain, all of the areas within the British Isles (including Ireland and Scotland), and the British European possessions of Gibraltar and Minorca comprise this category.

5. *Canadian Symbols* This category includes all of the colonies, cities, or regions now comprising part of Canada whether, at any point in the eighteenth century, they were controlled by French or British authorities.

6. *Caribbean Symbols* This category has two parts. "Florida and Gulf Port" symbols include references to places (Florida, Mobile, New Orleans, and Louisiana) that, until the Treaty of Paris of 1763, were in French or Spanish hands. After the peace settlement, all of the territory east of the Mississippi belonged to Great Britain. Since these areas were administered separately from the thirteen colonies by the English government, and since even the colonists tended not to include them in their references to "America" and "Americans," these areas are considered apart from the rest of British North America. "Caribbean and South American" symbols include all of the Caribbean islands, whether owned by the French, Spanish, or British, and the entire continent of South America (including the Falkland Islands). For the purposes of this inquiry, and in view of eighteenth-century political divisions, both California and Mexico are considered to be in this category.

7. *Other Symbols* It had originally been intended to consider references to Europe, to countries in continental Europe, to provinces, and to cities, in addition to references to the Ottoman Empire and Persia, Asia, and Africa (including Madeira and St. Helena), as separate subcategories in this final group. The pretest indicated, however, that an accurate

breakdown of European symbols alone would consume an inordinate amount of time, even though it might be quite useful in pinpointing the focus of attention in American newspapers on European wars, affairs of state, and gossip. The pretest showed, for example, that a steady flow of information reached America about such Italian cities as Genoa and Leghorn (Livorno), and that brief flurries of attention focused on particular areas in time of war. It is to be hoped that further studies of this type will center upon the specific areas of attention in Europe. But for the purposes of the present inquiry it seemed best to contract this category into one item, including all place-names outside the New World and the British Isles (and Gibraltar and Minorca).

Symbols of Common Identity Perhaps the most important symbol of community is that used to designate the community as a whole, its members and the land they inhabit. Symbols of common identity, as they are termed in this study, reflect the image that the members of a community have of themselves. When a person calls himself a "German," he identifies himself with the German political community, with the land called "Germany," and with the German people. Thus the French live in France, the Italians in Italy, and the Japanese in Japan. But what about the inhabitants of colonial America?

Group identity in eighteenth-century America has two separate facets: the identification of the colonists with a political community (did they consider themselves to be Englishmen living in the extensive British realm, or Americans inhabiting a new world? When did they stop referring to themselves as "British subjects" and begin to use the symbol "American" consistently?) and the image of the members of the British community living in the British Isles (did the people of London use the term "His Majesty's subjects" to cover Bostonians as well as Londoners? Or did they utilize symbols that differentiated the colonists from themselves? Did the English recognition of the separation of the two communities come before that of the colonists themselves, or were the colonists aware of their separation first? Or did the changeover in symbol usage occur simultaneously in both countries?).

One way to approach such questions, and the means that I used in this study, is through an analysis of the symbols of common identity used in the colonial newspapers. The symbols designating the geographic entity comprising the thirteen American colonies as well as the symbols referring to the inhabitants of that country are categorized in three different ways: according to their primary identification content, their symbolic identification content, and the source of the news item in which they appeared.

By differentiating the symbols according to their primary identification, that is, whether they denote the geographic entity or the population inhabiting the land, it is possible to learn whether the symbolic separation of the American continent from the British realm preceded or followed a recognition of the existence of two separate peoples—Englishmen and Americans—or whether the two processes took place simultaneously. Such a categorization as this poses practically no methodological problems, as it is always possible to tell whether a particular symbol refers to the land or to its inhabitants. A term used ambiguously, such as "American," can be classified by considering its context: Patrick Henry's famous statement, "I am not a Virginian, but an American," clearly uses the symbol to refer to a group of people; while a phrase like "the American seas" equally clearly refers to the waters in or around the territory of America.

The secondary identification differentiates the symbols according to their symbolic content, that is, whether they associate the land or its inhabitants with the British political community or with a distinctly American community. Viewed

Appendices

in this way, the symbols of common identity in the colonial press may be divided roughly into five groups: (1) Symbols of explicit British common identity: "British North America," "the English colonies," "British America" or "English America," "British Americans" or "English Americans," "British colonists," "English provincials"; (2) Symbols of identification with the British Crown: "His Majesty's colonies," "royal colonies" or "crown colonies," "His Majesty's subjects in America," "Royal Americans"; (3) Symbols of implicit British common identity: the "colonies" or "provinces," "our colonies in America" (only when used in the British press), "colonists," or "provincials"; (4) Symbols of implicit American common identity: the "continent" or "country," the "American colonies" or the "colonies in America," the "United Colonies," the "continentals," "American colonists"; and (5) Symbols of explicit American common identity: "America" or "North America," "Americans" or "North Americans."

Such a division raises two problems, one of definition and the other of method. The first lies in differentiating between implicit British and implicit American symbols. Although the separation of the content of the two categories is somewhat arbitrary—there does, after all, have to be a dividing line somewhere—there is nonetheless some rationale behind it. The terms "colonies" or "provinces" pose no real problem, for the use of these symbols calls to mind the mother country and the imperial system, and associates the territory of America with the mother country. The symbols "continent" and "country" are more neutral in this respect, but in fact seem to imply an entity separate from the mother country. More arbitrary, perhaps, is the decision to include "the American colonies" or "the colonies in America" among the symbols of implicit American common identity; in this instance, however, the more important symbolic identification in the terms seems to emphasize the American rather than the colonial tie.

The second problem lies in the process of tabulating the occasionally ambiguous symbols. The term "country," for example, was used by colonial writers to differentiate the rural from the urban areas, to specify a particular county or colony, or to designate the continent as a whole. Again, the terms "the colonies in America" or even "America" might refer to Spanish America, French America, or British America, depending upon the source of the news item using the symbol. In such instances, however, the context generally clarifies the sense in which the symbols are used.

The important question of whether the British or the colonists first recognized the separateness of the colonies from the mother country is best answered by tabulating the symbols of common identity according to the source of the news item using them: one tabulation for symbols in articles with British datelines, a second for symbols stemming from American sources, and a third for symbols of foreign (e.g. West Indian or French) origin.

The relationship of the primary identification (that is, the land or its population) to the symbolic identification (British or American common identity) can be represented by a matrix containing four boxes:

TABLE A-1. The Classification of Symbols
of Common Identity

Primary Identification	*Symbolic Identification*	
	British	American
The Land	1 E.g. British America, British Colonies	2 E.g. America, American Colonies
The Population	3 E.g. British Americans, British Colonists	4 E.g. Americans, American Colonists

Appendices

Thus, for example, the terms "British America" or "British colonies" refer to the geographic entity comprising all of the colonies, and symbolically assert that the geographic entity is a part of the British realm. The term "Americans" refers clearly to the inhabitants of the colonies, and symbolically differentiates them from the members of the British political community. For any single year, or any group of years, it would be possible to set up three such matrices, one representing the distribution of symbols for each of the three possible sources. Into the boxes themselves would be put the frequency of the appearance of the symbols fitting into the boxes. By comparing the distributions over the whole of the 41-year time period, it would be possible to discover what trends existed in colonial America in the usage of symbols of common identity, and to compare the trends representing symbol usage in news items from British, American, and foreign sources.

THE SYMBOL LIST

American Symbols
 1.0.00 *Symbols of Common Identity (or Continental Symbols):* [11] symbols referring collectively to the entire area that later became the United States of America or to the inhabitants of that area
 1.1.00 Symbols explicitly identifying the area as British ("British colonies," "English colonies," "British provinces," "English provinces," "British North America," "English North America," "British America," "English America")
 1.1.01 Indirect symbols explicitly identifying the area as

11. The symbols in category 1 are differentiated according to the source of the symbols, that is, whether they appear in articles with American datelines, British datelines, or foreign datelines.

British (that is, "they," "them," or "this area," when the referent is clearly a symbol explicitly identifying the area as British)

1.1.10 Symbols explicitly identifying the population as British ("British colonists," "English colonists," "British provincials," "English provincials," "British Americans," "English Americans," "British North Americans," "English North Americans," "British subjects," "English subjects")

1.1.11 Indirect symbols explicitly identifying the population as British (that is, "they," "them," "this people," etc., when the referent is clearly a symbol explicitly identifying the population as British)

1.2.00 Symbols explicitly identifying the area with the British Crown ("His Majesty's colonies," "His Majesty's provinces," "royal colonies")

1.2.01 Indirect symbols explicitly identifying the area with the British Crown

1.2.10 Symbols explicitly identifying the population with the British Crown ("His Majesty's subjects," "His Majesty's colonists," "His Majesty's Liege People in America," "His Majesty's American subjects," "Royal Americans")

1.2.11 Indirect symbols explicitly identifying the population with the British Crown

1.3.00 Symbols implicitly identifying the area as British ("colonies," "provinces," "our colonies in America [only when appearing in items with British datelines]")

1.3.01 Indirect symbols implictly identifying the area as British

1.3.10 Symbols implicitly identifying the population as British ("colonists," "provincials," "our colonists in

America [only when appearing in items with British datelines]")

1.3.11 Indirect symbols implicitly identifying the population as British

1.4.00 Symbols implicitly identifying the area as American ("continent," "American colonies," "colonies in America," "country," "United Colonies")

1.4.01 Indirect symbols implicitly identifying the area as American

1.4.10 Symbols implicitly identifying the population as American ("continentals," "American subjects," "countrymen")

1.4.11 Indirect symbols implicitly identifying the population as American

1.5.00 Symbols explicitly identifying the area as American ("America," "North America")

1.5.01 Indirect symbols explicitly identifying the area as American

1.5.10 Symbols explicitly identifying the population as American ("Americans," "North Americans")

1.5.11 Indirect symbols explicitly identifying the population as American

2.0.00 *Symbols of the Newspaper's Colony of Publication*

2.1.00 Home Colony

2.1.01 Indirect symbols of the Home Colony ("here," "this colony," etc.)

2.2.00 Home City

2.2.01 Indirect symbols of the Home City ("here," "this city," etc.)

2.3.00 Other place-names in the Home Colony

2.3.01 Indirect symbols of other place-names in the Home Colony

3.0.00 *Northern Colonies*

3.0.01 Indirect symbols of the Northern Colonies ("here," "these colonies," etc.)

3.0.10 New England

3.0.11 Indirect symbols of New England

3.1.00 New Hampshire and all place-names in New Hampshire

3.1.01 Indirect symbols of New Hampshire place-names

3.2.00 Vermont and all place-names in Vermont

3.2.01 Indirect symbols of Vermont place-names

3.3.00 Massachusetts and all place-names in Massachusetts (excluding Boston)

3.3.01 Indirect symbols of Massachusetts place-names (excluding Boston)

3.3.10 Boston

3.3.11 Indirect symbols of Boston

3.4.00 Rhode Island and all place-names in Rhode Island (excluding Newport)

3.4.01 Indirect symbols of Rhode Island place-names (excluding Newport)

3.4.10 Newport

3.4.11 Indirect symbols of Newport

3.5.00 Connecticut and all place-names in Connecticut

3.5.01 Indirect symbols of Connecticut place-names

4.0.00 *Middle Colonies*

4.0.01 Indirect symbols of the Middle Colonies

4.1.00 New York and all place-names in New York (excluding New York City)

4.1.01 Indirect symbols of New York place-names (excluding New York City)

4.1.10 New York City

4.1.11 Indirect symbols of New York City

4.2.00 New Jersey and all place-names in New Jersey

4.2.01 Indirect symbols of New Jersey place-names

Appendices

as Detroit and Ohio, and unidentified place-names that are definitely somewhere in the American colonies)

6.0.01   Indirect symbols of other American place-names

British Symbols

7.0.00   *British symbols* (including England, Scotland, Wales, Ireland, Minorca, and Gibraltar, as well as all place-names within those areas)

Other Symbols

8.0.00   *Canada and all place-names in Canada*

9.0.00   *Caribbean symbols*

9.1.00   Florida and Gulf Port symbols (including St. Augustine, Mobile, Louisiana, New Orleans, and other place-names in that area)

9.2.00   Caribbean and South American symbols (including the Caribbean islands, Central America, California, Mexico, South America, the Falkland Islands, and all other place-names in those areas)

10.0.00   *Other symbols*: non-British symbols outside the Western Hemisphere (including Europe, Africa, the Ottoman Empire, Persia, Asia, and Australasia)

The Distribution of Symbols

A. THE GLOBAL DISTRIBUTION OF SYMBOLS, 1735–1775
(includes explicit symbols only)
Composite (excluding *Boston Gazette*)

Year	No. of Issues in Sample	American Symbols No.	%	British Symbols No.	%	Other Symbols No.	%	Total Symbols No.	%
1735	16	112	9.7	236	20.4	810	70.0	1,158	100.1
1736	20	174	12.9	269	19.9	910	67.3	1,353	100.1
1737	20	233	16.3	345	24.1	854	59.6	1,432	100.0
1738	20	246	20.7	260	21.9	684	57.5	1,190	100.1
1739	20	141	9.9	361	25.4	919	64.7	1,421	100.0
1740	20	392	21.2	425	23.0	1,029	55.7	1,846	99.9
1741	16	110	8.4	224	17.0	982	74.6	1,316	100.0
1742	16	170	11.2	252	16.6	1,097	72.2	1,519	100.0
1743	16	176	11.2	204	13.0	1,190	75.8	1,570	100.0
1744	16	134	9.0	287	19.2	1,072	71.8	1,493	100.0
1745	20	385	12.9	509	17.0	2,094	70.1	2,988	100.0
1746	20	229	7.9	896	31.1	1,758	61.0	2,883	100.0
1747	16	254	10.9	376	16.1	1,707	73.0	2,337	100.0
1748	16	204	11.1	267	14.5	1,373	74.5	1,844	100.1
1749	16	191	12.4	332	21.6	1,017	66.0	1,540	100.0
1750	16	134	10.0	299	22.3	909	67.7	1,342	100.0
1751	19	236	16.8	289	20.6	880	62.6	1,405	100.0
1752	20	306	15.1	464	22.9	1,259	62.1	2,029	100.1
1753	17	356	21.6	381	23.1	912	55.3	1,649	100.0
1754	18	508	22.8	399	17.9	1,321	59.3	2,228	100.0
1755	20	711	26.9	669	25.3	1,266	47.9	2,646	100.1
1756	18	697	22.0	735	23.2	1,738	54.8	3,170	100.0
1757	18	712	19.5	724	19.8	2,216	60.7	3,652	100.0
1758	16	579	15.9	527	14.5	2,528	69.6	3,634	100.0
1759	17	666	16.1	547	13.3	2,911	70.6	4,124	100.0
1760	16	740	17.8	644	15.5	2,772	66.7	4,156	100.0
1761	17	454	15.6	566	19.4	1,896	65.0	2,916	100.0
1762	17	434	10.7	626	15.4	3,008	73.9	4,068	100.0
1763	17	528	15.4	702	20.5	2,191	64.1	3,421	100.0
1764	16	519	27.5	388	20.5	982	52.0	1,889	100.0
1765	16	722	26.7	658	24.4	1,322	48.9	2,702	100.0
1766	20	1,453	42.2	859	24.9	1,133	32.9	3,445	100.0
1767	20	837	26.2	755	23.6	1,602	50.2	3,194	100.0
1768	20	1,000	33.1	1,007	33.3	1,019	33.7	3,026	100.1
1769	20	1,215	27.7	1,187	27.1	1,984	45.2	4,386	100.0
1770	20	1,412	40.3	916	26.2	1,173	33.5	3,501	100.0
1771	20	773	23.9	908	28.1	1,552	48.0	3,233	100.0
1772	20	727	22.2	893	27.3	1,652	50.5	3,272	100.0
1773	20	794	23.4	730	21.5	1,875	55.2	3,399	100.1
1774	20	1,605	51.3	693	22.2	829	26.5	3,127	100.0
1775	20	2,245	56.4	826	20.8	911	22.9	3,982	100.1
Total	746	23,514	22.3	22,635	21.5	59,337	56.3	105,486	100.1

Symbols of American Community

Massachusetts Gazette, 1735–1775

Year	No. of Issues in Sample	American Symbols No.	American Symbols %	British Symbols No.	British Symbols %	Other Symbols No.	Other Symbols %	Total Symbols No.	Total Symbols %
1735	4	34	12.0	85	30.0	164	58.0	283	100.0
1736	4	60	15.8	101	26.7	218	57.5	379	100.0
1737	4	69	21.6	56	17.5	195	60.9	320	100.0
1738	4	70	22.5	61	19.6	180	57.9	311	100.0
1739	4	69	23.3	74	25.0	153	51.7	296	100.0
1740	4	170	36.7	97	21.0	196	42.3	463	100.0
1741	4	42	14.8	52	18.3	190	66.9	284	100.0
1742	4	53	16.3	79	24.3	193	59.4	325	100.0
1743	4	64	18.8	66	19.4	211	61.9	341	100.1
1744	4	43	11.4	91	24.1	244	64.6	378	100.1
1745	4	184	24.8	180	24.2	379	51.0	743	100.0
1746	4	54	9.2	206	35.0	328	55.8	588	100.0
1747	4	84	17.9	92	19.6	294	62.6	470	100.1
1748	4	57	12.5	98	21.4	302	66.1	457	100.0
1749	4	90	17.5	132	25.6	293	56.9	515	100.0
1750	4	58	13.2	103	23.5	277	63.2	438	99.9
1751	4	89	33.1	54	20.1	126	46.8	269	100.0
1752	4	51	12.2	82	19.7	284	68.1	417	100.0
1753	4	113	28.3	92	23.0	195	48.8	400	100.1
1754	4	77	18.6	63	15.3	273	66.1	413	100.0
1755	4	147	26.9	123	22.5	277	50.6	547	100.0
1756	4	202	35.4	112	19.6	257	45.0	571	100.0
1757	4	199	22.7	169	19.3	509	58.0	877	100.0
1758	4	199	22.5	153	17.3	533	60.2	885	100.0
1759	4	127	17.1	136	18.4	478	64.5	741	100.0
1760	4	141	12.5	181	16.1	802	71.4	1,124	100.0
1761	4	158	18.5	234	27.3	464	54.2	856	100.0
1762	4	165	18.5	136	15.3	590	66.2	891	100.0
1763	4	164	17.1	243	25.4	550	57.5	957	100.0
1764	4	181	43.7	80	19.3	153	37.0	414	100.0
1765	4	219	39.4	141	25.4	196	35.3	556	100.1
1766	4	404	48.3	222	26.5	211	25.2	837	100.0
1767	4	254	45.0	135	23.9	175	31.0	564	99.9
1768	4	206	53.0	66	17.0	117	30.1	389	100.1
1769	4	232	50.0	132	28.5	100	21.6	464	100.1
1770	4	385	51.1	198	26.3	171	22.7	754	100.1
1771	4	232	39.3	155	26.2	204	34.5	591	100.0
1772	4	266	47.7	151	27.1	141	25.3	558	100.1
1773	4	259	54.2	106	22.2	113	23.6	478	100.0
1774	4	319	59.2	99	18.4	121	22.5	539	100.1
1775	4	471	61.3	191	24.9	106	13.8	768	100.0
Total	164	6,461	28.8	5,027	22.4	10,963	48.8	22,451	100.0

Appendices

New-York Weekly Journal (1735–51) and New-York Mercury (1752–75)

Year	No. of Issues in Sample	American Symbols No.	%	British Symbols No.	%	Other Symbols No.	%	Total Symbols No.	%
1735	4	13	5.2	41	16.5	194	78.2	248	99.9
1736	4	10	9.7	28	27.2	65	63.1	103	100.0
1737	4	27	8.9	48	15.8	228	75.3	303	100.0
1738	4	49	15.5	46	14.6	221	69.9	316	100.0
1739	4	19	9.6	38	19.2	141	71.2	198	100.0
1740	4	28	9.5	89	30.3	177	60.2	294	100.0
1741	4	23	9.0	59	23.1	173	67.8	255	99.9
1742	4	40	12.5	42	13.1	239	74.5	321	100.1
1743	4	39	10.5	46	12.4	286	77.1	371	100.0
1744	4	40	11.0	80	21.9	245	67.1	365	100.0
1745	4	37	7.7	67	13.9	378	78.4	482	100.0
1746	4	35	5.8	144	23.7	428	70.5	607	100.0
1747	4	66	8.9	123	16.6	552	74.5	741	100.0
1748	4	96	20.4	53	11.3	322	68.4	471	100.1
1749	4	44	16.6	70	26.4	151	57.0	265	100.0
1750	4	16	5.8	84	30.3	177	63.9	277	100.0
1751	3	14	11.5	33	27.1	75	61.5	122	100.1
1752	4	120	24.1	141	28.3	238	47.7	499	100.1
1753	4	81	15.6	124	23.9	313	60.4	518	99.9
1754	4	142	24.4	119	20.4	322	55.2	583	100.0
1755	4	256	38.4	105	15.7	306	45.9	667	100.0
1756	4	180	22.9	162	20.6	443	56.4	785	99.9
1757	4	202	19.0	211	19.8	652	61.2	1,065	100.0
1758	4	166	18.2	114	12.5	634	69.4	914	100.1
1759	4	162	15.2	165	15.5	737	69.3	1,064	100.0
1760	4	160	16.3	160	16.3	660	67.4	980	100.0
1761	4	43	5.6	126	16.5	594	77.9	763	100.0
1762	4	91	7.6	233	19.4	875	73.0	1,199	100.0
1763	4	150	18.0	182	21.8	502	60.2	834	100.0
1764	4	130	27.6	115	24.4	226	48.0	471	100.0
1765	4	189	18.1	286	27.3	571	54.6	1,046	100.0
1766	4	257	37.0	175	25.2	262	37.8	694	100.0
1767	4	191	23.1	198	23.9	438	52.9	827	99.9
1768	4	255	45.4	185	32.9	122	21.7	562	100.0
1769	4	291	26.2	248	22.3	571	51.4	1,110	99.9
1770	4	343	39.4	234	26.9	294	33.8	871	100.1
1771	4	177	25.5	249	35.9	268	38.6	694	100.0
1772	4	122	14.7	211	25.5	496	59.8	829	100.0
1773	4	145	21.9	125	18.9	391	59.2	661	100.0
1774	4	379	45.5	229	27.5	225	27.0	833	100.0
1775	4	561	45.6	174	14.2	495	40.2	1,230	100.0
Total	163	5,389	21.2	5,362	21.1	14,687	57.7	25,438	100.0

Symbols of American Community

Pennsylvania Gazette, 1735–1775

Year	No. of Issues in Sample	American Symbols No.	%	British Symbols No.	%	Other Symbols No.	%	Total Symbols No.	%
1735	4	41	8.1	79	15.5	389	76.4	509	100.0
1736	4	31	9.2	40	11.9	266	78.9	337	100.0
1737	4	58	18.2	84	26.3	177	55.5	319	100.0
1738	4	69	36.7	49	26.1	70	37.2	188	100.0
1739	4	22	8.3	76	28.6	168	63.2	266	100.1
1740	4	65	18.6	84	24.0	201	57.4	350	100.0
1741	4	24	6.3	56	14.6	304	79.2	384	100.1
1742	4	27	4.4	102	16.5	491	79.2	620	100.1
1743	4	50	10.1	55	11.1	391	78.8	496	100.0
1744	4	26	4.4	83	14.1	479	81.5	588	100.0
1745	4	67	7.8	102	11.9	691	80.4	860	100.1
1746	4	71	7.7	300	32.4	555	59.9	926	100.0
1747	4	79	9.9	110	13.7	613	76.4	802	100.0
1748	4	46	5.7	89	11.0	675	83.3	810	100.0
1749	4	41	7.9	89	17.1	391	75.0	521	100.0
1750	4	34	8.3	68	16.6	309	75.2	411	100.1
1751	4	84	23.0	56	15.3	225	61.7	365	100.0
1752	4	83	13.3	136	21.7	407	65.0	626	100.0
1753	4	115	22.2	105	20.3	298	57.5	518	100.0
1754	4	186	25.6	115	15.8	426	58.6	727	100.0
1755	4	165	21.9	218	28.9	372	49.3	755	100.1
1756	4	217	21.6	193	19.2	597	59.3	1,007	100.1
1757	4	174	17.1	217	21.4	624	61.5	1,015	100.0
1758	4	124	8.6	228	15.9	1,086	75.5	1,438	100.0
1759	4	163	10.2	185	11.6	1,247	78.2	1,595	100.0
1760	4	239	20.4	166	14.1	769	65.5	1,174	100.0
1761	4	133	18.2	135	18.5	461	63.2	729	99.9
1762	4	108	8.8	169	13.7	953	77.5	1,230	100.0
1763	4	154	11.9	212	16.3	934	71.8	1,300	100.0
1764	4	100	15.8	110	17.4	424	66.9	634	100.1
1765	4	226	26.8	169	20.1	447	53.1	842	100.0
1766	4	342	33.9	243	24.1	425	42.1	1,010	100.1
1767	4	181	19.9	209	23.0	518	57.1	908	100.0
1768	4	264	32.2	361	44.1	194	23.7	819	100.0
1769	4	288	20.2	329	23.1	810	56.8	1,427	100.1
1770	4	340	35.5	239	24.9	380	39.6	959	100.0
1771	4	197	17.8	240	21.6	676	60.7	1,113	100.1
1772	4	193	18.5	220	21.1	630	60.4	1,043	100.0
1773	4	228	20.3	221	19.7	675	60.1	1,124	100.1
1774	4	337	50.2	107	16.0	227	33.8	671	100.0
1775	4	458	68.3	125	18.6	88	13.1	671	100.0
Total	164	5,850	18.2	6,174	19.2	20,063	62.5	32,087	99.9

Appendices

Virginia Gazette, 1736–1775

Year	No. of Issues in Sample	American Symbols No.	%	British Symbols No.	%	Other Symbols No.	%	Total Symbols No.	%
1735	—			(Not published)					
1736	4	70	20.1	79	22.7	199	57.2	348	100.0
1737	4	55	13.9	125	31.7	215	54.4	395	100.0
1738	4	51	16.2	94	29.8	170	54.0	315	100.0
1739	4	16	2.9	152	27.7	380	69.3	548	99.9
1740	4	92	16.1	110	19.3	369	64.6	571	100.0
1741	—								
1742	—								
1743	—								
1744	—								
1745	4	48	8.7	105	19.1	398	72.2	551	100.0
1746	4	18	4.3	189	44.8	215	51.0	422	100.1
1747	—								
1748	—								
1749	—								
1750	—								
1751	4	40	8.1	87	17.6	367	74.3	494	100.0
1752	4	24	7.1	79	23.3	236	69.6	339	100.0
1753	1	3	9.1	16	48.5	14	42.4	33	100.0
1754	2	36	25.7	33	23.6	71	50.7	140	100.0
1755	4	91	23.8	124	32.5	167	43.7	382	100.0
1756	2	75	21.7	96	27.8	174	50.4	345	99.9
1757	2	30	11.5	54	20.7	177	67.8	261	100.0
1758	—								
1759	1	6	4.2	6	4.2	131	91.6	143	100.0
1760	—								
1761	1	39	25.2	12	7.7	104	67.1	155	100.0
1762	1	20	9.0	29	13.0	174	78.0	223	100.0
1763	1	23	29.5	6	7.7	49	62.8	78	100.0
1764	—								
1765	—								
1766	4	193	50.4	97	25.3	93	24.3	383	100.0
1767	4	163	27.2	140	23.4	296	49.4	599	100.0
1768	4	125	17.2	249	34.3	353	48.6	727	100.1
1769	4	166	21.7	260	34.0	338	44.2	764	99.9
1770	4	78	15.9	116	23.7	296	60.4	490	100.0
1771	4	94	15.2	203	32.7	323	52.1	620	100.0
1772	4	64	11.6	203	36.7	286	51.7	553	100.0
1773	4	98	10.4	229	24.3	615	65.3	942	100.0
1774	4	351	48.2	159	21.8	218	30.0	728	100.0
1775	4	343	59.7	145	25.2	87	15.1	575	100.0
Total	91	2,412	19.9	3,197	26.4	6,515	53.7	12,124	100.0

Symbols of American Community

South-Carolina Gazette, 1735–1775

Year	No. of Issues in Sample	American Symbols No.	American Symbols %	British Symbols No.	British Symbols %	Other Symbols No.	Other Symbols %	Total Symbols No.	Total Symbols %
1735	4	24	20.3	31	26.3	63	53.4	118	100.0
1736	4	3	1.6	21	11.3	162	87.1	186	100.0
1737	4	24	25.3	32	33.7	39	41.1	95	100.1
1738	4	7	11.7	10	16.7	43	71.7	60	100.1
1739	4	15	13.3	21	18.6	77	68.1	113	100.0
1740	4	37	22.0	45	26.8	86	51.2	168	100.0
1741	4	21	5.3	57	14.5	315	80.2	393	100.0
1742	4	50	19.8	29	11.5	174	68.8	253	100.1
1743	4	23	6.4	37	10.2	302	83.4	362	100.0
1744	4	25	15.4	33	20.4	104	64.2	162	100.0
1745	4	49	13.9	55	15.6	248	70.5	352	100.0
1746	4	51	15.0	57	16.8	232	68.2	340	100.0
1747	4	25	7.7	51	15.7	248	76.6	324	100.0
1748	4	5	4.7	27	25.5	74	69.8	106	100.0
1749	4	16	6.7	41	17.2	182	76.2	239	100.1
1750	4	26	12.0	44	20.4	146	67.6	216	100.0
1751	4	9	5.8	59	38.1	87	56.1	155	100.0
1752	4	28	18.9	26	17.6	94	63.5	148	100.0
1753	4	44	24.5	44	24.5	92	51.1	180	100.1
1754	4	67	18.4	69	18.9	229	62.7	365	100.0
1755	4	52	17.6	99	33.6	144	48.8	295	100.0
1756	4	23	5.0	172	37.2	267	57.8	462	100.0
1757	4	107	24.7	73	16.8	254	58.5	434	100.0
1758	4	90	22.7	32	8.1	275	69.3	397	100.1
1759	4	208	35.8	55	9.5	318	54.7	581	100.0
1760	4	200	22.8	137	15.6	541	61.6	878	100.0
1761	4	81	19.6	59	14.3	273	66.1	413	100.0
1762	4	50	9.5	59	11.2	416	79.2	525	99.9
1763	4	37	14.7	59	23.4	156	61.9	252	100.0
1764	4	108	29.2	83	22.4	179	48.4	370	100.0
1765	4	88	34.1	62	24.0	108	41.9	258	100.0
1766	4	257	49.3	122	23.4	142	27.3	521	100.0
1767	4	48	16.2	73	24.7	175	59.1	296	100.0
1768	4	150	28.4	146	27.6	233	44.1	529	100.1
1769	4	238	38.3	218	35.1	165	26.6	621	100.0
1770	4	266	62.3	129	30.2	32	7.5	427	100.0
1771	4	73	34.0	61	28.4	81	37.7	215	100.1
1772	4	82	28.4	108	37.4	99	34.3	289	100.1
1773	4	64	33.0	49	25.3	81	41.8	194	100.1
1774	4	219	61.5	99	27.8	38	10.7	356	100.0
1775	4	412	55.8	191	25.9	135	18.3	738	100.0
Total	164	3,402	25.4	2,875	21.5	7,109	53.1	13,386	100.0

Appendices

Boston Gazette, 1762–1775

Year	No. of Issues in Sample	American Symbols No.	%	British Symbols No.	%	Other Symbols No.	%	Total Symbols No.	%
1762	4	90	12.6	167	23.3	459	64.1	716	100.0
1763	4	158	23.4	158	23.4	360	53.3	676	100.1
1764	4	146	40.6	102	28.3	112	31.1	360	100.0
1765	4	246	54.7	141	31.3	63	14.0	450	100.0
1766	4	221	50.8	145	33.3	69	15.9	435	100.0
1767	4	104	42.6	78	32.0	62	25.4	244	100.0
1768	4	284	51.9	138	25.2	125	22.9	547	100.0
1769	4	487	70.6	136	19.7	67	9.7	690	100.0
1770	4	281	64.2	83	19.0	74	16.9	438	100.1
1771	4	184	33.3	177	32.1	191	34.6	552	100.0
1772	4	372	60.7	137	22.4	104	17.0	613	100.1
1773	4	221	52.7	102	24.3	96	22.9	419	99.9
1774	4	441	71.1	107	17.3	72	11.6	620	100.0
1775	4	472	56.7	260	31.2	101	12.2	833	100.1
Total	56	3,707	48.8	1,931	25.4	1,955	25.7	7,593	99.9

B. THE DISTRIBUTION OF AMERICAN SYMBOLS,
1735-1775
(includes implicit and explicit symbols)
Composite (excluding *Boston Gazette*)

Year	No. of Issues in Sample	Cont. Symbols No.	%	Home Col. Symbols No.	%	Home Reg. Symbols No.	%	Other Col. Symbols No.	%	Total Symbols No.	%
1735	16	8	4.3	68	36.6	71	38.2	39	21.0	186	100.1
1736	20	5	1.8	146	53.3	55	20.1	68	24.8	274	100.0
1737	20	19	5.4	137	39.0	55	15.7	140	39.9	351	100.0
1738	20	15	3.6	161	39.1	116	28.2	120	29.1	412	100.0
1739	20	16	7.4	123	57.2	27	12.6	49	22.8	215	100.0
1740	20	50	9.6	175	33.5	105	20.1	192	36.8	522	100.0
1741	16	13	7.3	70	39.1	44	24.6	52	29.1	179	100.1
1742	16	7	2.4	137	46.8	71	24.2	78	26.6	293	100.0
1743	16	11	4.2	78	30.0	40	15.4	131	50.4	260	100.0
1744	16	12	4.6	96	37.1	67	25.9	84	32.4	259	100.0
1745	20	8	1.5	266	51.3	78	15.1	166	32.0	518	99.9
1746	20	15	4.5	128	38.4	70	21.0	120	36.0	333	99.9
1747	16	10	2.4	145	34.4	95	22.5	172	40.8	422	100.1
1748	16	19	6.1	115	37.1	35	11.3	141	45.5	310	100.0
1749	16	21	8.2	94	36.6	58	22.6	84	32.7	257	100.1
1750	16	6	3.3	91	49.5	39	21.2	48	26.1	184	100.1
1751	19	23	7.0	111	33.7	84	25.5	111	33.7	329	99.9
1752	20	18	3.8	144	30.1	98	20.5	218	45.6	478	100.0
1753	17	36	6.1	192	32.8	107	18.3	251	42.8	586	100.0
1754	18	29	4.0	189	26.1	147	20.3	359	49.6	724	100.0
1755	20	121	12.3	307	31.3	188	19.2	365	37.2	981	100.0
1756	18	127	12.7	310	30.9	240	23.9	326	32.5	1,003	100.0
1757	18	91	8.1	430	38.1	219	19.4	389	34.5	1,129	100.1
1758	16	48	5.4	213	24.1	159	18.0	464	52.5	884	100.0
1759	17	50	5.4	247	26.7	196	21.2	432	46.7	925	100.0
1760	16	79	8.1	253	26.0	107	11.0	535	54.9	974	100.0
1761	17	26	3.9	253	37.5	182	27.0	214	31.7	675	100.1
1762	17	50	7.8	206	31.9	142	22.0	247	38.3	645	100.0
1763	17	99	13.5	223	30.4	175	23.8	237	32.3	734	100.0
1764	16	134	18.4	166	22.8	168	23.1	260	35.7	728	100.0
1765	16	234	22.5	268	25.8	162	15.6	375	36.1	1,039	100.0
1766	20	717	37.3	445	23.1	233	12.1	530	27.5	1,925	100.0
1767	20	296	25.5	265	22.9	209	18.0	390	33.6	1,160	100.0
1768	20	345	25.6	373	27.6	199	14.7	433	32.1	1,350	100.0
1769	20	524	31.7	397	24.0	190	11.5	541	32.8	1,652	100.0
1770	20	462	25.2	442	24.1	263	14.3	669	36.4	1,836	100.0
1771	20	137	12.6	331	30.5	264	24.4	352	32.5	1,084	100.0
1772	20	96	9.0	439	41.3	166	15.6	361	34.0	1,062	99.9
1773	20	200	17.2	449	38.6	169	14.5	345	29.7	1,163	100.0
1774	20	654	27.4	648	27.1	201	8.4	887	37.1	2,390	100.0
1775	20	1,097	39.6	535	19.3	376	13.6	764	27.6	2,772	100.1
Total	746	5,928	17.9	9,866	29.7	5,670	17.1	11,739	35.4	33,203	100.1

Appendices

Massachusetts Gazette, 1735–1775

Year	No. of Issues in Sample	Cont. Symbols No.	%	Home Col. Symbols No.	%	Home Reg. Symbols No.	%	Other Col. Symbols No.	%	Total Symbols No.	%
1735	4	3	6.4	21	44.7	18	38.3	5	10.6	47	100.0
1736	4	2	2.1	61	64.2	15	15.8	17	17.9	95	100.0
1737	4	3	2.8	57	53.8	21	19.8	25	23.6	106	100.0
1738	4	2	1.8	38	34.2	22	19.8	49	44.1	111	99.9
1739	4	5	5.0	64	64.0	18	18.0	13	13.0	100	100.0
1740	4	21	9.2	97	42.5	53	23.2	57	25.0	228	99.9
1741	4	1	1.3	39	50.7	12	15.6	25	32.5	77	100.1
1742	4	4	4.0	55	55.0	24	24.0	17	17.0	100	100.0
1743	4	5	5.3	36	38.3	13	13.8	40	42.6	94	100.0
1744	4	2	2.9	36	51.4	15	21.4	17	24.3	70	100.0
1745	4	4	1.7	157	68.0	29	12.6	41	17.7	231	100.0
1746	4	—	—	33	44.6	16	21.6	25	33.8	74	100.0
1747	4	3	2.2	66	48.5	14	10.3	53	39.0	136	100.0
1748	4	6	7.1	46	54.1	15	17.6	18	21.2	85	100.0
1749	4	8	7.0	49	42.6	19	16.5	39	33.9	115	100.0
1750	4	3	4.2	39	54.9	10	14.1	19	26.8	71	100.0
1751	4	8	6.7	51	42.5	40	33.3	21	17.5	120	100.0
1752	4	4	4.8	49	59.0	10	12.0	20	24.1	83	99.9
1753	4	8	4.1	74	38.3	20	10.4	91	47.2	193	100.0
1754	4	3	2.6	35	30.4	5	4.3	72	62.6	115	99.9
1755	4	16	8.4	46	24.1	15	7.9	114	59.7	191	100.1
1756	4	27	9.8	68	24.7	28	10.2	152	55.3	275	100.0
1757	4	17	6.3	72	26.8	32	11.9	148	55.0	269	100.0
1758	4	8	2.8	59	20.7	37	13.0	181	63.5	285	100.0
1759	4	7	3.8	34	18.4	21	11.4	123	66.5	185	100.1
1760	4	19	9.7	69	35.2	7	3.6	101	51.5	196	100.0
1761	4	9	4.0	74	33.2	31	13.9	109	48.9	223	100.0
1762	4	16	6.0	81	30.6	51	19.2	117	44.2	265	100.0
1763	4	33	14.7	57	25.3	41	18.2	94	41.8	225	100.0
1764	4	36	14.0	59	22.9	71	27.5	92	35.7	258	100.1
1765	4	89	26.3	90	26.6	51	15.1	108	32.0	338	100.0
1766	4	219	43.7	65	13.0	47	9.4	170	33.9	501	100.0
1767	4	58	17.0	75	22.0	71	20.8	137	40.2	341	100.0
1768	4	48	15.8	95	31.4	61	20.1	99	32.7	303	100.0
1769	4	72	21.4	63	18.7	30	8.9	172	51.0	337	100.0
1770	4	102	19.5	156	29.8	87	16.6	179	34.2	524	100.1
1771	4	16	5.0	131	40.9	90	28.1	83	25.9	320	99.9
1772	4	32	8.0	166	41.4	80	20.0	123	30.7	401	100.1
1773	4	34	9.0	197	52.3	61	16.2	85	22.5	377	100.0
1774	4	86	15.9	318	58.9	59	10.9	77	14.3	540	100.0
1775	4	224	39.9	236	42.1	31	5.5	70	12.5	561	100.0
Total	164	1,263	13.8	3,314	36.2	1,391	15.2	3,198	34.9	9,166	100.1

Symbols of American Community

New-York Weekly Journal (1735–51) and
New-York Mercury (1752–75)

Year	No. of Issues in Sample	Cont. Symbols No.	%	Home Col. Symbols No.	%	Home Reg. Symbols No.	%	Other Col. Symbols No.	%	Total Symbols No.	%
1735	4	1	4.2	9	37.5	6	25.0	8	33.3	24	100.0
1736	4	—	—	18	78.3	1	4.3	4	17.4	23	100.0
1737	4	4	9.1	19	43.2	3	6.8	18	40.9	44	100.0
1738	4	9	13.6	13	19.7	15	22.7	29	43.9	66	99.9
1739	4	2	6.9	17	58.6	1	3.4	9	31.0	29	99.9
1740	4	10	26.3	17	44.7	1	2.6	10	26.3	38	99.9
1741	4	1	3.8	5	19.2	2	7.7	18	69.2	26	99.9
1742	4	—	—	7	13.7	11	21.6	33	64.7	51	100.0
1743	4	3	5.4	12	21.4	1	1.8	40	71.4	56	100.0
1744	4	2	2.6	31	40.3	7	9.1	37	48.1	77	100.1
1745	4	—	—	22	42.3	7	13.5	23	44.2	52	100.0
1746	4	2	3.4	14	23.7	17	28.8	26	44.1	59	100.0
1747	4	1	.8	26	21.7	31	25.8	62	51.7	120	100.0
1748	4	12	9.1	32	24.2	8	6.1	80	60.6	132	100.0
1749	4	5	8.9	15	26.8	7	12.5	29	51.8	56	100.0
1750	4	1	4.5	14	63.6	5	22.7	2	9.1	22	99.9
1751	3	2	8.3	5	20.8	—	—	17	70.8	24	99.9
1752	4	4	2.0	37	18.7	32	16.2	125	63.1	198	100.0
1753	4	3	1.9	68	43.9	37	23.9	47	30.3	155	100.0
1754	4	7	3.3	49	23.3	68	32.4	86	41.0	210	100.0
1755	4	28	7.8	118	32.8	79	21.9	135	37.5	360	100.0
1756	4	24	8.2	81	27.6	123	42.0	65	22.2	293	100.0
1757	4	12	3.8	100	31.8	86	27.4	116	36.9	314	99.9
1758	4	14	5.1	89	32.7	44	16.2	125	46.0	272	100.0
1759	4	9	3.7	85	35.0	58	23.9	91	37.5	243	100.1
1760	4	12	6.1	55	27.8	8	4.0	123	62.1	198	100.0
1761	4	3	4.0	31	41.3	14	18.7	27	36.0	75	100.0
1762	4	11	7.9	51	36.4	35	25.0	43	30.7	140	100.0
1763	4	18	8.5	42	19.7	85	39.9	68	31.9	213	100.0
1764	4	47	26.1	41	22.8	36	20.0	56	31.1	180	100.0
1765	4	67	26.3	45	17.6	39	15.3	104	40.8	255	100.0
1766	4	84	24.2	63	18.2	68	19.6	132	38.0	347	100.0
1767	4	50	19.2	68	26.2	62	23.8	80	30.8	260	100.0
1768	4	114	33.6	57	16.8	51	15.0	117	34.5	339	99.9
1769	4	114	27.9	97	23.7	83	20.3	115	28.1	409	100.0
1770	4	92	20.8	161	36.4	56	12.7	133	30.1	442	100.0
1771	4	30	11.6	48	18.6	43	16.7	137	53.1	258	100.0
1772	4	19	11.0	63	36.4	29	16.8	62	35.8	173	100.0
1773	4	23	10.7	80	37.2	48	22.3	64	29.8	215	100.0
1774	4	181	30.9	121	20.7	41	7.0	242	41.4	585	100.0
1775	4	213	29.5	93	12.9	150	20.8	266	36.8	722	100.0
Total	163	1,234	15.9	2,019	26.0	1,498	19.3	3,004	38.7	7,755	99.9

224

Appendices

Pennsylvania Gazette, 1735–1775

Year	No. of Issues in Sample	Cont. Symbols No.	%	Home Col. Symbols No.	%	Home Reg. Symbols No.	%	Other Col. Symbols No.	%	Total Symbols No.	%
1735	4	3	3.8	14	17.5	37	46.3	26	32.5	80	100.1
1736	4	1	2.3	4	9.1	8	18.2	31	70.5	44	100.1
1737	4	9	10.7	11	13.1	21	25.0	43	51.2	84	100.0
1738	4	2	1.4	53	38.4	75	54.3	8	5.8	138	99.9
1739	4	5	12.2	20	48.8	—	—	16	39.0	41	100.0
1740	4	4	4.2	19	20.0	18	18.9	54	56.8	95	99.9
1741	4	8	17.8	9	20.0	21	46.7	7	15.6	45	100.1
1742	4	3	4.8	33	53.2	8	12.9	18	29.0	62	99.9
1743	4	3	3.9	9	11.8	18	23.7	46	60.5	76	99.9
1744	4	2	2.6	5	6.6	39	51.3	30	39.5	76	100.0
1745	4	4	4.2	19	19.8	33	34.4	40	41.7	96	100.1
1746	4	5	5.4	26	28.0	22	23.7	40	43.0	93	100.1
1747	4	6	5.3	33	28.9	38	33.3	37	32.5	114	100.0
1748	4	—	—	30	38.5	12	15.4	36	46.2	78	100.1
1749	4	5	8.1	18	29.0	23	37.1	16	25.8	62	100.0
1750	4	—	—	13	25.0	20	38.5	19	36.5	52	100.0
1751	4	4	3.3	22	18.2	43	35.5	52	43.0	121	100.0
1752	4	6	5.4	25	22.3	41	36.6	40	35.7	112	100.0
1753	4	21	12.6	22	13.2	44	26.3	80	47.9	167	100.0
1754	4	16	6.5	39	15.9	45	18.4	145	59.2	245	100.0
1755	4	22	9.4	71	30.3	61	26.1	80	34.2	234	100.0
1756	4	52	17.5	126	42.4	65	21.9	54	18.2	297	100.0
1757	4	11	3.7	162	54.4	53	17.8	72	24.2	298	100.1
1758	4	16	8.2	47	24.2	62	32.0	69	35.6	194	100.0
1759	4	20	9.7	69	33.5	78	37.9	39	18.9	206	100.0
1760	4	22	7.3	30	10.0	51	17.0	197	65.7	300	100.0
1761	4	3	1.5	80	41.0	63	32.3	49	25.1	195	99.9
1762	4	12	8.1	39	26.2	22	14.8	76	51.0	149	100.1
1763	4	45	22.0	71	34.6	36	17.6	53	25.9	205	100.1
1764	4	30	22.6	36	27.1	33	24.8	34	25.6	133	100.1
1765	4	45	14.6	41	13.3	63	20.5	159	51.6	308	100.0
1766	4	158	38.3	81	19.6	65	15.7	109	26.4	413	100.0
1767	4	39	16.4	65	27.3	56	23.5	78	32.8	238	100.0
1768	4	71	20.0	107	30.1	53	14.9	124	34.9	355	99.9
1769	4	135	38.6	65	18.6	51	14.6	99	28.3	350	100.1
1770	4	102	25.1	56	13.8	86	21.1	163	40.1	407	100.1
1771	4	26	10.2	55	21.6	73	28.6	101	39.6	255	100.0
1772	4	21	8.6	80	32.8	48	19.7	95	38.9	244	100.0
1773	4	58	17.0	106	31.0	38	11.1	140	40.9	342	100.0
1774	4	109	23.3	76	16.3	71	15.2	211	45.2	467	100.0
1775	4	197	35.3	47	8.4	99	17.7	215	38.5	558	99.9
Total	164	1,301	16.2	1,934	24.1	1,793	22.3	3,001	37.4	8,029	100.0

Symbols of American Community

Virginia Gazette, 1736–1775

Year	No. of Issues in Sample	Cont. Symbols No.	Cont. Symbols %	Home Col. Symbols No.	Home Col. Symbols %	Home Reg. Symbols No.	Home Reg. Symbols %	Other Col. Symbols No.	Other Col. Symbols %	Total Symbols No.	Total Symbols %
1735	—					(Not published)					
1736	4	2	1.9	56	53.3	31	29.5	16	15.2	105	99.9
1737	4	2	2.6	26	34.2	3	4.0	45	59.2	76	100.0
1738	4	—	—	32	47.8	1	1.6	34	50.7	67	100.1
1739	4	3	13.0	13	56.5	3	13.0	4	17.4	23	99.9
1740	4	5	4.9	18	17.5	15	14.6	65	63.1	103	100.1
1741	—										
1742	—										
1743	—										
1744	—										
1745	4	—	—	26	43.3	1	1.7	33	55.0	60	100.0
1746	4	3	14.3	12	57.1	—	—	6	28.6	21	100.0
1747	—										
1748	—										
1749	—										
1750	—										
1751	4	7	14.3	21	42.9	1	2.0	20	40.8	49	100.0
1752	4	4	9.8	16	39.0	5	12.2	16	39.0	41	100.0
1753	1	—	—	3	100.0	—	—	—	—	3	100.0
1754	2	—	—	28	62.2	4	8.9	13	28.9	45	100.0
1755	4	30	27.0	43	38.7	16	14.4	22	19.8	111	99.9
1756	2	21	22.3	22	23.4	2	2.1	49	52.1	94	99.9
1757	2	8	21.6	11	29.7	1	2.7	17	45.9	37	99.9
1758	—										
1759	1	—	—	8	57.1	—	—	6	42.9	14	100.0
1760	—										
1761	1	3	6.7	6	13.3	27	60.0	9	20.0	45	100.0
1762	1	8	38.1	9	42.9	3	14.3	1	4.8	21	100.1
1763	1	1	4.0	11	44.0	2	8.0	11	44.0	25	100.0
1764	—										
1765	—										
1766	4	56	22.6	91	36.7	35	14.1	66	26.6	248	100.0
1767	4	139	55.2	12	4.8	10	4.0	91	36.1	252	100.1
1768	4	36	24.5	65	44.2	2	1.4	44	29.9	147	100.0
1769	4	56	27.2	76	36.9	17	8.3	57	27.7	206	100.1
1770	4	22	26.2	22	26.2	1	1.2	39	46.4	84	100.0
1771	4	54	47.0	45	39.1	4	3.5	12	10.4	115	100.0
1772	4	21	20.6	27	26.5	3	2.9	51	50.0	102	100.0
1773	4	61	51.7	17	14.4	8	6.8	32	27.1	118	100.0
1774	4	169	35.1	67	13.9	18	3.7	227	47.2	481	99.9
1775	4	187	46.9	88	22.1	23	5.8	101	25.3	399	100.1
Total	91	898	29.0	871	28.2	236	7.6	1,087	35.2	3,092	100.0

Appendices

South-Carolina Gazette, 1735–1775

Year	No. of Issues in Sample	Cont. Symbols No.	%	Home Col. Symbols No.	%	Home Reg. Symbols No.	%	Other Col. Symbols No.	%	Total Symbols No.	%
1735	4	1	2.9	24	68.6	10	28.6	—	—	35	100.1
1736	4	—	—	7	100.0	—	—	—	—	7	100.0
1737	4	1	2.4	24	58.5	7	17.1	9	22.0	41	100.0
1738	4	2	6.7	25	83.3	3	10.0	—	—	30	100.0
1739	4	1	4.5	9	40.9	5	22.7	7	31.8	22	99.9
1740	4	10	17.2	24	41.4	18	31.0	6	10.3	58	99.9
1741	4	3	9.7	17	54.8	9	29.0	2	6.5	31	100.0
1742	4	—	—	42	52.5	28	35.0	10	12.5	80	100.0
1743	4	—	—	21	61.8	8	23.5	5	14.7	34	100.0
1744	4	6	16.7	24	66.7	6	16.7	—	—	36	100.1
1745	4	—	—	42	53.2	8	10.1	29	36.7	79	100.0
1746	4	5	5.8	43	50.0	15	17.4	23	26.7	86	99.9
1747	4	—	—	20	38.5	12	23.1	20	38.5	52	100.1
1748	4	1	6.7	7	46.7	—	—	7	46.7	15	100.1
1749	4	3	12.5	12	50.0	9	37.5	—	—	24	100.0
1750	4	2	5.1	25	64.1	4	10.3	8	20.5	39	100.0
1751	4	2	13.3	12	80.0	—	—	1	6.7	15	100.0
1752	4	—	—	17	38.6	10	22.7	17	38.6	44	99.9
1753	4	4	5.9	25	36.8	6	8.8	33	48.5	68	100.0
1754	4	3	2.8	38	34.9	25	22.9	43	39.5	109	100.1
1755	4	25	29.4	29	34.1	17	20.0	14	16.5	85	100.0
1756	4	3	6.8	13	29.5	22	50.0	6	13.6	44	99.9
1757	4	43	20.4	85	40.3	47	22.3	36	17.1	211	100.1
1758	4	10	7.5	18	13.5	16	12.0	89	66.9	133	99.9
1759	4	14	5.1	51	18.4	39	14.1	173	62.5	277	100.1
1760	4	26	9.3	99	35.4	41	14.6	114	40.7	280	100.0
1761	4	8	5.8	62	45.3	47	34.3	20	14.6	137	100.0
1762	4	3	4.3	26	37.1	31	44.3	10	14.3	70	100.0
1763	4	2	3.0	42	63.6	11	16.7	11	16.7	66	100.0
1764	4	21	13.4	30	19.1	28	17.8	78	49.7	157	100.0
1765	4	33	23.9	92	66.7	9	6.5	4	2.9	138	100.0
1766	4	200	48.1	145	34.9	18	4.3	53	12.7	416	100.0
1767	4	10	14.5	45	65.2	10	14.5	4	5.8	69	100.0
1768	4	76	36.9	49	23.8	32	15.5	49	23.8	206	100.0
1769	4	147	42.0	96	27.4	9	2.6	98	28.0	350	100.0
1770	4	144	38.0	47	12.4	33	8.7	155	40.9	379	100.0
1771	4	11	8.1	52	38.2	54	39.7	19	14.0	136	100.0
1772	4	3	2.1	103	72.5	6	4.2	30	21.1	142	99.9
1773	4	24	21.6	49	44.1	14	12.6	24	21.6	111	99.9
1774	4	109	34.4	66	20.8	12	3.8	130	41.0	317	100.0
1775	4	276	51.9	71	13.3	73	13.7	112	21.1	532	100.0
Total	164	1,232	23.9	1,728	33.5	752	14.6	1,449	28.1	5,161	100.1

Symbols of American Community

Boston Gazette, 1762–1775

Year	No. of Issues in Sample	Cont. Symbols No.	%	Home Col. Symbols No.	%	Home Reg. Symbols No.	%	Other Col. Symbols No.	%	Total Symbols No.	%
1762	4	7	4.6	87	57.2	12	7.9	46	30.3	152	100.0
1763	4	27	13.1	65	31.6	32	15.5	82	39.8	206	100.0
1764	4	30	14.9	87	43.1	29	14.4	56	27.7	202	100.1
1765	4	136	41.2	99	30.0	28	8.5	67	20.3	330	100.0
1766	4	78	26.4	114	38.5	25	8.4	79	26.7	296	100.0
1767	4	37	20.7	101	56.4	9	5.0	32	17.9	179	100.0
1768	4	110	28.3	168	43.2	38	9.8	73	18.8	389	100.1
1769	4	142	23.7	403	67.4	9	1.5	44	7.4	598	100.0
1770	4	84	19.6	222	51.9	39	9.1	83	19.4	428	100.0
1771	4	77	28.9	132	49.6	9	3.4	48	18.0	266	99.9
1772	4	73	15.7	341	73.3	19	4.1	32	6.9	465	100.0
1773	4	73	20.3	213	59.3	43	12.0	30	8.4	359	100.0
1774	4	152	23.2	373	56.9	52	7.9	78	11.9	655	99.9
1775	4	195	32.8	241	40.5	31	5.2	128	21.5	595	100.0
Total	56	1,221	23.8	2,646	51.7	375	7.3	878	17.1	5,120	99.9

C. THE COLONIES LOOK AT EACH OTHER
(BY FIVE-YEAR PERIODS)
(includes implicit and explicit symbols)

Massachusetts Gazette, 1735–1775

Symbols devoted to

Years	Massa- chusetts No.	%	New York No.	%	Penn- sylvania No.	%	Virginia No.	%	South Carolina No.	%	Total American Symbols
1735–39	241	52.5	22	4.8	16	3.5	13	2.8	33	7.2	459
1740–44	263	46.2	52	9.1	23	4.0	17	3.0	31	5.4	569
1745–49	351	54.8	84	13.1	34	5.3	12	1.9	19	3.0	641
1750–54	248	42.6	69	11.9	53	9.1	13	2.2	34	5.8	582
1755–59	279	23.2	303	25.1	144	12.0	97	8.1	53	4.4	1,205
1760–64	340	29.1	219	18.8	105	9.0	32	2.7	71	6.1	1,167
1765–69	388	21.3	199	10.9	179	9.8	109	6.0	75	4.1	1,820
1770–75	1,204	44.2	215	7.9	125	4.6	46	1.7	69	2.5	2,723
Total	3,314	36.2	1,163	12.7	679	7.4	339	3.7	385	4.2	9,166

New-York Weekly Journal (1735–51) and
New-York Mercury (1752–75)

Symbols devoted to

Years	Massa- chusetts No.	%	New York No.	%	Penn- sylvania No.	%	Virginia No.	%	South Carolina No.	%	Total American Symbols
1735–39	23	12.4	76	40.9	11	5.9	4	2.2	3	1.6	186
1740–44	35	14.1	72	29.0	12	4.8	13	5.2	22	8.9	248
1745–49	91	21.7	109	26.0	41	9.8	29	6.9	36	8.6	419
1750–54	82	13.5	173	28.4	89	14.6	19	3.1	91	14.9	609
1755–59	160	10.8	473	31.9	254	17.1	71	4.8	94	6.3	1,482
1760–64	74	9.2	220	27.3	126	15.6	23	2.9	89	11.0	806
1765–69	154	9.6	330	20.5	173	10.8	54	3.4	91	5.7	1,610
1770–75	402	16.8	566	23.6	265	11.1	66	2.8	71	3.0	2,395
Total	1,021	13.2	2,019	26.0	971	12.5	279	3.6	497	6.4	7,755

Symbols of American Community

Pennsylvania Gazette, 1735–1775

Symbols devoted to

Years	Massachusetts No.	%	New York No.	%	Pennsylvania No.	%	Virginia No.	%	South Carolina No.	%	Total American Symbols
1735–39	15	3.9	71	18.4	102	26.4	9	2.3	36	9.3	387
1740–44	32	9.0	41	11.6	75	21.2	14	4.0	67	18.9	354
1745–49	73	16.5	97	21.9	126	28.4	20	4.5	31	7.0	443
1750–54	106	15.2	91	13.1	121	17.4	90	12.9	43	6.2	697
1755–59	115	9.4	229	18.6	475	38.7	53	4.3	33	2.7	1,229
1760–64	91	9.3	135	13.8	256	26.1	57	5.8	122	12.4	982
1765–69	241	14.5	183	11.0	359	21.6	66	4.0	34	2.0	1,664
1770–75	325	14.3	226	9.9	420	18.5	200	8.8	43	1.9	2,273
Total	998	12.4	1,073	13.4	1,934	24.1	509	6.3	409	5.1	8,029

Virginia Gazette, 1736–1775

Symbols devoted to

Years	Massachusetts No.	%	New York No.	%	Pennsylvania No.	%	Virginia No.	%	South Carolina No.	%	Total American Symbols
1735–39	26	9.6	38	14.0	12	4.4	127	46.9	19	7.0	271
1740–44	7	6.8	6	5.8	16	15.5	18	17.5	5	4.9	103
1745–49	2	2.5	7	8.6	10	12.4	38	46.9	1	1.2	81
1750–54	1	.7	15	10.9	9	6.5	68	49.3	4	2.9	138
1755–59	7	2.7	58	22.7	20	7.8	84	32.8	12	4.7	256
1760–64	—	—	4	4.4	11	12.1	26	28.6	23	25.3	91
1765–69	60	7.0	64	7.5	56	6.6	244	28.6	16	1.9	853
1770–75	276	21.3	44	3.4	38	2.9	266	20.5	25	1.9	1,299
Total	379	12.3	236	7.6	172	5.6	871	28.2	105	3.4	3,092

Appendices

South-Carolina Gazette, 1735–1775

Symbols devoted to

Years	Massa-chusetts No.	%	New York No.	%	Penn-sylvania No.	%	Virginia No.	%	South Carolina No.	%	Total American Symbols
1735–39	6	4.4	2	1.5	4	3.0	5	3.7	89	65.9	135
1740–44	8	3.3	4	1.7	3	1.3	6	2.5	128	53.6	239
1745–49	33	12.9	11	4.3	20	7.8	11	4.3	124	48.4	256
1750–54	31	11.3	20	7.3	23	8.4	34	12.4	117	42.6	275
1755–59	49	6.5	112	14.9	99	13.2	33	4.4	196	26.1	750
1760–64	31	4.4	103	14.5	55	7.8	21	3.0	259	36.5	710
1765–69	77	6.5	52	4.4	21	1.8	21	1.8	427	36.2	1,179
1770–75	202	12.5	84	5.2	67	4.1	74	4.6	388	24.0	1,617
Total	437	8.5	388	7.5	292	5.7	205	4.0	1,728	33.5	5,161

D. THE DISTRIBUTION OF SYMBOLS OF COMMON IDENTITY: THE LAND, 1735–1775
By Symbolic Content and Dateline Source (includes implicit and explicit symbols)

Composite (excluding *Boston Gazette*)

Year	Explicit British Symbols (AM	BR	FOR)	Explicit Crown Symbols (AM	BR	FOR)	Implicit British Symbols (AM	BR	FOR)	Implicit American Symbols (AM	BR	FOR)	Explicit American Symbols (AM	BR	FOR)	Total No. of Symbols (AM	BR	FOR)
1735	1						1	1				1				2	4	
1736		2			2								1	2		1	4	
1737	4	2			1								8	1		12	5	
1738							1	3		1			2	1		4	5	
1739				1	1		4						2	5		6	6	1
1740				7	2		7	1		1	1		14	8		29	12	
1741			1	4	2		2						2		2	8	2	2
1742				1			2							1		3	1	1
1743	1			1	1					1			4			7	2	
1744				2	2		1	1					3	1		6	3	
1745	2			2			1						2	1	1	7	3	1
1746	1	1			1		4						4	1		9	4	
1747	1	1			1		3			1	1		1	2		5	6	
1748	4	1		1	3		4						2	5	2	11	11	2
1749		3		2			3					3	2	2	2	7	2	3
1750							1		1					6	2	1	11	3
1751	1	1			1		5	2		1	1	1	2	6	2	9	7	5
1752				2	1					1			2	6	5	5	7	3
1753	1			10	2		9			1	1			2	4	21	4	4
1754		2		6			2	6		1			2	4	5	10	13	5

Year																	
1755	7	4	4	18	4		24			5			12	21	10	66	30	16
1756	2	3	1	6	2	1	16	1		4		1	17	31	10	45	56	11
1757	5	1		6			12	18		3	2		11	30	8	37	31	8
1758	1			1			12			2			5	15	3	21	15	3
1759		3	2	1			7			1	1		9	16	2	18	19	2
1760	2			5			10			7			9	21	6	33	22	8
1761				2			3		5	2			4	6	2	11	6	2
1762		3		1			6	4		5	3		9	12	2	21	22	2
1763	1	18		1			7	8	1	2	5		11	40	1	22	71	1
1764	2	13		2	20		15	14	4	10	4		13	31		42	82	
1765	6	17		4	2		53	19		5	17	7	29	59		97	114	9
1766	18	26	1	1	5		105	120		43	18		79	170	1	246	339	
1767	1	8		2	4		15	96		7	9		33	96		58	213	
1768	11	10		1	2		51	7		20	9		125	52		208	80	
1769	14	11		9	2		76	59		25	19		113	108		237	199	
1770	7	8		3	3	1	96	37	5	58	7		118	61		282	116	5
1771	2	5			4		20	3		6	2		36	30		64	44	1
1772	2	5			1		6	6		7	5		27	28		42	45	
1773	9	2	2	1	1		38	2	1	27	4	1	55	34	2	130	43	5
1774	23	7	2	3	10		116	48	1	61	7	1	137	127	2	340	199	6
1775	15	15	2	1	8	2	155	122	4	98	29	2	162	263	2	431	437	12
Total	143	172	15	106	88	4	893	578	11	405	150	13	1,067	1,300	75	2,614	2,288	118

Massachusetts Gazette, 1735–1775

Year	Explicit British Symbols (datelined in)			Explicit Crown Symbols (datelined in)			Implicit British Symbols (datelined in)			Implicit American Symbols (datelined in)			Explicit American Symbols (datelined in)			Total No. of Symbols (datelined in)		
	AM	BR	FOR	AM	BR	FOR	AM	BR	FOR	AM	BR	FOR	AM	BR	FOR	AM	BR	FOR
1735									1			1		1			3	
1736		2															2	
1737													1			1	2	
1738									1									
1739															1			1
1740				2	1		3	1		1			1	3		1	5	
1741				1									6			12		
1742							2	1								1	1	
1743										1			3	1		2	1	
1744				1				1								4		
1745				2			1	1					1			1	1	
1746					1		1										5	
1747		1			2		1									1	5	1
1748							2							2	1		1	2
1749											2			3	1	2	5	3
1750					1				1					1	2		1	2
1751								2				1	2	2	2		5	2
1752														1	2			2
1753														1	2	3	3	2
1754	1			2	2		1						1	1	1	1	1	1

Year																		
1755	5	9	2	4	8	1									1			1
1756	5	3	16	5	3	7									2	1	1	
1757	2	10	2	2	10	2			3			3			1			1
1758	1	4	2	1	4							1					1	
1759	1	5		1	4	1									1			1
1760		5	8	1	5				5						1			
1761		6	1		6	5						1						
1762		3	10		3	6		2	4		5	3						
1763		20	9		11	1		1	2		1						2	
1764		26	8		18				4								6	
1765		38	39		21	12		5	2		7	21					4	3
1766		109	85		55	21		5	10		43	50				1	6	4
1767		39	17		29	6			6		8	5		1	1		2	
1768			44			22		1	6			13						3
1769		26	32		13	19			9		12	2					2	1
1770		19	76		12	32			21		5	21			1			1
1771		4	3		4	1			1			1			1			
1772		14	14		10	7		2	7		1						3	1
1773		10	18		6	6		2	8		1	3					1	4
1774		27	44		9	15		1	10		9	14		6	1		1	2
1775	8	104	76	1	57	27	2		22	3	42	25	2	3			1	
Total	35	517	539	25	304	204	3	22	122	4	140	173	2	17	18	1	34	22

235

New-York Weekly Journal (1735–51) and New-York Mercury (1752–75)

Year	Explicit British Symbols datelined in AM	BR	FOR	Explicit Crown Symbols datelined in AM	BR	FOR	Implicit British Symbols datelined in AM	BR	FOR	Implicit American Symbols datelined in AM	BR	FOR	Explicit American Symbols datelined in AM	BR	FOR	Total No. of Symbols datelined in AM	BR	FOR
1735							1									1		
1736	2																	
1737							1			1			1	1		3	1	
1738								2								2	3	
1739														2			2	
1740				1			2				1		3	1		6	2	
1741															1			1
1742																		
1743													1			1		
1744				1												1		
1745							1						1			2		
1746																1		
1747										1						11		
1748	4			1			4						2	1		2	2	
1749		1					1				1		1	1	1			1
1750											1			1			1	
1751														2			2	
1752						1	2							1	1	2	3	
1753														1	1	2	1	1
1754				4									1	1		5	1	

Year	C1	C2	C3	C4	C5	C6	C7	C8	C9	C10	C11	C12	C13	C14	C15	C16	C17	C18
1755	1	3	23	1	2	5			2			11			3		1	2
1756	1	16	5	1	6			1				4		2				1
1757	3	7	2	3	7				1		7				1			1
1758		2	6		2							1						
1759		1	4		1	1						4				2		
1760		1	5		1	3			1			4						
1761	1		1	1		1		2				1						
1762	3	7	2	1	4	1					2	2					1	
1763	2	14	4	2	6	2					5	1					6	
1764	1	37	7	1	8	3		2	2					20	1		2	
1765		50	14		25	7		5	1		9	5		1			10	
1766		39	25		16	14		2	4		15	5		1			5	
1767		27	17		14	10		2	1		5	3		3			3	
1768		31	70		20	55		4	4		3	10		2			2	
1769		25	87		15	53		3	4		5	24					2	
1770		25	51		18	20			5	5	3	25	1	3	2		1	
1771		22	3		13	3	1	1						4			4	
1772	5	16	1		5	1		5			4					2	2	
1773	1	7	10	2	6	7		1				3						
1774	5	71	82		48	24		2	6		20	45		1		2		7
1775	4	117	65	1	65	32		7	10	1	41	21			1		4	2
Total	30	536	521	16	292	252	1	41	43	6	121	181	1	38	14	6	44	31

Pennsylvania Gazette, 1735–1775

Year	Explicit British Symbols — datelined in AM	BR	FOR	Explicit Crown Symbols — datelined in AM	BR	FOR	Implicit British Symbols — datelined in AM	BR	FOR	Implicit American Symbols — datelined in AM	BR	FOR	Explicit American Symbols — datelined in AM	BR	FOR	Total No. of Symbols — datelined in AM	BR	FOR
1735	1															1		
1736													1			1		
1737	2				1								5	1		7	2	
1738																		
1739							4						1			5		
1740													1	2		1	2	
1741				3		2	2						1			6	2	2
1742			1	1												1		1
1743	1			1		1										2	1	
1744							1									1		
1745	2						1								1	3		1
1746	1						2						1	1		3	1	
1747		1										1	1	1		3	3	
1748																		
1749		1		1									1	1		2	2	
1750																		
1751	1						2						1			4		
1752				2									1	2		3	2	
1753	1			8			3								2	12		2
1754		1					1		6			1		3	4	1		11

Year																	
1755	6	3	11	2	2	1						5		4	3	1	1
1756	4	32	11	3	17	4						6		1	1	3	
1757	1	2	7	1	2	3						4					
1758	2	7	6	2	7	1						5					
1759		13	5		11	3					11	2				2	
1760	4	10	6	4	10	3	1					3		1			
1761			3			1						1					
1762	1	4	6	1	4	2						3					
1763	1	37	6	1	23	2		3			1	3				10	
1764		18	11		4	3		1	1		8	6		1		5	2
1765	13	26	6	6	6	2	9	2		3	16				2	2	
1766	124	22	62	8	62	8	9	4		44	9		1		8	1	
1767	27	8	20	7	20	2			4	1			3		1		
1768	6	48	4	30	4		6		1	8			1		1	3	
1769	88	24	53	11	53	11	1		22	8					1	1	
1770	22	74	13	41	13	2	7		7	21	1		1			4	
1771	14	1	11	1	11	1			1			1			1		
1772	8	13	8	12	8	1	3		1	17						1	
1773	8	42	6	18	6	1	8		2	20			1			3	
1774	19	69	16	36	16	1		1	2	62					1	5	
1775	14	152	10	64	10	1		21	2							4	
Total	28	495	607	22	300	272	1	37	53		113	216	6	30	5	39	36

Virginia Gazette, 1736–1775

Year	Explicit British Symbols — datelined in AM	BR	FOR	Explicit Crown Symbols — datelined in AM	BR	FOR	Implicit British Symbols — datelined in AM	BR	FOR	Implicit American Symbols — datelined in AM	BR	FOR	Explicit American Symbols — datelined in AM	BR	FOR	Total No. of Symbols — datelined in AM	BR	FOR
1735								(Not published)										
1736		1		2												2	1	
1737													1			1		
1738																		
1739																		
1740				1			1						3	3		5	3	
1741																		
1742																		
1743																		
1744																		
1745																		
1746	1						1									1	1	
1747																		
1748																		
1749																		
1750																		
1751	1						2								1			
1752										1			1	2		4	3	
1753										1			1	1		2	1	
1754																		1

Year																		
1755	3	11	15	2	7	4			1		1	2			5			3
1756	1	3	12	1	3	5			1			3			3			2
1757	2	2	4	2	2										2			
1758																		
1759																		
1760																	1	
1761			3			1						2						
1762		7	1		1	1											2	
1763			1				1											
1764											4	1		2				1
1765	6	11	13	2	6	6		1	6		6	4					1	2
1766		28	24		20	12		5			79	5	1				2	1
1767		118	10		32	6		3	1		1	4					3	2
1768		20	12		13	6		2			15	4					3	1
1769		33	13		13	8					2	2			1		3	3
1770		15	4		10	2			3	1	2	2						5
1771		4	48		2	26					1	17		1				4
1772		6	12		4	6						5		1			1	
1773		17	40		15	17			14			6				2		
1774		24	117		22	52			28		2	30						
1775		65	75		41	23		5	30		13	18		2	2		4	
Total	13	364	404	8	191	175	1	16	86	1	126	105	1	8	14	2	23	24

South-Carolina Gazette, 1735–1775

Year	Explicit British Symbols (datelined in) AM	BR	FOR	Explicit Crown Symbols (datelined in) AM	BR	FOR	Implicit British Symbols (datelined in) AM	BR	FOR	Implicit American Symbols (datelined in) AM	BR	FOR	Explicit American Symbols (datelined in) AM	BR	FOR	Total No. of Symbols (datelined in) AM	BR	FOR
1735																		
1736		1															1	
1737																	1	
1738													2			2	1	
1739				3	1								1			5	1	
1740					1			1					1	2		5	3	
1741													1			1		
1742																		
1743															1			1
1744					2								3	1		3	3	
1745																		
1746					1			1					2	1		3	1	
1747					1													
1748	1																1	
1749				1										1		1	2	
1750								1						1	1	1		1
1751								1						1		1	1	
1752																		
1753								3		1						4		
1754				2				1								3		1

1755	1			5	2		6			2			1	2	1	15	4	1
1756													1	2		1	2	
1757	3	1		3			8			3			5	9		22	10	
1758							5			1			1	2		7	2	
1759				1			1			1			6			9		
1760	1			4			3			2	1		4	5		14	6	
1761										1			2			3		
1762				1			1				1					2	1	
1763							1						1			2		
1764				1			5			4			6	1		16	1	
1765		1		3			11				5		4	7		18	13	
1766	10	6	1	1	3		36	12		19	1	7	24	17	1	90	39	9
1767					1		2						4	1		6	2	
1768	2	4					16	2		4	2		12	15		34	23	
1769	5	5		4	1		40	5		10	2		22	14		81	27	
1770	1	2		1			27	20		25	5		23	8		77	35	
1771							2			2			5			9		
1772							1						1	1		2	1	
1773	2						9			2			7	1		20	1	
1774	2	6			3		7	15		9	2		10	32		28	58	
1775	3	5			3		29	24		15	15		16	90		63	137	
Total	30	32	1	30	19		218	78		101	34	7	164	213	4	543	376	12

Boston Gazette, 1762–1775

Year	Explicit British Symbols datelined in			Explicit Crown Symbols datelined in			Implicit British Symbols datelined in			Implicit American Symbols datelined in			Explicit American Symbols datelined in			Total No. of Symbols datelined in		
	AM	BR	FOR	AM	BR	FOR	AM	BR	FOR	AM	BR	FOR	AM	BR	FOR	AM	BR	FOR
1762	1						1			2	1		2	1		5	1	
1763		3					1	8		7			3	5		12	14	
1764						1	5	6		1	6		1	4		7	20	
1765	1	6		3			11	22		21	2		32	15		68	45	
1766	1	3			2		9	6	1	11	2		17	18		38	31	1
1767	7	3					6	1		5			4	3		22	7	
1768	6	3		1	1		23	17		13	1		18	12		61	34	
1769	2	1		1	1		40	2		23			39	11	1	105	15	1
1770		1					19	7		22	3		12	18		53	29	
1771				2			10	4		17			23	5		52	9	
1772	3						12	1		17	1		20	3		52	5	
1773	3						17			17			21	3		58	3	
1774	7			1			40	1		54	1		40	2		142	4	1
1775	1		1				13	9		46	4		49	43	1	109	57	
Total	32	21	1	8	5	1	207	84	1	256	21		281	143	2	784	274	3

245

E. THE DISTRIBUTION OF SYMBOLS OF COMMON IDENTITY: THE POPULATION, 1735–1775
By Symbolic Content and Dateline Source (includes implicit and explicit symbols)

Composite (excluding *Boston Gazette*)

Year	Explicit British Symbols datelined in			Explicit Crown Symbols datelined in			Implicit British Symbols datelined in			Implicit American Symbols datelined in			Explicit American Symbols datelined in			Total No. of Symbols datelined in		
	AM	BR	FOR	AM	BR	FOR	AM	BR	FOR	AM	BR	FOR	AM	BR	FOR	AM	BR	FOR
1735				2												2		
1736																		
1737				2												2		
1738				4	2											4	2	
1739				3												3		
1740		2		5		1							2			7		2
1741																	1	
1742				2												2		
1743				2												2		
1744				3												3		
1745																		
1746				3												3		
1747				1												1		
1748				1	1											1	1	
1749				1												1		
1750																		
1751																		
1752				1												1		
1753				7												7		
1754				1												1		

Year	1	2	3	4	5	6	7	8	9	10	11	12	13	14	15	16	17	18
1755	1			8												9		
1756	1			10	4		4									11	4	
1757				9	1		2									14	1	
1758				7			4									9		
1759				7			5									11		
1760				10	1								1			15	1	
1761				5		4	2									6	1	4
1762				2												4	1	
1763	1			1			3	1								5		
1764	1			1	3	1	3						1			6	4	1
1765	2			9	2		2	11		5			4	4		17	6	
1766	1	3		16	2		5	5					50	26		77	42	
1767	2	1		3	6		3			14			2	9		5	20	
1768	2			13	3		1	2		3			17	3		49	7	
1769	2			36	7		1	1	1	4			12	25		54	34	
1770	1	1		5	5		2	10					12	28	1	24	34	
1771			1	2	1		2						2	9		7	20	
1772	2			3			1			2			3			8	1	1
1773	2	2		5		2		8		2			11	1		21	1	1
1774	5	1	2	14	12		5	13		1			28	35		51	57	1
1775			1	28	16		25				12		33	80	1	92	122	3
Total	23	8	3	232	68	7	70	52	1	32	12		178	220	2	535	360	13

Massachusetts Gazette, 1735–1775

Year	Explicit British Symbols datelined in			Explicit Crown Symbols datelined in			Implicit British Symbols datelined in			Implicit American Symbols datelined in			Explicit American Symbols datelined in			Total No. of Symbols datelined in		
	AM	BR	FOR	AM	BR	FOR	AM	BR	FOR	AM	BR	FOR	AM	BR	FOR	AM	BR	FOR
1735																		
1736																		
1737				2												2		
1738																		
1739				3												3		
1740				3									1			4		
1741				1												1		
1742																1		
1743																		
1744				1												1		
1745																		
1746																		
1747				1												1		
1748						1											1	
1749																		
1750																		
1751																		
1752				1												1		
1753																		
1754																		

Year	1	2	3	4	5	6	7	8	9	10	11	12
1755		2	1									
1756		1	2						2	1		
1757			1			2			1	1		
1758			1									
1759		1	4			1			1	3		
1760		1	1			1				1		
1761		1	2						1	1		
1762			4			1						
1763			2			3						1
1764				1	1	1						
1765		4	8	4	4	1				3		1
1766		9	16	5	3	3	4			8		
1767		1	1	1						1		
1768			4		2					2		
1769		7	7	3	1	2			2	6	1	
1770		2	5	2	5							
1771		9		4		5						
1772			4		3					1		
1773		1	5	1	4			2		1		
1774	2	8	7	2	2		1		6	4		1
1775		27	7	21	3	4			2	3		
Total	2	75	95	43	29	15	15	2	16	48	1	3

New-York Weekly Journal (1735–51) and New-York Mercury (1752–75)

Year	Explicit British Symbols datelined in AM	BR	FOR	Explicit Crown Symbols datelined in AM	BR	FOR	Implicit British Symbols datelined in AM	BR	FOR	Implicit American Symbols datelined in AM	BR	FOR	Explicit American Symbols datelined in AM	BR	FOR	Total No. of Symbols datelined in AM	BR	FOR
1735																		
1736																		
1737																		
1738				4												4		
1739				1												2		
1740														1				
1741																		
1742																		
1743				2												2		
1744				1												1		
1745																		
1746																		
1747																		
1748				1												1		
1749																		
1750																		
1751																		
1752																		
1753																		
1754				1												1		

Year																
1755	1		1											1		
1756	2		2											2		
1757																
1758	4			2									6			
1759	3			2									3			
1760	1												3			
1761				1												
1762													1			
1763															1	
1764		3												3	1	
1765	2	2	1			2				3	12		2	1		
1766		1								1			4	16		
1767	1	1	4							4	2		2	4		
1768		1	3					1					7	6	1	
1769		2								3			2			
1770		3	2				1	1			1		7	3		
1771		1	1	1							1		1	2		
1772	1	1											1	1		
1773		1											1			
1774	2	3	3					1		1	13		5	23		
1775		5	4	1		5	7		1	3	6	1	9	17	1	
Total	6	42	21	6	1	7	7	3	1	16	35	1	68	76	3	

251

Pennsylvania Gazette, 1735–1775

Year	Explicit British Symbols datelined in			Explicit Crown Symbols datelined in			Implicit British Symbols datelined in			Implicit American Symbols datelined in			Explicit American Symbols datelined in			Total No. of Symbols datelined in		
	AM	BR	FOR	AM	BR	FOR	AM	BR	FOR	AM	BR	FOR	AM	BR	FOR	AM	BR	FOR
1735				2												2		
1736																		
1737																		
1738					2												2	
1739																		
1740				1												1		
1741				1												1		
1742																		
1743				1												1		
1744																		
1745				1												1		
1746																		
1747																		
1748																		
1749				1												1		
1750																		
1751																		
1752																		
1753				7												7		
1754																		

Year											
1755				2						2	
1756				3	2					3	2
1757				1						1	
1758				1						1	
1759				2						2	
1760				2						2	
1761											
1762				1						1	
1763				1						1	
1764			1				1				1
1765	1			3	1	1				5	1
1766			2	2	1	2	2		7	2	10
1767				1					3	1	3
1768	1			7	1			7		17	
1769				14				1	7	15	8
1770				1		2		4	1	5	1
1771			5				5		4	2	9
1772											
1773	1			3		1		3		8	
1774				4					9	12	9
1775	1	1	2	13	1	2		11	2	27	4
Total	4	1	8	75	8	8	8	34	33	121	50

Virginia Gazette, 1736–1775

Year	Explicit British Symbols datelined in			Explicit Crown Symbols datelined in			Implicit British Symbols datelined in			Implicit American Symbols datelined in			Explicit American Symbols datelined in			Total No. of Symbols datelined in		
	AM	BR	FOR	AM	BR	FOR	AM	BR	FOR	AM	BR	FOR	AM	BR	FOR	AM	BR	FOR
1735									(Not published)									
1736																		
1737																		
1738																		
1739																		
1740																		
1741																		
1742																		
1743																		
1744																		
1745																		
1746					1												1	
1747																		
1748																		
1749																		
1750																		
1751																		
1752																		
1753																		
1754																		

1755			1									1		
1756			4									5		
1757														
1758														
1759														
1760									1					
1761														
1762														
1763														1
1764														
1765									3	2		1		
1766					1				1	5		3	3	
1767						1						2	11	
1768			1	1		5			2		1			
1769										8			8	
1770										3			3	
1771												2		
1772			1		2				4			3		
1773												4		
1774		1	3	2	4		1		11	1		20	1	1
1775	1		2		6		1	4	11	21		20	27	
Total	1	1	13	3	13	6	2	4	33	40	1	62	53	2

South-Carolina Gazette, 1735–1775

Year	Explicit British Symbols datelined in			Explicit Crown Symbols datelined in			Implicit British Symbols datelined in			Implicit American Symbols datelined in			Explicit American Symbols datelined in			Total No. of Symbols datelined in		
	AM	BR	FOR	AM	BR	FOR	AM	BR	FOR	AM	BR	FOR	AM	BR	FOR	AM	BR	FOR
1735																		
1736																		
1737																		
1738																		
1739																		
1740			2															2
1741						1											1	
1742																		
1743																		
1744																		
1745																		
1746				1												1		
1747																		
1748																		
1749																		
1750																		
1751																		
1752																		
1753																		
1754																		

Year															
1755	1		4										5		
1756	1		8			2							11		
1757			1										1		
1758			2			3							5		
1759			4			2							6		
1760			4						1				5		
1761						2									
1762															
1763															
1764	1												4		4
1765	1		1	1					5		44		2	4	
1766			5	1			3				1		54	1	
1767					4						1		1	1	
1768			3			1			13				18	11	
1769	2		13	4		1	1		3		9	1	28	25	
1770	2		1	3		1	1		3			7	7		
1771	1		1									21	2		
1772									2						
1773	1			3		1	3				6	10	3		
1774	4			7		15	9				5	30	7	16	
1775		2	5					1		1			29	47	
Total	14	2	54	20	4	28	16	1	27	1	66	69	189	106	6

Boston Gazette, 1762–1775

Year	Explicit British Symbols datelined in			Explicit Crown Symbols datelined in			Implicit British Symbols datelined in			Implicit American Symbols datelined in			Explicit American Symbols datelined in			Total No. of Symbols datelined in		
	AM	BR	FOR	AM	BR	FOR	AM	BR	FOR	AM	BR	FOR	AM	BR	FOR	AM	BR	FOR
1762				1												1		
1763				1												1		
1764							1	1					1			2	1	
1765		3		5			5	5					5			15	8	
1766	1			2				1					2	2		5	3	
1767				4			1						3			8		
1768				3			4						5	2		12	2	
1769		1		3			3						13	1	1	19	2	1
1770				1												1	1	
1771	2			5			1						8			16		
1772		1		2			2						11	1		15	1	
1773				3			3						5			11		
1774													6			6		
1775	3					2	3	2		1			6	15	1	10	19	1
Total	3	5		30		2	23	9		1			65	21	1	122	37	1

F. THE GLOBAL DISTRIBUTION OF SYMBOLS
BY MONTH, 1762–1766
(includes explicit symbols only)

Composite (*Boston Gazette* and *New-York Mercury*)

Year	Month	American Symbols No.	%	British Symbols No.	%	Other Symbols No.	%	Total Symbols No.	%
1762	Jan	40	9.1	78	17.8	321	73.1	439	100.0
	Feb	31	9.0	45	13.1	267	77.8	343	99.9
	Mar	32	10.2	71	22.6	211	67.2	314	100.0
	Apr	63	11.4	78	17.9	295	67.7	436	100.0
	May	37	5.3	109	15.8	546	78.9	692	100.0
	Jun	28	4.6	80	13.3	495	82.1	603	100.0
	Jul	45	9.2	91	18.6	353	72.2	489	100.0
	Aug	52	9.7	117	21.9	366	68.4	535	100.0
	Sep	63	11.1	83	14.6	424	74.4	570	100.1
	Oct	32	6.2	76	14.8	406	79.0	514	100.0
	Nov	26	9.1	64	22.4	196	68.6	286	100.1
	Dec	50	11.8	68	16.1	304	72.0	422	99.9
1763	Jan	56	13.1	59	13.8	313	73.1	428	100.0
	Feb	69	24.0	49	17.1	169	58.9	287	100.0
	Mar	71	22.7	63	20.1	179	57.2	313	100.0
	Apr	38	9.2	102	24.8	271	66.0	411	100.0
	May	49	9.6	144	28.2	317	62.2	510	100.0
	Jun	25	9.0	105	37.9	147	53.1	277	100.0
	Jul	66	26.9	65	26.5	114	46.5	245	99.9
	Aug	72	48.3	37	24.8	40	26.8	149	99.9
	Sep	76	43.9	17	9.8	80	46.2	173	99.9
	Oct	69	26.3	69	26.3	124	47.3	262	99.9
	Nov	76	28.0	96	35.4	99	36.5	271	99.9
	Dec	67	23.2	75	26.0	147	50.9	289	100.1
1764	Jan	103	33.8	67	22.0	135	44.3	305	100.1
	Feb	152	44.6	68	19.9	121	35.5	341	100.0
	Mar	93	60.8	23	15.0	37	24.2	153	100.0
	Apr	52	25.0	52	25.0	104	50.0	208	100.0
	May	74	34.7	52	24.4	87	40.8	213	99.9
	Jun	178	54.1	32	9.7	119	36.2	329	100.0
	Jul	63	30.1	62	29.7	84	40.2	209	100.0
	Aug	97	28.2	87	25.3	160	46.5	344	100.0
	Sep	76	26.8	40	14.1	168	59.2	284	100.1
	Oct	72	21.9	64	19.5	193	58.7	329	100.1
	Nov	42	16.2	57	22.0	160	61.8	259	100.0
	Dec	54	34.4	61	38.9	42	26.8	157	100.1
1765	Jan	99	38.8	58	22.7	98	38.4	255	99.9
	Feb	134	38.1	59	16.8	159	45.2	352	100.1

Appendices

Year	Month	American Symbols No.	%	British Symbols No.	%	Other Symbols No.	%	Total Symbols No.	%
1765	Mar	81	27.5	68	23.1	146	49.5	295	100.1
	Apr	71	37.6	45	23.8	73	38.6	189	100.0
	May	107	26.4	113	27.8	186	45.8	406	100.0
	Jun	238	61.5	72	18.6	77	19.9	387	100.0
	Jul	69	28.0	56	22.8	121	49.2	246	100.0
	Aug	136	42.2	78	24.2	108	33.5	322	99.9
	Sep	129	49.8	62	23.9	68	26.3	259	100.0
	Oct	116	41.9	86	31.0	75	27.1	277	100.0
	Nov	53	46.9	34	30.1	26	23.0	113	100.0
	Dec	143	58.6	63	25.8	38	15.6	244	100.0
1766	Jan	85	29.9	53	18.7	146	51.4	284	100.0
	Feb	145	47.1	70	22.7	93	30.2	308	100.0
	Mar	156	52.9	65	22.0	74	25.1	295	100.0
	Apr	230	65.2	94	26.6	29	8.2	353	100.0
	May	179	53.8	52	15.6	102	30.6	333	100.0
	Jun	79	32.1	62	25.2	105	42.7	246	100.0
	Jul	119	35.7	82	24.6	132	39.6	333	99.9
	Aug	119	42.3	54	19.2	108	38.4	281	99.9
	Sep	108	28.6	102	27.1	167	44.3	377	100.0
	Oct	72	28.8	60	24.0	118	47.2	250	100.0
	Nov	98	26.1	132	35.2	145	38.7	375	100.0
	Dec	90	41.3	57	26.1	71	32.6	218	100.0
Total		5,145	26.5	4,183	21.6	10,059	51.9	19,387	100.0

Boston Gazette, 1762–1766

Year	Month	American Symbols No.	%	British Symbols No.	%	Other Symbols No.	%	Total Symbols No.	%
1762	Jan	23	31.5	16	21.9	34	46.6	73	100.0
	Feb	15	6.6	26	11.4	188	82.1	229	100.1
	Mar	17	11.6	27	18.5	102	69.9	146	100.0
	Apr	29	13.2	41	18.6	150	68.2	220	100.0
	May	25	11.8	44	20.8	143	67.4	212	100.0
	Jun	16	5.6	29	10.2	240	84.2	285	100.0
	Jul	33	18.5	27	15.2	118	66.3	178	100.0
	Aug	20	15.2	26	19.7	86	65.2	132	100.1
	Sep	37	12.2	46	15.2	220	72.6	303	100.0
	Oct	15	5.7	35	13.2	215	81.1	265	100.0
	Nov	22	13.7	29	18.0	110	68.3	161	100.0
	Dec	29	15.0	28	14.4	137	70.6	194	100.0

Symbols of American Community

Year	Month	American Symbols No.	American Symbols %	British Symbols No.	British Symbols %	Other Symbols No.	Other Symbols %	Total Symbols No.	Total Symbols %
1763	Jan	32	17.6	12	6.6	138	75.8	182	100.0
	Feb	45	44.6	13	12.9	43	42.6	101	100.1
	Mar	51	41.8	35	28.7	36	29.5	122	100.0
	Apr	21	17.4	39	32.2	61	50.4	121	100.0
	May	32	16.4	48	24.6	115	59.0	195	100.0
	Jun	3	2.7	53	47.8	55	49.6	111	100.1
	Jul	37	55.2	6	9.0	24	35.8	67	100.0
	Aug	33	47.1	21	30.0	16	22.9	70	100.0
	Sep	47	62.7	7	9.3	21	28.0	75	100.0
	Oct	38	20.3	45	24.1	104	55.6	187	100.0
	Nov	40	33.6	53	44.5	26	21.9	119	100.0
	Dec	47	20.9	54	24.0	124	55.1	225	100.0
1764	Jan	46	68.7	10	14.9	11	16.4	67	100.0
	Feb	41	91.1	2	4.4	2	4.4	45	99.9
	Mar	31	86.1	5	13.9	—	—	36	100.0
	Apr	27	31.8	9	10.6	49	57.7	85	100.1
	May	13	65.0	4	20.0	3	15.0	20	100.0
	Jun	153	89.0	8	4.7	11	6.4	172	100.1
	Jul	56	60.9	18	19.6	18	19.6	92	100.1
	Aug	27	23.1	20	17.1	70	59.8	117	100.0
	Sep	50	52.1	22	22.9	24	25.0	96	100.0
	Oct	54	62.8	19	22.1	13	15.1	86	100.0
	Nov	17	11.5	40	27.0	91	61.5	148	100.0
	Dec	46	42.2	23	21.1	40	36.7	109	100.0
1765	Jan	76	45.0	41	24.3	52	30.8	169	100.1
	Feb	72	51.4	17	12.1	51	36.4	140	99.9
	Mar	50	34.7	47	32.6	47	32.6	144	99.9
	Apr	43	58.9	22	30.1	8	11.0	73	100.0
	May	41	40.2	29	28.4	32	31.4	102	100.0
	Jun	187	71.4	39	14.9	36	13.7	262	100.0
	Jul	38	40.9	12	12.9	43	46.2	93	100.0
	Aug	70	53.0	25	18.9	37	28.0	132	99.9
	Sep	52	67.5	13	16.9	12	15.6	77	100.0
	Oct	22	24.2	57	62.6	12	13.2	91	100.0
	Nov	29	51.8	19	33.9	8	14.3	56	100.0
	Dec	56	54.4	30	29.1	17	16.5	103	100.0
1766	Jan	62	57.4	22	20.4	24	22.2	108	100.0
	Feb	78	58.2	38	28.4	18	13.4	134	100.0
	Mar	79	64.2	25	20.3	19	15.5	123	100.0

Appendices

Year	Month	American Symbols No.	%	British Symbols No.	%	Other Symbols No.	%	Total Symbols No.	%
1766	Apr	99	67.4	45	30.6	3	2.0	147	100.0
	May	102	70.3	23	15.9	20	13.8	145	100.0
	Jun	32	43.2	29	39.2	13	17.6	74	100.0
	Jul	7	70.0	3	30.0	—	—	10	100.0
	Aug	62	45.9	22	16.3	51	37.8	135	100.0
	Sep	32	37.7	21	24.7	32	37.7	85	100.1
	Oct	46	54.8	18	21.4	20	23.8	84	100.0
	Nov	47	31.8	47	31.8	54	36.5	148	100.1
	Dec	30	27.0	39	35.1	42	37.8	111	99.9
Total		2,680	34.4	1,623	20.8	3,489	44.8	7,792	100.0

New-York Mercury, 1762–1766

Year	Month	American Symbols No.	%	British Symbols No.	%	Other Symbols No.	%	Total Symbols No.	%
1762	Jan	17	4.6	62	16.9	287	78.4	366	99.9
	Feb	16	14.0	19	16.7	79	69.3	114	100.0
	Mar	15	8.9	44	26.2	109	64.9	168	100.0
	Apr	34	15.7	37	17.1	145	67.1	216	99.9
	May	12	2.5	65	13.5	403	84.0	480	100.0
	Jun	12	3.8	51	16.0	255	80.2	318	100.0
	Jul	12	3.9	64	20.6	235	75.6	311	100.1
	Aug	32	7.9	91	22.6	280	69.5	403	100.0
	Sep	26	9.7	37	13.9	204	76.4	267	100.0
	Oct	17	6.8	41	16.5	191	76.7	249	100.0
	Nov	4	3.2	35	28.0	86	68.8	125	100.0
	Dec	21	9.2	40	17.5	167	73.3	228	100.0
1763	Jan	24	9.8	47	19.1	175	71.1	246	100.0
	Feb	24	12.9	36	19.4	126	67.7	186	100.0
	Mar	20	10.5	28	14.7	143	74.9	191	100.1
	Apr	17	5.9	63	21.7	210	72.4	290	100.0
	May	17	5.4	96	30.5	202	64.1	315	100.0
	Jun	22	13.3	52	31.3	92	55.4	166	100.0
	Jul	29	16.3	59	33.1	90	50.6	178	100.0
	Aug	39	49.4	16	20.3	24	30.4	79	100.1
	Sep	29	29.6	10	10.2	59	60.2	98	100.0
	Oct	31	41.3	24	32.0	20	26.7	75	100.0
	Nov	36	23.7	43	28.3	73	48.0	152	100.0
	Dec	20	31.3	21	32.8	23	35.9	64	100.0

Symbols of American Community

Year	Month	American Symbols		British Symbols		Other Symbols		Total Symbols	
		No.	%	No.	%	No.	%	No.	%
1764	Jan	57	23.9	57	23.9	124	52.1	238	99.9
	Feb	111	37.5	66	22.3	119	40.2	296	100.0
	Mar	62	53.0	18	15.4	37	31.6	117	100.0
	Apr	25	20.3	43	35.0	55	44.7	123	100.0
	May	61	31.6	48	24.9	84	43.5	193	100.0
	Jun	25	15.9	24	15.3	108	68.8	157	100.0
	Jul	7	6.0	44	37.6	66	56.4	117	100.0
	Aug	70	30.8	67	29.5	90	39.6	227	99.9
	Sep	26	13.8	18	9.6	144	76.6	188	100.0
	Oct	18	7.4	45	18.5	180	74.1	243	100.0
	Nov	25	22.5	17	15.3	69	62.2	111	100.0
	Dec	8	16.7	38	79.2	2	4.2	48	100.1
1765	Jan	23	26.7	17	19.8	46	53.5	86	100.0
	Feb	62	29.2	42	19.8	108	50.9	212	99.9
	Mar	31	20.5	21	13.9	99	65.6	151	100.0
	Apr	28	24.1	23	19.8	65	56.0	116	99.9
	May	66	21.7	84	27.6	154	50.7	304	100.0
	Jun	51	40.8	33	26.4	41	32.8	125	100.0
	Jul	31	20.3	44	28.8	78	51.0	153	100.1
	Aug	66	34.7	53	27.9	71	37.4	190	100.0
	Sep	77	42.3	49	26.9	56	30.8	182	100.0
	Oct	94	50.5	29	15.6	63	33.9	186	100.0
	Nov	24	42.1	15	26.3	18	31.6	57	100.0
	Dec	87	61.7	33	23.4	21	14.9	141	100.0
1766	Jan	23	13.1	31	17.6	122	69.3	176	100.0
	Feb	67	38.5	32	18.4	75	43.1	174	100.0
	Mar	77	44.8	40	23.3	55	32.0	172	100.1
	Apr	131	63.6	49	23.8	26	12.6	206	100.0
	May	77	41.0	29	15.4	82	43.6	188	100.0
	Jun	47	27.3	33	19.2	92	53.5	172	100.0
	Jul	112	34.7	79	24.5	132	40.9	323	100.1
	Aug	57	39.0	32	21.9	57	39.0	146	99.9
	Sep	76	26.0	81	27.7	135	46.2	292	99.9
	Oct	26	15.7	42	25.3	98	59.0	166	100.0
	Nov	51	22.5	85	37.5	91	40.1	227	100.1
	Dec	60	56.1	18	16.8	29	27.1	107	100.0
Total		2,465	21.3	2,560	22.1	6,570	56.7	11,595	100.1

(includes implicit and explicit symbols)

Composite (*Boston Gazette* and *New-York Mercury*)

Year	Month	Cont. Symbols No.	%	Home Col. Symbols No.	%	Home Reg. Symbols No.	%	Other Col. Symbols No.	%	Total Symbols No.	%
1762	Jan	—	—	45	52.9	14	16.5	26	30.6	85	100.0
	Feb	1	1.7	24	41.4	7	12.1	26	44.8	58	100.0
	Mar	11	24.4	12	26.7	11	24.4	11	24.4	45	99.9
	Apr	5	5.0	31	31.0	34	34.0	30	30.0	100	100.0
	May	17	29.8	21	36.8	6	10.5	13	22.8	57	99.9
	Jun	1	1.8	28	50.9	11	20.0	15	27.3	55	100.0
	Jul	3	4.1	17	23.0	4	5.4	50	67.6	74	100.1
	Aug	4	5.3	27	35.5	14	18.4	31	40.8	76	100.0
	Sep	2	2.1	38	40.4	14	14.9	40	42.6	94	100.0
	Oct	4	8.2	23	46.9	12	24.5	10	20.4	49	100.0
	Nov	2	5.0	12	30.0	4	10.0	22	55.0	40	100.0
	Dec	2	2.6	29	38.2	11	14.5	34	44.7	76	100.0
1763	Jan	8	9.9	22	27.2	17	21.0	34	42.0	81	100.1
	Feb	8	7.8	38	37.3	21	20.6	35	34.3	102	100.0
	Mar	10	9.3	25	23.1	41	38.0	32	29.6	108	100.0
	Apr	2	2.6	30	38.5	19	24.4	27	34.6	78	100.1
	May	15	23.4	18	28.1	9	14.1	22	34.4	64	100.0
	Jun	2	4.3	13	27.7	8	17.0	24	51.1	47	100.1
	Jul	—	—	22	21.8	20	19.8	59	58.4	101	100.0
	Aug	3	2.9	33	32.0	38	36.9	29	28.2	103	100.0
	Sep	4	3.9	11	10.7	23	22.3	65	63.1	103	100.0
	Oct	15	14.4	24	23.1	17	16.3	48	46.2	104	100.0
	Nov	19	17.8	25	23.4	12	11.2	51	47.7	107	100.1
	Dec	35	38.5	22	24.2	5	5.5	29	31.9	91	100.1
1764	Jan	12	7.4	46	28.4	43	26.5	61	37.7	162	100.0
	Feb	80	41.5	29	15.0	14	7.3	70	36.3	193	100.1
	Mar	6	3.7	34	21.1	82	50.9	39	24.2	161	99.9
	Apr	6	7.2	28	33.7	27	32.5	22	26.5	83	99.9
	May	24	21.1	36	31.6	13	11.4	41	36.0	114	100.1
	Jun	6	3.1	151	77.4	16	8.2	22	11.3	195	100.0
	Jul	3	2.9	38	37.3	27	26.5	34	33.3	102	100.0
	Aug	60	48.8	25	20.3	15	12.2	23	18.7	123	100.0
	Sep	14	9.9	28	19.7	41	28.9	59	41.6	142	100.1
	Oct	41	41.8	18	18.4	18	18.4	21	21.4	98	100.0
	Nov	3	5.1	14	23.7	15	25.4	27	45.8	59	100.0
	Dec	8	9.6	31	37.3	11	13.3	33	39.8	83	100.0
1765	Jan	31	18.9	78	47.6	17	10.4	38	23.2	164	100.1
	Feb	4	2.0	86	43.9	36	18.4	70	35.7	196	100.0

Year	Month	Cont. Symbols No.	%	Home Col. Symbols No.	%	Home Reg. Symbols No.	%	Other Col. Symbols No.	%	Total Symbols No.	%
1765	Mar	31	23.0	17	12.6	16	11.9	71	52.6	135	100.1
	Apr	6	7.4	19	23.5	22	27.2	34	42.0	81	100.1
	May	75	52.1	32	22.2	18	12.5	19	13.2	144	100.0
	Jun	47	16.7	168	59.8	35	12.5	31	11.0	281	100.0
	Jul	22	24.2	17	18.7	10	11.0	42	46.2	91	100.1
	Aug	80	45.2	22	12.4	23	13.0	52	29.4	177	100.0
	Sep	34	16.2	41	19.5	48	22.9	87	41.4	210	100.0
	Oct	45	25.7	44	25.1	14	8.0	72	41.1	175	99.9
	Nov	13	13.7	31	32.6	15	15.8	36	37.9	95	100.0
	Dec	53	21.0	82	32.5	78	31.0	39	15.5	252	100.0
1766	Jan	54	41.5	39	30.0	18	13.8	19	14.6	130	99.9
	Feb	41	19.3	90	42.5	49	23.1	32	15.1	212	100.0
	Mar	88	41.3	26	12.2	21	9.9	78	36.6	213	100.0
	Apr	226	75.8	34	11.4	10	3.4	28	9.4	298	100.0
	May	152	65.5	18	7.8	28	12.1	34	14.7	232	100.1
	Jun	25	18.4	45	33.1	26	19.1	40	29.4	136	100.0
	Jul	73	40.6	26	14.4	30	16.7	51	28.3	180	100.0
	Aug	36	20.9	30	17.4	21	12.2	85	49.4	172	99.9
	Sep	53	39.0	20	14.7	30	22.1	33	24.3	136	100.1
	Oct	11	9.2	52	43.7	21	17.6	35	29.4	119	99.9
	Nov	28	20.1	55	39.6	13	9.4	43	30.9	139	100.0
	Dec	12	8.6	57	41.0	20	14.4	50	36.0	139	100.0
Total		1,676	22.3	2,197	29.2	1,313	17.5	2,334	31.0	7,520	100.0

Boston Gazette, 1762–1766

Year	Month	Cont. Symbols No.	%	Home Col. Symbols No.	%	Home Reg. Symbols No.	%	Other Col. Symbols No.	%	Total Symbols No.	%
1762	Jan	—	—	31	59.6	11	21.2	10	19.2	52	100.0
	Feb	—	—	7	31.8	4	18.2	11	50.0	22	100.0
	Mar	2	8.7	10	43.5	7	30.4	4	17.4	23	100.0
	Apr	1	2.1	22	46.8	6	12.8	18	38.3	47	100.0
	May	9	23.7	14	36.8	4	10.5	11	29.0	38	100.0
	Jun	1	3.6	14	50.0	5	17.9	8	28.6	28	100.1
	Jul	3	5.5	13	23.6	1	1.8	38	69.1	55	100.0
	Aug	3	11.1	8	29.6	7	25.9	9	33.3	27	99.9
	Sep	—	—	21	41.2	6	11.8	24	47.1	51	100.1
	Oct	2	10.0	13	65.0	1	5.0	4	20.0	20	100.0

Appendices

Year	Month	Cont. Symbols No.	%	Home Col. Symbols No.	%	Home Reg. Symbols No.	%	Other Col. Symbols No.	%	Total Symbols No.	%
1762	Nov	2	6.7	6	20.0	3	10.0	19	63.3	30	100.0
	Dec	—	—	17	39.5	4	9.3	22	51.2	43	100.0
1763	Jan	7	14.3	11	22.5	11	22.5	20	40.8	49	100.1
	Feb	3	4.4	33	48.5	12	17.7	20	29.4	68	100.0
	Mar	10	13.7	20	27.4	22	30.1	21	28.8	73	100.0
	Apr	2	5.0	22	55.0	11	27.5	5	12.5	40	100.0
	May	12	26.7	13	28.9	5	11.1	15	33.3	45	100.0
	Jun	—	—	1	25.0	—	—	3	75.0	4	100.0
	Jul	—	—	10	18.2	—	—	45	81.8	55	100.0
	Aug	2	4.2	22	45.8	9	18.8	15	31.3	48	100.1
	Sep	—	—	8	13.1	9	14.8	44	72.1	61	100.0
	Oct	7	13.0	15	27.8	1	1.9	31	57.4	54	100.1
	Nov	4	6.3	18	28.1	1	1.6	41	64.1	64	100.1
	Dec	24	36.9	12	18.5	5	7.7	24	36.9	65	100.0
1764	Jan	3	4.1	14	18.9	14	18.9	43	58.1	74	100.0
	Feb	—	—	13	20.0	7	10.8	45	69.2	65	100.0
	Mar	3	5.4	23	41.1	3	5.4	27	48.2	56	100.1
	Apr	3	5.6	23	42.6	8	14.8	20	37.0	54	100.0
	May	—	—	21	75.0	1	3.6	6	21.4	28	100.0
	Jun	4	2.5	144	88.3	8	4.9	7	4.3	163	100.0
	Jul	3	3.5	28	32.2	23	26.4	33	37.9	87	100.0
	Aug	10	23.8	15	35.7	9	21.4	8	19.1	42	100.0
	Sep	14	14.0	20	20.0	28	28.0	38	38.0	100	100.0
	Oct	35	51.5	17	25.0	7	10.3	9	13.2	68	100.0
	Nov	3	12.5	8	33.3	9	37.5	4	16.7	24	100.0
	Dec	2	3.2	18	29.0	9	14.5	33	53.2	62	99.9
1765	Jan	31	24.4	67	52.8	10	7.9	19	15.0	127	100.1
	Feb	—	—	66	64.7	23	22.6	13	12.7	102	100.0
	Mar	20	23.0	12	13.8	14	16.1	41	47.1	87	100.0
	Apr	2	4.3	12	25.5	13	27.7	20	42.6	47	100.1
	May	38	61.3	16	25.8	8	12.9	—	—	62	100.0
	Jun	32	15.4	155	74.5	10	4.8	11	5.3	208	100.0
	Jul	12	22.2	8	14.8	7	13.0	27	50.0	54	100.0
	Aug	56	67.5	10	12.1	10	12.1	7	8.4	83	100.1
	Sep	19	22.1	27	31.4	26	30.2	14	16.3	86	100.0
	Oct	12	29.3	24	58.5	3	7.3	2	4.9	41	100.0
	Nov	11	17.7	24	38.7	5	8.1	22	35.5	62	100.0
	Dec	20	21.7	15	16.3	25	27.2	32	34.8	92	100.0

Symbols of American Community

Year	Month	Cont. Symbols No.	Cont. Symbols %	Home Col. Symbols No.	Home Col. Symbols %	Home Reg. Symbols No.	Home Reg. Symbols %	Other Col. Symbols No.	Other Col. Symbols %	Total Symbols No.	Total Symbols %
1766	Jan	49	47.6	35	34.0	16	15.5	3	2.9	103	100.0
	Feb	31	27.0	63	54.8	12	10.4	9	7.8	115	100.0
	Mar	33	30.3	14	12.8	10	9.2	52	47.7	109	100.0
	Apr	75	58.6	23	18.0	8	6.3	22	17.2	128	100.1
	May	113	91.9	6	4.9	1	.8	3	2.4	123	100.0
	Jun	15	22.4	28	41.8	11	16.4	13	19.4	67	100.0
	Jul	7	58.3	5	41.7	—	—	—	—	12	100.0
	Aug	31	38.3	20	24.7	2	2.5	28	34.6	81	100.1
	Sep	16	39.0	8	19.5	7	17.1	10	24.4	41	100.0
	Oct	9	11.4	42	53.2	12	15.2	16	20.3	79	100.1
	Nov	23	37.7	25	41.0	3	4.9	10	16.4	61	100.0
	Dec	9	20.9	17	39.5	4	9.3	13	30.2	43	99.9
Total		838	21.5	1,427	36.6	511	13.1	1,122	28.8	3,898	100.0

New-York Mercury, 1762–1766

Year	Month	Cont. Symbols No.	Cont. Symbols %	Home Col. Symbols No.	Home Col. Symbols %	Home Reg. Symbols No.	Home Reg. Symbols %	Other Col. Symbols No.	Other Col. Symbols %	Total Symbols No.	Total Symbols %
1762	Jan	—	—	14	42.4	3	9.1	16	48.5	33	100.0
	Feb	1	2.8	17	47.2	3	8.3	15	41.7	36	100.0
	Mar	9	40.9	2	9.1	4	18.2	7	31.8	22	100.0
	Apr	4	7.6	9	17.0	28	52.8	12	22.6	53	100.0
	May	8	42.1	7	36.8	2	10.5	2	10.5	19	99.9
	Jun	—	—	14	51.9	6	22.2	7	25.9	27	100.0
	Jul	—	—	4	21.1	3	15.8	12	63.2	19	100.1
	Aug	1	2.0	19	38.8	7	14.3	22	44.9	49	100.0
	Sep	2	4.7	17	39.5	8	18.6	16	37.2	43	100.0
	Oct	2	6.9	10	34.5	11	37.9	6	20.7	29	100.0
	Nov	—	—	6	60.0	1	10.0	3	30.0	10	100.0
	Dec	2	6.1	12	36.4	7	21.2	12	36.4	33	100.1
1763	Jan	1	3.1	11	34.4	6	18.8	14	43.8	32	100.1
	Feb	5	14.7	5	14.7	9	26.5	15	44.1	34	100.0
	Mar	—	—	5	14.3	19	54.3	11	31.4	35	100.0
	Apr	—	—	8	21.1	8	21.1	22	57.9	38	100.1
	May	3	15.8	5	26.3	4	21.1	7	36.9	19	100.1
	Jun	2	4.7	12	27.9	8	18.6	21	48.8	43	100.0
	Jul	—	—	12	26.1	20	43.5	14	30.4	46	100.0
	Aug	1	1.8	11	20.0	29	52.7	14	25.5	55	100.0
	Sep	4	9.5	3	7.1	14	33.3	21	50.0	42	99.9

Appendices

Year	Month	Cont. Symbols No.	%	Home Col. Symbols No.	%	Home Reg. Symbols No.	%	Other Col. Symbols No.	%	Total Symbols No.	%
1763	Oct	8	16.0	9	18.0	16	32.0	17	34.0	50	100.0
	Nov	15	34.9	7	16.3	11	25.6	10	23.3	43	100.1
	Dec	11	42.3	10	38.5	—	—	5	19.2	26	100.0
1764	Jan	9	10.2	32	36.4	29	33.0	18	20.3	88	99.9
	Feb	80	62.5	16	12.5	7	5.5	25	19.5	128	100.0
	Mar	3	2.9	11	10.5	79	75.2	12	11.4	105	100.0
	Apr	3	10.3	5	17.2	19	65.5	2	6.9	29	99.9
	May	24	27.9	15	17.4	12	14.0	35	40.7	86	100.0
	Jun	2	6.3	7	21.9	8	25.0	15	46.9	32	100.1
	Jul	—	—	10	66.7	4	26.7	1	6.7	15	100.1
	Aug	50	61.7	10	12.4	6	7.4	15	18.5	81	100.0
	Sep	—	—	8	19.1	13	31.0	21	50.0	42	100.1
	Oct	6	20.0	1	3.3	11	36.7	12	40.0	30	100.0
	Nov	—	—	6	17.1	6	17.1	23	65.7	35	99.9
	Dec	6	28.6	13	61.9	2	9.5	—	—	21	100.0
	Jan	—	—	11	29.7	7	18.9	19	51.4	37	100.0
	Feb	4	4.3	20	21.3	13	13.8	57	60.6	94	100.0
	Mar	11	22.9	5	10.4	2	4.2	30	62.5	48	100.0
	Apr	4	11.8	7	20.6	9	26.5	14	41.2	34	100.1
	May	37	45.2	16	19.5	10	12.2	19	23.2	82	100.1
	Jun	15	20.6	13	17.8	25	34.3	20	27.4	73	100.1
1765	Jul	10	27.0	9	24.3	3	8.1	15	40.5	37	99.9
	Aug	24	25.5	12	12.8	13	13.8	45	47.9	94	100.0
	Sep	15	12.1	14	11.3	22	17.7	73	58.9	124	100.0
	Oct	33	24.6	20	14.9	11	8.2	70	52.2	134	‹9.9
	Nov	2	6.1	7	21.2	10	30.3	14	42.4	33	100.0
	Dec	33	20.6	67	41.9	53	33.1	7	4.4	160	100.0
1766	Jan	5	18.5	4	14.8	2	7.4	16	59.3	27	100.0
	Feb	10	10.3	27	27.8	37	38.1	23	23.7	97	99.9
	Mar	55	52.9	12	11.5	11	10.6	26	25.0	104	100.0
	Apr	151	88.8	11	6.5	2	1.2	6	3.5	170	100.0
	May	39	35.8	12	11.0	27	24.8	31	28.5	109	100.1
	Jun	10	14.5	17	24.6	15	21.7	27	39.1	69	99.9
	Jul	66	39.3	21	12.5	30	17.9	51	30.4	168	100.1
	Aug	5	5.5	10	11.0	19	20.9	57	62.6	91	100.0
	Sep	37	38.9	12	12.6	23	24.2	23	24.2	95	99.9
	Oct	2	5.0	10	25.0	9	22.5	19	47.5	40	100.0
	Nov	5	6.4	30	38.5	10	12.8	33	42.3	78	100.0
	Dec	3	3.1	40	41.7	16	16.7	37	38.6	96	100.1
Total		838	23.1	770	21.3	802	22.1	1,212	33.5	3,622	100.0

Index

Index

symbols, 54–56; by months, 75–81; in individual newspapers, 65–73; shift in, 60–65, 73
levels, in American community, 170 f.
patterns, 43 f., 46; cyclical nature, 55; increasing congruence among colonies, 67 n., 70 n., 87 n., 101, 109 f., 136; parallel, 16; shared, 16; symmetrical, 16
relative, acceptance from other colonies, 98–111; from one colony to another, 103–07
self-perception: hypotheses about interaction with events, 184 f.; shifts in, 78 f.
Austrian Succession, War of, 63; as formative event, 29. *See also* Jenkins' Ear, War of; King George's War
Awareness, American community, 40–53; and Albany Congress, 156 f.; and colonial wars, 148–57; and formative events, 161–69, 181; and French and Indian War, 167 f.; and functional amalgamation, 145–47; and intercolonial communication, 174 f., 180–82; and King George's War, 165 f.; and Molasses Act, 158–60; and Pontiac's Conspiracy, as formative event, 162–65, 167; and Royal Proclamation of October 1763, as formative event, 168 f; and Stamp Act, 79–81, 157–60, 179; and theory of revolution, 64 n.; and Treaty of Paris, as formative event, 161 f.; changing levels, 170–75, and formative events, 175–79; growth, 142 f.; patterns, 41 f., 57–59, 229–59; rise, 81; symbols of self-identification, 112–41; timing and patterns of growth in, 179

Anglo-American community, xiv
community, xv, 6, 8 f., 13 f., 21 f.; curves of, 24–26; generalization of hypotheses about, 189; indicators of growth of, as tests of theories of political integration, 46; patterns, as indicators of internalized community interests, 52 f. (*See also* Community, sense of)
group, 16, 18, 24; internalization of group interests as concomitant of, 50

Bancroft, George, 12
Battle of Bloody Marsh, 102; as formative event, 29
Beard, Charles, 13
Becker, Carl Lotus, 8 f., 155
Beer, George Louis, 155, 159 n.
Behavior, and demands for change, xi
Bernd, Joseph L., xiv n.
Boorstin, Daniel J., 33 n., 34 n.
Boston Massacre, 61; and British image of American land, 117 f.; as formative event, 31
Boston Tea Party, as formative event, 31
Boucher, Jonathan, 5 n., 48
Bouchier, Jonathan, 5 n.
Bougainville, Louis Antoine de, 167
Braddock, General: defeat of, 61; expedition, 155
Bradford, Andrew, 192
Bridenbaugh, Carl, 9 f., 13 n., 73 n.
Brigham, Clarence S., 171 n., 194 n., 195
British: colonial system, 31–33; image of American land, 115–22; image of American people, 130–33; mercantile policies as formative event, 81; parliament and American sense of community, 176–79

Index

273

Index

Index

Index

internalization of, 16 f., 50–53; internalization of, 22
Internalization. *See* preceding entry
Intolerable Acts, 36, 61; as formative event, 31
Iron Bill, 160

Janis, Irving L., 178
Jenkins' Ear, War of, 8; and community awareness, 148–57, 165; and continental symbols, 86; as formative event, 29; Battle of Bloody Marsh, 102, as formative event, 29. *See also* Austrian Succession, War of; King George's War
Jensen, Merrill, 5 n., 147
Johnson, Sir William, and Pontiac's Conspiracy, 164 f.

Kalm, Peter de, 161 n.
Kann, Robert A., 11 n.
Keimer, Samuel, 192, 195
Kelley, Harold H., 178
Kelman, Herbert C., 158 n.
King George's War, 8; and community awareness, 148–57, 165 f.; as formative event, 29. *See also* Austrian Succession, War of; Jenkins' Ear, War of
King James II, 33
King William's War, 33
Knollenberg, Bernhard, 9, 164 n., 165 n.
Kraus, Michael, 12, 34 n.

Labaree, Leonard W., xvii
La Demoiselle, 167
Lamb, Robert K., 12 f.
Lane, Wheaton J., 13
Lasswell, Harold D., xii n., xvi f., 49 n., 178 n.
League of Augsburg, War of the, 33
Learning curve, 126, 131
Lee, James Melvin, 195
Lee, Maurice, 11 n.
Leffman, Henry, 38

Lerner, Daniel, xii n., 49 n.
Lexington, Battle of, as formative event, 31
Lichterman, Martin, 11 n.
Lindgren, Raymond E., 11 n.
Livingston, William, and Pontiac's Conspiracy, 164
Loewenheim, Francis L., 11 n.
Louisburg, capture and return, as formative event, 29; conquest, 102
McCreary, Eugene C., xvii
Macmahon, Arthur W., 6 n.
Malaysia, implications of this study for, 189
Mann-Whitney U Test, 78 n., 199 n.
Mars, 7 f.
Massachusetts: as "idea-man," 139 f.; House of Representatives, 34 f.; importance in last colonial decade, 102 f.; self-centeredness, 57, 111
Meredith, Hugh, 192, 195 f.
Merritt, Richard L., xii n., xiv n., 42 n., 158 n., 182 n., 195 n.
Middle colonies: as "decision makers," 140; pluralistic outlook of, 57, 110 f.
Miller, John C., 9
Miller, William, 13 n.
Mobility, 1, 11; intercolonial, 173
Molasses Act, and community awareness, 158–60
Montreal, capture of, as formative event, 30
Morgan, Edmund S., xvi f., 9, 28, 175 n.
Morgan, Helen M., 28, 175 n.
Morison, Samuel Eliot, 32 n., 37 n.
Mosteller, Frederick, 126 n.
Mott, Frank Luther, 195
Multiple loyalties, 113 f.; Anglo-American, 155 f.

Name, common, 22
National community, 1 f.

Index

Nationalistic outlook of southern colonies, 57

Neale, Thomas, 34

Needs of the people, vii

Nevins, Allan, 9

New England Confederation, 33

New Englanders, 5 n.

New York, as most important colony to others, 102 f.

Newspapers: as basis for symbol analysis, 191–201; as source of data on patterns of community awareness, 42 f.; choice of, for this study, 194–98; growth, 171; political alignment and symbol distribution, 71 f.; significance in colonial America, 42–44; Tory orientation, 198 f.; Whig orientation, 198 f.

Newsworthiness of colonies, 101–03

Nonparametric statistics, xvi

North Atlantic Treaty Organization, implications of this study for, 189

Oglethorpe, General James, 29, 102

Opinion change, psychological basis of, 177

Paine, Thomas, 43

Pakistan, implications of this study for, 189

Paris, Treaty of, 55; as formative event, 30; and community awareness, 161 f.

Parkman, Francis, 161 n., 166 n., 167 n.

Parks, William, 44 n., 195

Peace race, 8

Peckham, Howard H., 12, 165 n.

People, American: American image of, 130–33, British image of, 130–33

Petition of Rights (1774), 36

Pitcairn, Major John, 38

Place-name symbols: general comments about, 44–46; quality of, 48 f.

Pluralistic outlook of middle colonies, 57

Political change. *See* Change; Community; Integration

Politics, 20

Pontiac's Conspiracy, as formative event, 30, 81; and community awareness, 162–65, 167

Pool, Ithiel de Sola, xii n., 49 n.

Population growth, 172

Post Office, 34, 36; service, 173

Potter, David, 21 n., 52 n.

Public opinion and formative events, 158 n.

Purdie, Alexander, 195

Qualitative inferences, xii

Quantitative indicators, 24

Quebec, capture of, as formative event, 30

Quebec Act, as formative event, 31

Quincy, Josiah, 5 n.

RAND Corporation, 200 n.

Ranney, John C., 5 n., 50 f., 147

Religion, before the Revolution, 6 n. *See also* Great Awakening

Revolution, American, 5 n., 6, 13, 19, 29, 38, 60

Revolution, theory of, and data on American self-awareness, 64 n.

Rewards and deprivations, and conscious basis of demands for change, x f.

Rich, William E., 34 n.

Rigaud, Pierre François de, Marquis de Vaudreuil, 166 f.

Royal Proclamation of *October 7, 1763*: and community awareness, 168 f.; as formative event, 30, 81

Royle, Joseph, 195

Royster, Eugene, xvii

St. Augustine, 102; Spanish defense of, as formative event, 29

Sampling procedure, 199 f.; coding reliability, 200 f.; geographic

Index

direct and indirect, 83 f., 115, 202

European and other, 204 f.

home colony, 92–96, 203, 222–28, 265–69; in individual newspapers, 96 f.; intensive analysis, 93–96

list of, for this study, 209–14

neutral, shift in, 128–30

of common identity, 45 f., 112–41, 203, 205–09, 232–59; according to origin, primary identification content, and symbolic identification, 114 f.; direct and indirect, 115; in individual newspapers, 134–39. *See also* Symbols, continental

of community, 22

of focus of attention, 201–14, categories, 203–05

other colony, 98–111, 203, 222–28, 265–69

place-name, general comments, 44–46; quality of, 48 f.

Tea Act, as formative event, 31
Thomas, Isaiah, 195
Thorndike, Edward L., 126 n.
Timothy, Lewis, 196
Timothy, Peter, 196 f., 198
Tocqueville, Alexis de, 189
Tory orientation of newspapers, 198 f.
Townshend Acts, 35, 61; as formative event, 31
Transaction: communication, 23; integration through, 25 f; flow analysis, 98–111; flows, Alker computer program for, 56 f.; mutual, 1
Transportation, intercolonial, 13

Unification of colonies, early efforts at, 32–34. *See also* Integration

Van Doren, Carl, 3
Van Wagenen, Richard W., 11 n.
Vernon, Admiral Edward, capture of Porto Bello, 29
Virginia House of Burgesses, 35

War: as formative event, 8; as social process, 152–56
Wars. *See* Austrian Succession, War of; French and Indian War; Jenkins' Ear, War of; King George's War; King William's War; League of Augsburg, War of; Revolution, American; Seven Years' War
Washington, George, 30, 155; and Continental Army, 38 f.
Wector, Dixon, 192 n.
Weeden, William B., 12
Wells, William V., 198 n.
Wheare, Kenneth C., 6, 147
Whig orientation of newspapers, 198 f.
Whitefield, George, 173
Whitmarsh, Thomas, 196
Whyte, William Foote, 139 f.
William and Mary, 34
Wolfe, General James, 30, 156
World government and political integration, 3 f.
Wright, Chester W., 159 f.
Wright, Esmond, 6, 147, 161 n., 165 n., 168 n.
Wynne, Marjorie, xvii

Zenger, Catherine, 197
Zenger, John, 197
Zenger, John Peter, 194, 197 f., 202

279